THE PATHWORK
OF SELF-
TRANSFORMATION

Other Bantam New Age Books of interest to readers of
THE PATHWORK OF SELF-TRANSFORMATION:

BEYOND SUPERNATURE by Lyall Watson
CHANNELING: HOW TO REACH OUT TO YOUR SPIRIT
GUIDE by Kathryn Ridall, Ph.D.
CREATIVE VISUALIZATION by Shakti Gawain
EDGAR CAYCE: THE SLEEPING PROPHET by Jess Stearn
EMMANUEL'S BOOK: A MANUAL FOR LIVING
COMFORTABLY IN THE COSMOS
compiled by Pat Rodegast and Judith Stanton
EMMANUEL'S BOOK II: THE CHOICE FOR LOVE
compiled by Pat Rodegast and Judith Stanton
FOCUSING by Eugene T. Gendlin, Ph.D.
GOING WITHIN by Shirley MacLaine
IF YOU MEET THE BUDDHA ON THE ROAD, KILL HIM!
by Sheldon Kopp
JOURNEY OF AWAKENING by Ram Dass
HANDS OF LIGHT by Barbara Ann Brennan
THE LAZY MAN'S GUIDE TO ENLIGHTENMENT
by Thaddeus Golas
LIFE AFTER LIFE by Raymond A. Moody, Jr., M.D.
OTHER LIVES, OTHER SELVES by Roger J. Woolger, Ph.D.
THE SETH BOOKS by Jane Roberts
SHAMBHALA by Chögyam Trungpa
SOULMATES by Jess Stearn
SPIRIT COMMUNICATION
by Kevin Ryerson and Stephanie Harolde

THE PATHWORK OF SELF-TRANSFORMATION

Eva Pierrakos

Compiled and edited by Judith Saly

A
BANTAM
TRADE
PAPERBACK

BANTAM BOOKS
NEW YORK · TORONTO · LONDON · SYDNEY · AUCKLAND

THE PATHWORK OF SELF-TRANSFORMATION
A Bantam Book / May 1990

Library of Congress Cataloging-in-Publication Data

Guide (Spirit)
   The pathwork of self-transformation / [channeled] by Eva
Pierrakos.
      p.   cm.   •
   ISBN 0-553-34896-5
   1. Spirit writings.   2. Self-realization—Miscellanea.
3. Spiritual life—Miscellanea.   I. Pierrakos, Eva, 1915–1979.
II. Title.
BF1301.G94   1990
133.9'3—dc20   89-27802
                                                              CIP

Published simultaneously in the United States and Canada

*Bantam Books are published by Bantam Books, a division of Bantam
Doubleday Dell Publishing Group, Inc. Its trademark, consisting of
the words "Bantam Books" and the portrayal of a rooster, is Registered
in U.S. Patent and Trademark Office and in other countries. Marca
Registrada. Bantam Books, 1540 Broadway, New York, New York
10036.*

PRINTED IN THE UNITED STATES OF AMERICA

OPM   0 9

Acknowledgment

The Pathwork Foundation wishes to thank the enthusiastic team who cooperated in preparing this volume for publication: Judith Saly, Donovan Thesenga, Jan Bresnick, John Saly, Susan Thesenga, Iris Connors, Rebecca Daniels, and Hedda Koehler.

Donovan Thesenga is the Editorial Director of the Pathwork Series.

Contents

Introduction

No matter where you are in life, what your profession is, what your problems are, whether you are young or old, this book will help you see yourself and life in a new light. This new light combines reason with love and illuminates a pathway leading into your innermost self.

This book is channeled material. Its true author is a discarnate being who did not give himself a name, but who came to be known as the Guide. He delivered, through Eva Pierrakos, 258 lectures on the nature of psychological and spiritual reality and on the process of personal spiritual development. This process came to be known as the Pathwork and the transmissions were called the Pathwork Lectures or the Guide Lectures.

There are many volumes of channeled material in print today, and it therefore seems right that we do our best to let the potential reader know what distinguishes this book from so many others. Let us introduce you to the two principal distinguishing features of the Pathwork guidance:

1. The channeled teachings of the Pathwork Guide outline a *complete path* for personal transformation and spiritual self-realization.

2. This path includes a profound understanding of personal negativity—its sources, consequences, and a process to meet and transform it. This process, as taught by the Guide, is unmatched anywhere else.

The goal of *personal psychological work* is to become self-actualized, to realize our individual human potential for meaningful work in the world and for loving relationships with others.

The goal of *spiritual practice* is to experience enlightenment, or unitive consciousness, our oneness with all things. The aim of spiritual work is to know our innermost identity as God-inspired beings, filled with love and light.

A *complete path* must help us address both the frustrations in the fulfillment of our personal lives and the limitations that prevent our spiritual awakening. Most approaches to personal and spiritual growth offer us help for only part of this journey. We still want to know: *How can I get from where I am to where I want to be?*

Most present-day channeled material, as well as the esoteric traditions of most religions, tell us that we create our own reality. *But if this is so and I am indeed the creator of my life, what part of me is it that creates events that I find quite unpleasant? Why don't I do a better job of creating the life that I believe I want? Why are some aspects of myself so hard to change?*

The most valuable contribution the Guide has made to the modern psychological-spiritual quest is a practical, rational, and honest way to get from where we are to where we want to be. All spiritual teachers describe the enlightened state of love and harmony in which one feels at one with everyone and surrenders joyfully to God. We have also read the descriptions from humanistic and transpersonal psychologists of the fulfilled life of the self-actualized, whole person.

But if we do not deceive ourselves, we will know that we fall short of these goals. We need a way to accept ourselves fully as we are now, and to work with whatever in us blocks our personal and spiritual evolution. We need maps of the psyche that do not idealize or gloss over our all-too-human failings. The Pathwork outlines a map of human consciousness that includes our devils as well as our angels, the vulnerable child as well as the competent adult, the petty ego concerns as well as the grand visionary longings.

We need guidance to give us support as we take steps

from where we are now to the larger, more fulfilled, more aware person that we can be. The Pathwork encourages us to stop trying to pretend we are an idealized image of ourselves, the person who we think we ought to be. The Guide helps us to relax into an acceptance of who we honestly are and what we honestly feel, moment to moment. Any one of us who is truthful can discover disagreeable, self-centered feelings and attitudes within ourselves.

And yet we do not feel like bad people. We would like to follow the Golden Rule. Most of us would even agree that if we could love ourselves, and then our neighbors as ourselves, we would feel a lot better. *Why is it so hard for me to do this? Why do I continue to be so self-centered, or, alternately, so self-degrading?*

Generally speaking, we are given very little real help on these issues. Most religions give us moral commandments, often reinforced by guilt or fear, threats or cajoling, so we won't act out our negativity. When we fail, as we inevitably will, we are admonished to try harder. We are told to give over our flaws to someone else—to Christ, the church, or the guru. Or, in much contemporary guidance, we are expected to "rise above" our own limitations and see our negativity as merely temporary ignorance of our divinity. *How can I acknowledge my negativity without either glossing over it or being devastated by it?*

Most psychologies don't answer these questions either. Instead, we are inadvertently discouraged from taking full responsibility for our negativity. Since guilt is such a debilitating emotion, we are often encouraged by the psychological approach to stop thinking of ourselves as sinful or even flawed. In one way or another we are allowed to blame someone else—our parents, our past lives, oppressive societal norms—for our negativity. We think of ourselves as victims. We discharge our bad feelings toward those whom we see as having hurt us and then we hope that bad thoughts and feelings will go away. But they do not.

Do I just have to live with my imperfections? If I cannot overcome them, am I condemned by them? We are left with the secret fear that we are intrinsically bad in a way that we cannot change. This is the source of much of our despair and discouragement.

The Pathwork Lectures provide the missing element in both contemporary and traditional approaches to personal growth. While giving us the spiritual perspective that we are fundamentally divine, that at our center we are one with all that is, the Guide teaches that we also each contain a layer of negativity which he calls the *lower self*. The lower self is that part of us which actively, though usually unconsciously, *chooses* negativity, separation, egotism, fear, and distrust. However, since the lower self is ultimately a distortion of the one divine energy that animates the universe, it can be transformed back into its original life-affirming vitality. In the Pathwork Lectures, the Guide shows us *how*.

It is very hard work to come face to face with the lower self and most of us would like to avoid it. That is why we cling to the idealized images of ourselves. That is why we avoid the deep emotional work where such negative feelings surface. Yet recognizing and acknowledging our negative emotions are not too hard when we have the spiritual perspective and experience that tell us that our essence is divine. The troubled feelings we find inside can be transformed when we acknowledge them without evasion and learn to reconvert them into their originally divine nature. As the Guide says:

Through the gateway of feeling your weakness lies your strength.
Through the gateway of feeling your pain lies your pleasure and joy.
Through the gateway of feeling your fear lies your security and safety.
Through the gateway of feeling your loneliness lies your capacity to have fulfillment, love, and companionship.
Through the gateway of feeling your hopelessness lies true and justified hope.
Through the gateway of accepting the lacks in your childhood lies your fulfillment now.

Not only does the Guide offer a spiritual approach to the

problem of evil, but also a systematic and thorough path to releasing the light hidden behind our distortions. He leads us gently and lovingly through our darkness. The practice of honest, compassionate confrontation of the lower self, while anchoring ourselves more and more solidly in the higher self, brings the greatest personal liberation. This is a path of empowerment through self-responsibility.

It is the most illuminating experience to finally be able to connect the events of one's life—both positive and negative—with those forces within that have created them. It brings us home to the unitive core in ourselves, to our true, creative identity.

* * *

The lectures in this volume were carefully chosen to represent the basic teachings of the Guide and give an overview. We recommend that you read them sequentially, because the concepts are introduced gradually and progressively. However, you will understand them even if you pick at first those titles that most intrigue you.

It is possible to work with the lectures by yourself, following through with whatever exercises for self-awareness the Guide proposes in the lectures themselves. It is also helpful to form a small group in which the lectures can be discussed and your self-work can be shared. The Pathwork Centers offer introductory workshops as well as ongoing teaching and training programs that help you apply the lecture material to your personal development. The Centers also have trained helpers available to work individually or with groups. You can also use the Pathwork Lectures in your sessions with a spiritually inspired therapist. Many psychotherapists and psychiatrists have already discovered that the Guide's lectures contain material on transforming negativity that is *nowhere else to be found*. And many clergy and other people doing spiritual service have found in these lectures practical help in fulfilling their calling. The important thing is commitment to your personal truth, to your own inner path.

The Guide's teachings help us to purify ourselves so that we can fulfill our task on earth, become self-realized people, and learn to love in the true sense of the word. As members of society our task is to transform the planet Earth, and create a global brother-sisterhood through the spreading of the new consciousness and developing new ways of communication, interaction, and problem-solving. Understanding our personal evolution as part of the evolution of the planet Earth, and becoming conscious co-creators of a new and expanded reality, are the most joyful and positive aims of this path.

To absorb these lectures is the beginning of *doing Pathwork*. Let them touch you deeply, not only in your mind, but also in your heart. May they inspire you.

JUDITH SALY and DONOVAN THESENGA

THE PATHWORK
OF SELF-
TRANSFORMATION

1

What Is the Path?

A journey through the known into the unknown regions of the soul is similar to the quest told in fairy tales. The ignorant hero or heroine sets out from the familiar, everyday world because of a longing to find a greater life than the ordinary routine of a limited existence. Frightening encounters, tests of all kinds follow. If you pass the tests, you find happiness. The reward is wealth and a life partner; you become king or queen: a fulfilled adult.

The inner quest, if taken seriously, also takes courage, also traverses dark regions, and also leads to maturity—and the treasure is also always found. Just as in the fairy tales the hero doesn't sneak around the dragon but fights him, and doesn't run away from the old witch but befriends her, you, too, must meet the destructive forces within yourself and deal with them.

In this lecture the Guide shows how to follow the longing and liberate the dormant powers within yourself, so that you come upon the treasure of your wise, loving, inner Godself.

∽

Greetings and welcome, my friends. Blessings for every one of you. In this lecture I would like to discuss the path to the fulfillment of your deepest longings.

1

Longing for a Larger and More Fulfilling State of Consciousness

Every human being senses an inner longing that goes deeper than the longings for emotional and creative fulfillment, although these are, of course, part of the deeper and more essential desire. This longing comes from sensing that *another, more fulfilling state of consciousness and a larger capacity to experience life must exist.*

As you translate this longing into conscious terms, you may become involved in confusion and contradiction. Confusions and apparent contradictions come from the dualistic consciousness of the human mind. The dualism is always present, for humans perceive reality in terms of either/or, good or bad, right or wrong, black or white. This way of perceiving life is at best only half true: One can perceive only fragments of reality; the full truth can never be found. Truth always comprises more than what the dualistic way of seeing reality can grasp.

One confusion might be: "Am I longing for something unreal? Would it be perhaps more realistic and more mature to give up this longing and accept that life is just this flat, dismal, gray place? Do we not hear over and over that acceptance is necessary in order to be at peace with oneself and life? Therefore I should really abandon this longing."

The way out of your confusion can only be found when you take a step beyond the dualism implicit in this dilemma. It is true that you must accept your present state. It is true that life, as it manifests, cannot be perfect. Yet this fact is not what truly makes you unhappy, rather it is your demand that life should be perfect and be handed to you in its perfection that creates a problem. If you go deeply enough, you will inevitably discover that there is a part of you that denies pain and frustration; a place where you are angry and spiteful because there is no loving authority who will eliminate undesirable experiences for you. Thus it is true that your longing for this utopian kind of happier state is unrealistic and should be abandoned.

The False Desire

But does this truly mean that the longing *per se* stems from immature, greedy, or neurotic attitudes? No, my friends, it does not. There is an inner voice telling you *there is much, much more to your life and yourself than you are capable of experiencing at this time*.

How then can we find clarity about what is real and what is false about your deepest longing? The desire is false when your personality wishes love and fulfillment, perfection and happiness, or pleasure and creative expansion without paying the price of strictest self-confrontation. It is false when you do not assume the responsibility for your present state, or the state you long for. For example, if you feel sorry for yourself because of your unfulfilled life, and if you in any way blame others for your present state, no matter how wrong those others may be, whether your parents, your peers, your associates, or life as a whole, then you do not assume responsibility. If this is the case, then in some way you also wish to receive the new and better state as an unearned reward. You may try to be a good little obedient follower of a powerful authority figure in order to be rewarded. Since the reward in reality can never come from the outside, no matter what you do, you must feel disappointed, resentful, cheated, and angry, and you will resort again and again to your old, destructive patterns that are in fact responsible for the state that creates your unfulfilled longing.

The Realistic Longing

The longing is realistic when you start from the premise that the *clue to fulfillment must lie in you;* when you wish to find the attitudes in you that prevent you from experiencing life in a fulfilled and meaningful way; when you interpret the longing as a message from the core of your inner being, sending you on a path that helps you to find your real self.

However, when the inner message of longing is misinterpreted by the negative, greedy, ungiving and demanding personality, confusion sets in. The longing is then put into channels of unrealizable fantasies of magic. You believe fulfillment is supposed to be given to you, rather than attained through the courage and honesty of looking at yourself as you now are, even at areas you would rather avoid. If a life situation is painful and you react with rage, complaints, and other defenses against cleanly experiencing this pain, you are not in truth about your present state. But if you just let the pain be and feel it, without playing games like "it will annihilate me," or "it will last forever," the experience will release powerful creative energies to increasingly work for you in your life and open the channels to your spiritual self. Feeling the pain will also yield a deeper, fuller, and wiser understanding of the connections between cause and effect. For instance, you will see how you attracted this particular pain. Such insight may not come immediately, for the more you force it, the more it will elude you. But it will come if you stop the inner fighting and resisting.

Do not abandon the longing itself. Take it seriously. In fact, cultivate it and learn to understand it, so that you will follow its message and take the inner path to your core; go through that part which you want to avoid, which is the real culprit solely responsible for your less than fulfilled and joyful state.

Do not abandon the longing that comes from the sense that your life could be much more, that there is a state in which you can live without painful, tortured confusions, where you can function on a level of inner resilience, contentment, and security, where you are capable of deep feelings, of blissful pleasure and can express them, where you are capable of meeting life without fear because you no longer fear yourself. You will, therefore, find life, even its problems, a joyful challenge. If your inner problems can become a challenge that gives spice to your life, the ensuing peace will be all the more sweet. The tackling of these problems will give you a sense of your own strength, resourcefulness, and creative ability. You will feel the spiritual self flowing through your veins, in your thoughts, in your vision and your perceptions, so that decisions will be made from the center of your being. When you live this way, occasional outer problems are the salt of your life and become almost pleasurable. But the times of outer problems will become less frequent, and peaceful, joyous, creative living will become the norm.

Learning to Endure the State of Bliss

Right now, the saddest part of your longing is that deep inside you know how your own body and soul are not even capable of accepting and sustaining intense pleasure at this time. Pleasure exists on all levels: spiritual, physical, emotional, and mental. However, spiritual pleasure, separated from the levels of everyday functioning, is an illusion, because true spiritual bliss encompasses the total personality. The personality must therefore learn to endure a state of bliss. This it cannot do unless it learns to endure whatever is locked inside the psyche now: pain, meanness, malice, hate, suffering, guilt, fear, terror. All these must be transcended. Then, and then only, can the human personality function in a blissful state. Your longing to experience more pleasure is a message for you to embark on a road that affords you the possibility of being in bliss.

The state of existence I described need not be given up as unrealistic or wishful thinking. It need not be given up because you will earn it and make it your own by going through whatever in you prevents you from experiencing it. This state already exists as a dormant potential within you. It is not something that can be given to you by others, or acquired through learning or effort. It unfolds organically as a byproduct of your going on a path such as I am privileged to show you.

This brings us to the whole question of what this path is. This path is not new: It has existed in many different forms for as long as human beings have lived on this earth. The forms and the ways must change as humanity evolves, but the fundamental path remains the same. The particular path—the "Pathwork"—in which I guide you is anchored in ancient and perennial wisdom and yet it is also new. It offers help for your psychological and spiritual growth at this present, critical stage in humanity's evolution.

The Pathwork and Psychotherapy

The pathwork is not psychotherapy, although aspects of it must necessarily deal with areas psychotherapy also deals with. In the framework of the pathwork, the psychological approach is only a side issue, a way of getting through obstructions. It is essential to deal with confusions, inner misconceptions, misunderstandings, destructive attitudes, alienating defenses, negative emotions, and paralyzed feelings, all of which psychotherapy also attempts to do and even posits as its ultimate goal. In contrast, the pathwork enters its most important phase only after this first stage is over. The second and most important phase consists of learning how to activate the greater consciousness dwelling within every human soul.

Often the second phase overlaps with the first phase that is concerned with overcoming the obstructions, because the second or spiritual phase of the pathwork is essential for truly executing the first. The first part of the work cannot truly be successful unless contact with the spiritual self is regularly cultivated and used. However, when and how this may be done varies greatly and is dependent on the personality and on the predisposition, prejudices, and blocks of the individual entering this path. The sooner you can use, explore, and activate the inexhaustible fountain of strength and inspiration within, the easier and faster will you deal with the obstructions. It is thus quite clear in what way this path differs from psychotherapy, although some of the emphases and, at times, even the methods may be similar.

The Pathwork and Spiritual Practice

Nor is this path a spiritual practice that aims simply at reaching higher spiritual consciousness. There are many methods and practices that attempt realization of the spiritual self. Though using valid methods to forcefully reach this goal, many spiritual disciplines do not pay sufficient attention to those areas of the ego-self that are steeped in negativity and destructiveness. Any success thus achieved is always short-lived and illusory, even though some of the experiences may be genuine enough. But a spiritual state reached in such a one-sided way is not solid and cannot be maintained unless the total personality is included. Since human beings shy away from accepting and dealing with certain parts of themselves, they often seek refuge in paths that promise that one can avoid facing these problematic inner areas. If you think of a spiritual path as the practice of meditation for its own sake, or for the sake of reaching blissful cosmic experiences and consciousness, then this path is not your way.

The temptation to use spiritual practices to grab happiness and fulfillment, and to avoid already existing negativities, confusions, and pain, is great. But this attitude defeats the purpose; it comes from and leads to further illusions. One illusion is that anything that exists in you can be avoided. Another illusion is the belief that what is in you needs to be feared and denied. No matter how destructive it is, any inner aspect of you can be transformed. Only when you avoid what is in you does your illusion truly become detrimental to you and others.

Let me recapitulate what I have said so far. This path is neither psychotherapy, nor a spiritual path in the usual sense of the word: and, at the same time, it is both. It will be helpful if you remember the following points as you consider the possibility of embarking on this journey.

How to Find Your Real Self

By doing the pathwork, you embark on a voyage leading you into the new territory of your inner universe. Whether you have had therapy—satisfactory and successful or not—or whether you are deeply troubled and need help in order to live your life in a fulfilling way, you will still need for quite a while to pay attention mainly to those areas within yourself that are negative, destructive, and in error. You may not like to do so, but if you truly wish to find your real self, that core of your being from which all good stems, this focus is necessary.

"How long will it take?" you may ask. That depends on your own state of mind or feeling and your outer life manifestation. When your inner negativities are overcome, this new state will express itself in your life: There will be no doubt. Your path will organically bring you into different emphases and concerns. The aim of this path is not to cure you of an emotional or mental illness, although it does this very well and it is bound to do so if you do the work. But you should not enter this path for that purpose.

Do not enter this path if you expect that it will make you forget your sadness and pain or let you gloss over those aspects of your personality you like least or even dislike outright. Your dislike may not be "neurotic." You may be quite right to dislike these aspects, but you are not right in believing yourself hopelessly bad because of them. So this path must teach you to face whatever is in you, for only when you do this can you truly love yourself. Only then can you find your essence and true Godself. If you wish to find your essence but refuse to face whatever is in you, this is not the path for you.

It cannot be denied that to expand the consciousness of a limited mind is a tremendously difficult task, for all human beings have only the limited mind available to them when they start out. This limited mind must transcend itself in order to realize its unlimited power and scope. Therefore this path constantly requires your mind to bridge the gap of its own limitations by considering new possibilities and by making room for other alternatives for the self, for life, and for expressing the self in life.

Make no mistake: This is not an easy path. But the difficulty is not fixed and immovable. It exists only to the degree the personality has a stake in avoiding aspects of the self. To the degree the commitment is made to be in truth with the self, the difficulty vanishes. And what first seemed a difficulty now begins to become a challenge, an exciting journey, a process that makes life so intensely real and wholesome, so secure and fulfilling, that you would not want to give it up for anything. In other words, the difficulty exists exclusively in the false belief that if you have a certain negative attitude, then all of you is bad. Such a belief makes facing the self difficult or even impossible. Hence it is necessary to find the underlying beliefs behind any strong resistance to looking at the dark areas of the self.

This path demands from you that which most people are least willing to give: *truthfulness with the self, exposure of what exists now, elimination of masks and pretenses, and the experience of one's naked vulnerability.* It is a tall order, and yet it is the only real way that leads to genuine peace and wholeness. But once you have committed yourself to it, it is no longer a tall order but rather an organic and natural process.

Positivity and Negativity Are One Energy Current

This path is simultaneously the most difficult and the easiest. It merely depends from what point of view you look at it and choose to experience it. The difficulty can be measured in terms of your truthfulness with yourself. To the degree you want to be in truth, the path will appear neither too difficult, nor will it appear as if it dealt, in the words of some of its critics, "too much with the negative side of life and self." For the negative is the positive, in essence. Negative and positive are not two aspects of energy and consciousness: they are one and the same. Whatever particles of energy and consciousness in your self have turned negative must be reconverted into their original positive way of being. This cannot be accomplished without fully taking responsibility for the negativity in you.

The reluctance to be truthful with oneself applies to even the most honest people. A person may be noted for his or her honesty and integrity on one level, yet there can be deeper levels where this is not so at all. This path leads into the as yet concealed, more subtle levels that are difficult to pinpoint but certainly ascertainable.

"Images," or Wrong Conclusions

On these concealed, unconscious levels, misconceptions are formed in early childhood. These distorted perceptions of reality continue to influence the behavior of the adult. They develop into firmly held conclusions about life, which I like to call "images," because they form rigid patterns as if engraved on the soul substance.

An image is made up of misconceptions, distorted feelings, and physical blocks. A conclusion drawn from distorted perception is a wrong conclusion; therefore images are actually wrong conclusions about the nature of reality that are so firmly embedded in a person's psyche that they become behavior-controlling signals in life situations. A person may have several images, but underlying them all is a main image, which is the key to the basic negative attitude toward life.

Let me give you some examples. An image formed because of a particular situation in the child's family might be that the display of emotion, especially of warm feelings, is a sign of weakness and will lead to one's being hurt. Although this is a personal image, it may be reinforced by the societal mass image that, especially for a man, the display and physical expression of warm feelings are unmanly and weak because they mean losing control. An individual with this image will then, in any situation where he could emotionally open himself, obey the signal of the images instead of spontaneously responding to the actual situation or to the other person, which would be the positive, life-affirming response. He will also act toward others in a way to which they will respond negatively and confirm his false belief. In this way he deprives himself of pleasure and restricts the flow of the life force, creating inner tensions and further feeding his image. Thus negative compulsive patterns, or self-perpetuating vicious circles, are created.

Or, a baby cries because she is hungry, but the mother does not respond. However, when she does not cry, the mother will come and feed her. So the little girl draws the conclusion that if she shows her need, she will not be heard, but if she does not, she will get attention. Then the following conclusion is drawn: "In order to have my need fulfilled, I must not show that I have a need." With this particular mother, perhaps not showing the need actually did work for a while, but, obviously, in later years such an attitude will produce the opposite result. Since no one will know that this woman has any specific needs, no one will fulfill them. However, since she is completely ignorant of her "image," that is, the wrong conclusion about showing needs, because it has long ago sunk into her unconscious, she will go through life showing her needs less and less, hoping that eventually someone will reward her for being so unassuming, and not understanding why she is so unfulfilled. She does not know that it is her behavior that makes life confirm her wrong belief. For images have a magnetic power.

The wrong conclusions that form an image are drawn in ignorance or half-knowledge and therefore cannot remain in the conscious mind, and could actually have been carried over from previous incarnations. As the child grows up, his or her newly learned intellectual knowledge contradicts the old emotional "knowledge." The person pushes the emotional knowledge down until it disappears from conscious sight. Yet *the more the emotional knowledge is hidden, the more potent it becomes*. These unconscious images then restrict the unfolding of the person's potential. Therefore, a conscious effort has to be made to bring these images into awareness and learn how to inactivate them.

To find out if such unconscious images exist in you on a deeper level you can use an infallible key that will give you faultless answers. This key is: How do you feel about yourself and about your life? How meaningful, fulfilled, and rich is your life? Do you feel secure with others? Do you feel comfortable about your most intimate self in the presence of others, or at least with certain people with whom you have a goal in common? How much joy are you capable of feeling, giving, and receiving? Are you plagued with resentments, anxiety, and tension, or with loneliness and a sense of isolation? Do you need a lot of overactivity in order to alleviate anxiety? Actually, the fact that you do not consciously feel anxious by no means proves that you are without anxiety. Many start out on the path without awareness of their anxiety, but they feel dead, numb, listless, and paralyzed. This may be a sign that the anxiety was overcome through an artificial deadening process. This path cannot skip the step of making you first feel your anxiety and then feel whatever the anxiety hides. Only then can real aliveness come.

Exhilaration, enthusiasm, joyousness, and the unique blend of excitement and peace that connotes spiritual wholeness are a result of inner truthfulness. When these states are absent, then truthfulness must be absent. It is as simple as that, my friends.

So if you are prepared to embark on the journey into yourself to find, acknowledge, and bring out whatever is in you, if you summon all your inner truthfulness and commitment for the journey, if you find the courage and humility not to appear other than you are even in your own eyes, then you have indeed every right to expect that this path will help you realize your full life, and fulfill your longing in every conceivable way. This is a realistic hope. You will increasingly know it to be so.

Progress on the Path

Little by little you will begin to function from your innermost center, which is a very different experience from functioning from your periphery. You are now so accustomed to the latter that you cannot even imagine how else it could be. Now you are constantly dependent on what happens around you. You depend on appreciation and approval from others, on being loved, and on being successful in terms of the outside world. Whether you are aware of it or not, you inwardly strive to make sure you will obtain all this outer support so as to have peace and fulfillment.

When you function from your center, security and joy spring from a deep well within you. This does not by any means imply that when this happens you are condemned to live without approval, appreciation, love, or success. This is another dualistic misunderstanding. You think: "Either I experience my center and then must forfeit all love and appreciation from others and be alone, or I must forfeit my inner self because I cannot contemplate such a lonely life." In reality, when you function from the liberated center of your innermost self, you attract all the abundance of life to you, but you do not depend on it. It enriches you and is a fulfillment of a legitimate need, but it is not the substance of life. The substance is within.

In the healthy life of every human being there must be exchange, intimacy, communication, sharing, mutual love, mutual pleasure, and the giving as well as the receiving of warmth and openness. Also, every human being needs recognition of what he or she does. But there is an enormous difference between wanting this recognition in a healthy way and depending on outside recognition to such an extent that you are unable to do without it at all times. In the latter case, the self begins to sacrifice its integrity in tragic ways that cost much too much. Then the real self is betrayed and the seeking of recognition defeats itself. This path is geared to finding your center, the deep, inner spiritual reality, and not some illusory religious escape. Quite the contrary, this path is immensely pragmatic, for the true spiritual life is never in contradiction to practical life on earth. There must be a harmony between these two aspects of the whole. Forsaking everyday living is not true spirituality. In most cases, it is merely another kind of escape. For

many it is easier to sacrifice something and to chastise themselves than to face and deal with their dark aspects. The guilt
for the latter is constantly atoned for by self-deprivations that
are supposedly doorways to heaven. Yet this guilt cannot be
wiped out unless the personality deals directly with the darkness within. Then sacrifice and deprivation become not only
unnecessary but even contradictory to true spiritual unfoldment. The universe is abundant in its joy, pleasure, and bliss:
Human beings are supposed to experience them, not forsake
them. No amount of forsaking will wipe out the guilt for
avoiding the purification of the soul.

I would like to mention another specific feature of the inner obstructions that must be met so they can be transcended.
It is necessary to first understand that all thoughts and feelings
are powerful agents of creative energy, regardless of whether
the thoughts are true and wise or false and limited. Likewise,
whether the feelings are loving or hateful, angry or benign,
fearful or peaceful, their energy must create according to their
nature. Thoughts and opinions create feelings, and both of
them together create attitudes, behaviors, and emanations,
which in turn create the life circumstances. These sequences
must be connected with, understood, and fully recognized.
This is an essential aspect of the pathwork.

Your fear of your negative feelings is unjustified. The
feelings in themselves are not terrible or unbearable. However, your beliefs and attitudes can make them so. This process is constantly being verified by those who follow this path,
because they find that the deepest pain is a revivifying experience. It releases contracted energy and paralyzed creativity. It
enables people to feel pleasure to the degree they are willing
to feel pain.

The same applies to fear. To experience fear in itself is not
devastating: once experienced, the fear instantly becomes a
tunnel through which you travel, not letting go of the feeling
of fear until it carries you to a deeper level of reality. The fear
is a denial of other feelings. When the original feeling is being
accepted and experienced, the knot dissolves. Thus, it is never

the feeling itself that is unbearable. However, your attitude
has the power to make it so.

Fear of your feelings makes you cut them off. Thus you
cut yourself off from life. Your spiritual center cannot evolve
and manifest and unify with your ego self unless you learn to
fully embrace all your feelings, allow yourself to be carried by
them, and learn to take responsibility for them. If you make
others responsible for your feelings, you will be in a bind because you will either deny them or act them out destructively
against others. Neither one of these two alternatives is desirable or can bring any solution.

Freeing Your Spiritual Self

Your spiritual self cannot be freed unless you learn to feel
all your feelings, unless you learn to accept every part of your
being no matter how destructive it may be right now. No matter how negative, mean, vain, or egotistical you may find a
corner of yourself to be—contrary to other, more developed
aspects of your personality—it is absolutely necessary that
every aspect of your being be accepted and dealt with. No aspect should be left out or covered over in the wishful hope that
it would no longer matter and would somehow just go away.
It does matter, my friends. Nothing that exists in you is power-
less. No matter how hidden a dark aspect might be, it creates
life conditions that you must deplore. This is one reason why
you must learn to accept the negatively creating aspects in
you. Another reason is that *no matter how destructive*, cruel,
and bad it may be, every aspect of energy and consciousness is
in its original essence both beautiful and positive. The distortions must be reconverted into their original essence. Energy
and consciousness can become creative again in a positive way
only when the light of cognizance and positive intentionality
are brought to bear on them. Unless you do this, you cannot
come into your creative core.

Giving Up Illusions

This is basically the pathwork. Your only difficulty is you cling to illusions about how you are and how you should be, and to another illusion that you should not have certain problems. Unless you give up these illusions and take stock of whatever is in you, you must remain alienated from your own spiritual essence. That essence is constantly self-renewing; it is constantly conciliating apparently insoluble conflicts. Your spiritual essence furnishes you with all that you could ever need for living your life and for completing the task you came to fulfill through your birth. It is your divine center. You are thus an expression of all that exists—the all-consciousness. As long as you remain disconnected from it because you are too afraid of giving up your little vanity, your longing can never be fulfilled, for there is no panacea that can give you what you need and rightfully wish for without taking the path into and through your own darkness. Spiritual practices alone cannot fulfill your longing, no matter how much you sit in meditation and concentration. Meditation, and creative visualization, however, can be very helpful tools when used in conjunction with self-confrontation.

Very, very few people on this earth are willing to undertake the kind of path I have described to you. But for those who have the courage to go all the way, relentlessly and patiently, what glory awaits them in their innermost center!

Being Lived Through by the Spirit

The path is glorious when you have progressed beyond the initial stages in which you battle with your own false ideas that always create two unacceptable alternatives. When the path opens up from within you, you begin to experience, maybe for the first time in your life, your own potential of being, your own divinity. You will feel your potential for pleasure and security, awareness of yourself and others, and therefore your infinitely greater power to relate to others, comprehend them and be with them without fear.

The initial decision to enter a path such as this must be made realistically if it is to work. Are you willing to give up your illusions about yourself and your expectations—which come from your resistance to giving up self-delusions—of what others should do for you? Are you willing to shed your false fears about what feelings you should or should not, could or could not experience? If you make your commitment to yourself to fully accept everything you now are and to proceed to get to know yourself where you do not yet know yourself, you will find it is the most exciting, significant, and meaningful journey into your own depth. You will have all the help you can possibly need, for no one can undertake this journey alone. The help will be given to you; it will come to you.

When your spiritual center begins to manifest, your ego-consciousness integrates with it and you begin to be "lived through," as it were, by the spirit. Your living becomes a spontaneous, effortless flow.

Now, are there any questions?

QUESTION: *In what way was this path different in former eras and cultures?*

ANSWER: Humanity's development in former times necessitated a different approach. For example, people in the Middle Ages were apt to act out their cruel impulses. They were not capable of separating themselves sufficiently from their impulses in order to identify them, own up to them, and assume responsibility for them. They felt compelled to give vent to them and became wholly enveloped by them. Therefore people required strict authority from the outside to keep their lower natures in check. Only when the human personality became capable of using self-control could the next evolutionary step be taken. That over-control must now be loosened up.

In former times the average person was too far removed from his or her core to seek spiritual life from inside; it had to be projected outside. This inability to assume responsibility for the self then led to the creation of an outer devil who would possess an individual and an outside God who would help.

Now all this has changed. For example, today humankind's greatest hindrance is egotistical pride. People have accomplished much with the powers of the ego. They needed to develop these powers so as to no longer be irresponsible, helpless children. But these powers must now be exercised from within by one's own spiritual center and not be ascribed to the ego. The pride of the ego makes this difficult. Questions arise such as: "What will others say? Will they think me naive, stupid, or unscientific?" It is everyone's task today to overcome this pride and this dependency on the opinions of others. How often do individuals betray their spiritual truth by mouthing what is supposed to be intelligent without ever even daring to let their divine selves inspire them! These are the criteria for the path today.

Every stage in the evolution of spiritual consciousness necessitates a different approach. However, there is one exception. In every era there always was a small minority of people who were developed way beyond the scope of the average person. For them the path was always the same. These few formed secret societies that were unknown and not in the least popular. A group such as yours can therefore not be a popular movement either, for even today there are very few people capable or willing to follow such a path. But there are certainly many more today who could do so than in former times; many could, but few will.

I will withdraw now from this instrument through which I am allowed to manifest. A great spiritual power protects you. This may seem incomprehensible for some of you, yet it is a reality, my friends. There is a whole world beyond the world you know and touch and see. Only as you explore yourself and go into your core will you meet this world, and then it will reveal itself in its stark reality and utter glory. This world exists within and around you and it will inspire you from its own complete wisdom as you reach for it.

Be blessed, every one of you. Those of you who want to make the commitment to your inner being, and want to avail yourselves of the help this particular path can give, are blessed and guided in all your moves; and those of you who do not yet wish to take this step or who are drawn elsewhere, they, too, are being blessed. Be in peace.

2

The Idealized Self-Image

Most of us grow up believing that we are not good enough to be loved for just being ourselves. So we try desperately to live up to a self-created image of how we should be. The constant struggle to uphold this idealized version of ourselves causes many of our difficulties. It is, therefore, important to discover on what assumptions you have created your own idealized image and how it has caused distress and frustration in your life. You will find that it has achieved the exact opposite of what you had hoped it would. This discovery may be painful, but will allow you to reevaluate the way you are presenting yourself to the world and help you to become your true, relaxed self.

ϲᴏ

Greetings. God bless all of you, my dearest friends.

The Higher Self, the Lower Self, and the Mask

In an effort to understand human nature better, imagine it as represented by three concentric spheres. The central sphere, the inmost core, is the *higher self*, which is part of the universal intelligence and love that pervades life; in short: God. It is the divine spark. The higher self is free, spontane-

ous, creative, loving, giving, all-knowing, and capable of uninterrupted joy and bliss. You can always get in touch with it
when you are in truth, when you give from your heart, and
through meditation and prayer.

The layer that surrounds the divine self is the hidden
world of egocentricity that we call the *lower self*. This is your
undeveloped part, which still contains negative emotions,
thoughts, and impulses such as fear, hate, or cruelty.

The outermost layer, with which people cover up their
lower selves and often even their higher selves as a protective
shield, is the *mask self*, or idealized self-image.

Needless to say, there are many degrees and stages within
each of these levels of consciousness. The way they overlap,
cancel each other out, and create confusion, along with indirect effects and chain reactions, needs to be explored and understood. This work of exploration is what you are engaged in
on this path. All these aspects of the personality can be conscious or unconscious to varying degrees. The less awareness
you have of any of them, the more conflict will be in your life
and the less you will be equipped to deal with the challenges
that come your way. If your awareness is low, it will slow
down the process of transformation by which you will eventually integrate your lower self and your mask self into your divine center.

It is about the mask self, or idealized self-image, that I
want to speak to you tonight.

Pain is part of the human experience, beginning with
birth. Though pleasurable experiences are bound to follow
the painful ones, the knowledge and fear of pain are always
present. The most significant countermeasure to which people
resort in the false belief that it will circumvent unhappiness,
pain, and even death, is the creation of the idealized self-
image as a universal pseudo-protection. It is supposed to be a
means of avoiding unhappiness. Unhappiness, insecurity,
and lack of belief in oneself are interconnected. By pretending what one is not, that is, by creating the idealized self, one
hopes to reestablish happiness, security, and self-confidence.

In truth and reality, healthy and genuine self-confidence

is peace of mind. It is security and healthy independence and allows one to achieve a maximum of happiness through developing one's inherent talents, leading a constructive life, and entering into fruitful human relationships. But since the self-confidence established through the idealized self is artificial, the result cannot possibly be what was expected. Actually, the consequence is quite the contrary and frustrating because cause and effect are not obvious to you.

You need to grasp the significance, the effects, the damages, and the links between your unhappiness and your idealized self-image and to fully recognize in what particular way does it manifest in your individual case. To find this requires a great deal of work. The dissolution of the idealized self is the only possible way to find your true self, to find serenity and self-respect, and to live your life fully.

Fear of Pain and Punishment

As a child, regardless of what your particular circumstances were, you were indoctrinated with admonitions on the importance of being good, holy, perfect. When you were not, you were often punished in one way or another. Perhaps the worst punishment was that your parents withdrew their affection from you; they were angry, and you had the impression you were no longer loved. No wonder "badness" associated itself with punishment and unhappiness, "goodness" with reward and happiness. Hence to be "good" and "perfect" became an absolute must; it became a question of life or death for you. Still, you knew perfectly well that you were not as good and as perfect as the world seemed to expect you to be. This fact had to be hidden; it became a guilty secret, and you started to build a false self. This, you thought, would be your protection and your means of attaining what you desperately wanted—life, happiness, security, self-confidence. The awareness of this false front began to vanish, but you were and are permanently permeated with the guilt of pretending to be something you are not. You strain harder and harder to become this false self, this idealized self. You were, and unconsciously still are, convinced that if you strain hard enough, one day you will be that self. But through this artificial attempt to squeeze yourself into something that you are not, you can never attain genuine self-improvement, self-purification, and growth. You started building an unreal self on a false foundation and left your real self out. In fact, you are desperately hiding it.

The Moral Mask of the Idealized Self

The idealized self-image may assume many forms. It does not always dictate standards of *generally recognized perfection*. Oh yes, the idealized self-image often does impose high moral standards, making it all the more difficult to question its validity. "But isn't it right to want to be always decent, loving, understanding, never angry, and to have no faults, but try to attain perfection? Isn't this what we are supposed to do?" Such considerations will make it difficult for you to discover the compulsive attitude that denies present imperfection, such as the pride and lack of humility that prevents you from accepting yourself as you are now. This includes the pretense and the shame that goes with it, fear of exposure, secretiveness, tension, strain, guilt, and anxiety. It will take some progress in this work before you begin to experience the difference in feeling between the genuine desire to gradually work toward growth, and the ungenuine pretense imposed upon you by the dictates of your idealized self. You will discover the deeply hidden fear that says your world will come to an end if you do not live up to its standards. You will sense and know many other aspects and differences between the genuine and the ungenuine self. And you will also discover what *your particular* idealized self demands.

There are also facets of the idealized self, depending on personality, life conditions, and early influences, which are not and cannot be considered good, ethical, or moral. Aggressive, hostile, proud, overambitious trends are glorified, or idealized. It is true that these negative tendencies exist behind all idealized self-images. But they are hidden, and since they

crassly contradict the morally high standards of the particular
idealized self, they cause additional anxiety, in that the idealized self will be exposed for the fraud it is. The person who
glorifies such negative tendencies, believing them to prove
strength and independence, superiority and aloofness, would
be deeply ashamed of the kind of goodness another person's
idealized self uses as a front, and would consider it as weakness, vulnerability, and dependency in an unhealthy sense.
Such a person entirely overlooks the fact that nothing makes a
person as vulnerable as pride; nothing causes so much fear.

In most cases there is a combination of these two tendencies: overexacting moral standards impossible to live up to and
pride in being invulnerable, aloof, and superior. The coexistence of these mutually exclusive ways presents a particular
hardship for the psyche. Needless to say, the conscious awareness of this contradiction is missing until this particular work
is well in progress.

There are many more facets, possibilities, and individual
pseudo-solutions combining all sorts of mutually exclusive behaviors. All this has to be found individually.

Let us now consider some of the general effects of the existence of the idealized self and some of the implications. Since
the standards and dictates of the idealized self are impossible
to realize, and yet you never give up the attempt to uphold
them, you cultivate within yourself an inner tyranny of the
worst order. You do not realize the impossibility of being as
perfect as your idealized self demands, and never give up
whipping yourself, castigating yourself, and feeling a complete failure whenever it is proven that you cannot live up to
its demands. A sense of abject worthlessness comes over you
whenever you fall short of these fantastic demands and engulfs
you in misery. This misery may at times be conscious but most
of the time it is not. Even if it is, you do not realize the entire
significance, the impossibility of what you expect from yourself. When you try to hide your reactions to your own "failure," you use special means to avoid seeing it. One of the most
common devices is to project the blame for "failure" into the
outer world, onto others, onto life.

The more you try to identify with your idealized self-image, the harder the disillusionment whenever life brings you into a position where this masquerade can no longer be maintained. Many a personal crisis is based on this dilemma, rather than on outer difficulties. These difficulties then become an added menace beyond their objective hardship. The existence of the difficulties is a proof to you that you are not your idealized self, and this robs you of the false self-confidence you tried to establish with the creation of the idealized self. There are personality types who know perfectly well that they cannot identify with their idealized self. But they do not know this in a healthy way. They despair. They believe they ought to be able to live up to it. Their whole life is permeated with a sense of failure, while the former type experiences it only on more conscious levels when outer and inner conditions culminate in showing up the phantom of the idealized self for what it really is: an illusion, a pretense, a dishonesty. It amounts to saying: "I know I am imperfect, but I make believe I am perfect." Not to recognize this dishonesty is comparatively easy when rationalized by conscientiousness, honorable standards and goals, and a desire to be good.

Self-Acceptance

The genuine desire to better oneself leads one to accept one's personality as it is now. If this basic premise is the main governing force of your motivation for perfection, any discovery of where you fall short of your ideals will not throw you into depression, anxiety, and guilt, but will rather strengthen you. You will not need to exaggerate the "badness" of the behavior in question, nor will you defend yourself against it with the excuse that it is the fault of others, of life, of fate. You will gain an objective view of yourself in this respect, and this view will liberate you. You will fully assume responsibility for the faulty attitude, being willing to take the consequences upon yourself. When you act out your idealized self, you dread nothing more than that, for taking the responsibility of your shortcomings upon yourself is tantamount to saying, "I am not my idealized self."

The Inner Tyrant

Feelings of failure, frustration, and compulsion, as well as guilt and shame, are the most outstanding indications that your idealized self is at work. These are the consciously felt emotions out of all those that lie hidden underneath. Actually, the basis of the tyranny of the idealized self-image is the sense of *false shame* and *false guilt* that this image produces when one cannot live up to it. In addition, the idealized self also manifests *false needs,* which are superimposed and artificially created, like the need for glory, the need to triumph, to satisfy vanity or pride. The pursuit of these needs never results in true fulfillment.

The idealized self has been called into existence in order to attain self-confidence and therefore, finally, happiness, pleasure supreme. The stronger its presence, the more genuine self-confidence fades away. Since you cannot live up to its standards, you think even less of yourself than you originally did. It is therefore obvious that genuine self-confidence can be established only when you remove the superstructure, which is this merciless tyrant, your idealized self.

Yes, you could have self-confidence if the idealized self were really you; and if you could live up to these standards. Since this is impossible and since, deep down, you know perfectly well you are not anything like what you think you are supposed to be, you build up additional insecurity with this "super self," and further vicious circles come into existence. The original insecurity, which was supposedly whisked away by the establishment of the idealized self, steadily increases. It snowballs, and becomes worse and worse. The more insecure you feel, the more stringent the demands of the superstructure or idealized self, the less you are able to live up to it, and the more insecure you feel. It is very important to see how this vicious circle works. But this cannot be done until and unless you become fully aware of the devious, subtle, unconscious ways in which this idealized self-image exists in your particular case. Ask yourself in what particular areas it manifests. What causes and effects are connected with it?

Estrangement from the Real Self

A further and drastic result of this problem is the constantly increasing estrangement from the real self. The idealized self is a falsity. It is a rigid, artificially constructed imitation of a live human being. You may invest it with many aspects of your real being; nevertheless, it remains an artificial construct. The more you invest your energies, your personality, your thought processes, concepts, ideas, and ideals into it, the more strength you take from the center of your being, which alone is amenable to growth. This center of your being is the only part of you, the real you, that can live, grow, and be. It is the only part that can properly guide you. It alone functions with all your capacities. It is flexible and intuitive. Its feelings alone are true and valid even if, for the moment, they are not yet fully in truth and reality, in perfection and purity. But the feelings of the real self function in perfection relative to what you are now. The more you take out of that live center in order to invest into the robot you have created, the more estranged you become from the real self and the more you weaken and impoverish it.

In the course of this work, you have sometimes come upon the puzzling and often frightening question: *"Who am I really?"* This is the result of the discrepancy and struggle between the real and the false self. Only upon solving this most vital and profound question will your live center respond and function to its full capacity, will your intuition begin to function to its full capacity, will you become spontaneous, free of all compulsions, will you trust in your feelings because they will have an opportunity to mature and grow. Feelings will become every bit as reliable to you as your reasoning power and your intellect.

All this is the final finding of self. Before this can be done, a great many hurdles have to be overcome. It seems to you that this is a life-or-death struggle. You still believe you need the idealized self in order to live and be happy. Once you understand that this is not so, you will be able to give up the pseudo-defense that makes the maintenance and cultivation of the idealized self seem so necessary. Once you understand that the idealized self was supposed to solve the particular problems in your life above and beyond your need for happiness, pleasure, and security, you will come to see the wrong conclusion of this theory. Once you go a step still further and recognize the damage the idealized self has brought into your life, you will shed it as the burden it is. No conviction, theory, or words you hear will make you give it up, but the recognition of what specifically it was supposed to solve and what damage it has done and is continuing to do will enable you to dissolve this image of all images.

Needless to say, you also have to recognize most particularly and in detail what your idealized self's specific demands and standards are, and, further, you have to see their unreasonableness, their impossibility. When you have a feeling of acute anxiety and depression, consider the fact that your idealized self may feel questioned and threatened, either by your own limitations, by others, or by life. Recognize the self-contempt that underlies the anxiety or depression. When you are compulsively angry at others, consider the possibility that this is but an externalization of your anger at yourself for not living up to the standards of your false self. Do not let it get away with using the excuse of outer problems to account for acute depression or fear. Look into the question from this new angle. Your private and personal work will help you in this direction, but it is almost impossible to do it alone. Only after you have made some substantial progress will you recognize that so many of these outer problems are directly or indirectly the result of the discrepancy between your capacities and the standards of your idealized self and how you deal with this conflict.

So, as you proceed in this particular phase of the work, you will come to understand the exact nature of your idealized self: Its demands, its requirements of self and others in order to maintain the illusion. Once you fully see that what you regarded as commendable is really pride and pretense, you will have gained a most substantial insight that enables you to weaken the impact of the idealized self. Then, and then only, will you realize the tremendous self-punishment you inflict upon yourself. For whenever you fall short, as you are bound to, you feel so impatient, so irritated, that your feelings can snowball into fury and wrath at yourself. This fury and wrath are often projected on others because it is too unbearable to be aware of self-hate, unless one unrolls this whole process and sees it entire, in the light. Nevertheless, even if this hate is unloaded upon others, the effect on the self is still there and it can cause disease, accident, loss, and outer failure in many ways.

Giving Up the Idealized Self

When you make the very first steps toward giving up the idealized self, you will feel a sense of liberation as never before. Then you will be truly born again; your real self will emerge. Then you will rest within your real self, centered within. Then you will truly grow, not only on the outer fringes that may have been free of the idealized self's dictatorship, but in every part of your being. This will change many things. First will come changes in your reactions to life, to incidents, to yourself and others. This changed reaction will be astounding enough, but, little by little, outer things are also bound to change. Your different attitude will have new effects. The overcoming of your idealized self means overcoming an important aspect of the duality between life and death.

At present you are not even aware of the pressure of your idealized self, of the shame, humiliation, exposure you fear and sometimes feel, of the tension, strain, and compulsion. If you have an occasional glimpse of such emotions, you do not as yet connect them with the fantastic demands of your idealized self. Only after fully seeing these fantastic expectations and their often contradictory imperatives will you relinquish them. The initial inner freedom gained in this way will allow you to deal with life and to stand in life. You will no longer have to hold on frantically to the idealized self. The mere inner activity of holding on so frantically generates a pervasive climate of holding on in general. This is sometimes lived out in external attitudes, but most often it is an inner quality or attitude. As you proceed in this new phase of your work, you will sense and feel this inner tightness and gradually you will recognize the basic damage it causes. It makes the letting go of many an attitude impossible. It makes it unduly difficult to go through any change that would allow life to bring forth joy and a spirit of vigor. You keep yourself contained within yourself and thereby you go against life in one of its most fundamental aspects.

The words are insufficient; you have to sense rather what I mean. You will know exactly when you have weakened your idealized self by fully understanding its function, its causes and effects. Then you will gain the great freedom of giving yourself to life because you no longer have to hide something from yourself and others. You will be able to squander yourself into life, not in an unhealthy, unreasonable way, but healthily as nature squanders herself. Then, and then only will you know the beauty of living.

You cannot approach this most important part of your inner work with a general concept. As usual, your most insignificant daily reactions, considered from this viewpoint, will yield the necessary results. So continue your self-search out of these new considerations and do not be impatient if it takes time and relaxed effort.

Coming Home

One more word: The difference between the real and the idealized self is often not a question of quantity, but rather of quality. That is, the original motivation is different in these two selves. This will not be easy to see, but as you recognize the demands, the contradictions, the cause-and-effect sequences, the difference in motivation will gradually become clear to you. Another important consideration is the time ele-

ment. The idealized self wants to be perfect, according to its
specific demands, right now. The real self knows this cannot
be and does not consider this fact painful.

Of course you are not perfect. Your present self is a com-
plex of everything you are at the moment. Of course you have
your basic egocentricity, but if you own up to it, you can cope
with it. You can learn to understand it and therefore diminish
it with each new insight. Then you will truly experience the
truth that the more egocentric you are, the less self-confident
you can be. The idealized self believes just the opposite. Its
claims for perfection are motivated by purely egocentric reasons, and this very egocentricity makes self-confidence impossible.

The great freedom of *coming home*, my friends, is finding your way back to the real you. The expression "coming
home" has often been used in spiritual literature and teachings, but it has been much misunderstood. It is often interpreted to mean the return into the spirit world after physical
death. Much more is meant by coming home. You may die
many deaths, one earth life after another, but if you have not
found your real self, you cannot come home. You may be lost
and remain lost until you do find the way into the center of
your being. On the other hand, you can find your way home
right here and right now while you are still in the body. When
you muster the courage to become your real self, even though
it would seem much less than the idealized self, you will find
out that it is much more. Then you will have the peace of being at home within yourself. Then you will find security. Then
you will function as a whole human being. Then you will have
broken the iron whip of a taskmaster whom it is impossible to
obey. Then you will know what peace and security really
mean. You will cease once and for all to seek them by false
means.

May you all find truth and help and further enlightenment through the words I gave you tonight. However, you
should understand and expect that a theoretical understanding will avail you nothing. As long as these words remain theory you will not be helped by them. When you begin or

continue to work in this direction and allow yourself to feel and observe your emotional reactions connected to your idealized self, then you will make substantial progress in your own liberation and self-finding in the truest sense of the word.

My dearest ones, each one of you, receive our love, our strength, and our blessings. Be in peace, be in God!

3

Compulsion to Recreate and Overcome Childhood Hurts

*The Guide says that depth psychology is a spir-
itual discipline, because only through knowing
yourself can you purify your soul, that is, cleanse it
of self-destructive patterns and make it ready to connect with the inner God. The "repetition compulsion" is well known in psychology; what this
repetition is supposed to achieve, however, has
never been as illuminatingly explained as in this lecture. Our repeated negative experiences are bound
up not only with our early childhood, but also with
previous incarnations. With the help of this lecture
we can discover why we keep running in our respective squirrel cages and how we can stop doing so.*

ᔕ

Greetings, my dearest friends. God bless all of you. May
the divine blessings extended to every one of you help you as-
similate the words I speak tonight, so that this will be a fruitful occasion for you.

The Lack of Mature Love

Because children so seldom receive sufficient mature love
and warmth, they continue to hunger for it throughout their

lives unless this lack and hurt is recognized and properly dealt with. If not, *as adults they will go through life unconsciously crying out for what they missed in childhood*. This will make them incapable of loving maturely. You can see how this condition continues from generation to generation.

The remedy cannot be found by wishing that things were different and that people would learn to practice mature love. The remedy lies solely in you. True, if you had received such love from your parents, you would be without this problem of which you are not really and fully aware. But this lack of receiving mature love need trouble neither you nor your life if you become aware of it, see it, and rearrange your former unconscious wishes, regrets, thoughts, and concepts by aligning them to the reality of each situation. As a consequence, you will not only become a happier person, but you will also be able to extend mature love to others—to your children, if you have any, or to other people in your environment—so that a benign chain reaction can start. Such realistic self-correction is very contrary to your present inner behavior, which we shall now consider.

All people, including even those few who have started to explore their own unconscious mind and emotions, habitually overlook the strong link between the child's longing and unfulfillment and the adult's present difficulties and problems, because only very few people experience personally—and not just recognize in theory—how strong this link is. Full awareness of it is essential.

There may be isolated, exceptional cases where one parent offers a sufficient degree of mature love. Even if one parent has it to some measure, very likely the other does not. Since mature love on this earth is only present to a degree, the child will suffer from the shortcomings of even a loving parent.

More often, however, both parents are emotionally immature and cannot give the love the child craves, or give it only in insufficient measure. During childhood, this need is rarely conscious. Children have no way of putting their needs into thoughts. They cannot compare what they have with what others have. They do not know that something else might exist. They believe this is the way it should be. Or, in extreme cases, they feel especially isolated, believing their lot is like no one else's. Both attitudes deviate from the truth. In both cases the real emotion is not conscious and therefore cannot be properly evaluated and come to terms with. Thus, children grow up never quite understanding why they are unhappy, nor even that they are unhappy. Many of you look back on childhood convinced that you had all the love you wanted just because you actually did have some love.

There are a number of parents who give great demonstrations of love. They may overindulge their children. Such spoiling and pampering may be an overcompensation and a sort of apology for a deeply suspected inability to love maturely. Children feel the truth very acutely. They may not consciously think about it, but inwardly children keenly feel the difference between mature, genuine love and the immature, over-demonstrative variety offered instead.

Proper guidance and security are the parents' responsibility and call for authority on their part. There are parents who never dare to punish or exert a healthy authority. This failing is due to guilt because real, giving, warming, comforting love is absent in their own immature personalities. Other parents may be too severe, too strict. They thereby exert a domineering authority by bullying the child, and not allowing his or her individuality to unfold. Both types fall short as parents, and their wrong attitudes, absorbed by the child, will cause hurt and unfulfillment.

In children of the strict parents, the resentment and rebellion will be open, and therefore more easily traced. In the other case, the rebellion is just as strong, but hidden, and therefore infinitely harder to trace. If you had a parent who smothered you with affection or pseudo-affection, yet lacked in genuine warmth, or if you had a parent who conscientiously did everything right but was also lacking in real warmth, unconsciously you knew it as a child and you resented it. Consciously you may not have been aware of it at all, because, when a child, you really could not put your finger on what was lacking. You were outwardly given everything you wanted and needed. How could you draw the subtle, fine borderline distinction between real affection and pseudo-affection with your child's intellect? The fact that something bothered you without your being able to explain it rationally made you feel guilty and uncomfortable. You therefore pushed it out of sight as far as possible.

As long as the hurt, disappointment, and unfulfilled needs of your early years remain unconscious, you cannot come to terms with them. No matter how much you may love your parents, an unconscious resentment exists in you, which prevents you from forgiving them for the hurt. You can only forgive and let go if you recognize your deeply hidden hurt and resentment. As an adult human being you will see that your parents, too, are just human beings. They were not as faultless and perfect as the child had thought and hoped them to be, yet they are not to be rejected now because they had their own conflicts and immaturities. The light of conscious reasoning has to be applied to these very emotions you never allowed yourself to be aware of fully.

Attempts to Remedy the Childhood Hurt in Adulthood

As long as you are unaware of the conflict between your longing for a perfect love from your parents and your resentment against them, you are bound to try remedying the situation in your later years. This striving may manifest in various aspects of your life. You run constantly into problems and repeated patterns that have their origin in your attempt to *reproduce the childhood situation so as to correct it.* This unconscious compulsion is a very strong factor, but is so deeply hidden from your conscious understanding!

The most frequent way of attempting to remedy the situation is in your *choice of love partners.* Unconsciously you will know how to choose in the partner aspects of the parent who has particularly fallen short in affection and love that is real and genuine. But you also seek in your partner aspects of the other parent who has come closer to meeting your demands.

Important as it is to find both parents represented in your partners, it is even more important and more difficult to find those aspects that represent the parent who has particularly disappointed and hurt you, the one more resented or despised and for whom you had little or no love. So you seek the parents again—in a subtle way that is not always easy to detect, in your marital partners, in your friendships, or in other human relationships. In your subconscious, the following reactions take place: Since the child in you cannot let go of the past, cannot come to terms with it, cannot forgive, cannot understand and accept, this very child in you always creates similar conditions, trying to win out in the end in order to finally master the situation instead of succumbing to it. Losing out means being crushed—this must be avoided at all costs. The costs are high indeed, for the entire strategy is unfeasible. What the child in you sets out to accomplish cannot ever come to realization.

The Fallacy of this Strategy

This entire procedure is utterly destructive. In the first place, it is an illusion that you were defeated. Therefore, it is an illusion that you can now be victorious. Moreover, it is an illusion that the lack of love, sad as that may have been when you were a child, is indeed the tragedy that your subconscious still feels it to be. The only tragedy lies in the fact that you obstruct your future happiness by continuing to reproduce the situation and then attempting to master it. My friends, this process is a deeply unconscious one. Of course, nothing is further from your mind as you focus on your conscious aims and wishes. It will take a great deal of digging to uncover the emotions that lead you again and again into situations where your secret aim is to remedy childhood woes.

In trying to reproduce the childhood situation, you unconsciously choose a partner with aspects similar to those of the parent. Yet it is these very aspects that will make it as impossible to receive the mature love you rightfully long for now as it was then. Blindly, you believe that by willing it more strongly and more forcefully, the parent-partner will now yield, whereas in reality love cannot come that way. Only when you are free of this ever-continuing repetition, will you no longer cry to be loved by the parent. Instead, you will look for a partner or for other human relationships with the aim of finding the maturity you really need and want. In not demanding to be loved as a child, you will be equally willing to love. However, the child in you finds this impossible, no matter how much you may otherwise be capable of it through development and progress. This hidden conflict eclipses your otherwise growing soul.

If you already have a partner, the uncovering of this conflict may show you how he or she is similar to your parents in certain immature aspects. But since you now know that there is hardly a really mature person, these immaturities in your partner will no longer be the tragedy they were while you constantly sought to find your parent or parents again, which of course could never come to pass. With your existing immaturity and incapacity, you may nevertheless build a more mature relationship, free of the childish compulsion to recreate and correct the past.

You have no idea how preoccupied your subconscious is with the process of reenacting the play, so to speak, only hoping that "this time it will be different." And it never is! As time goes on, each disappointment weighs heavier and your soul becomes more and more discouraged.

For those of my friends who have not yet reached certain depths of their unexplored subconscious, this may sound quite preposterous and contrived. However, those of you who have come to see the power of your hidden trends, compulsions, and images will not only readily believe it, but will soon experience the truth of these words in their own personal lives. You already know from other findings how potent are the workings of your subconscious mind, how shrewdly it goes about its destructive and illogical ways.

Reexperiencing the Childhood Hurt

If you learn to look at your problems and unfulfillment from this point of view and follow the usual process of allowing your emotions to come to the fore, you will gain much further insight. But it will be necessary, my friends, to reexperience the longing and the hurt of the crying child you were once, even though you were also a happy one. Your happiness may have been valid and without self-deception at all. For it is possible to be both happy and unhappy. You may now be perfectly aware of the happy aspects of your childhood, but that which hurt deeply and that certain something you greatly longed for—you did not even quite know what—you were not aware of. You took the situation for granted. You did not know what was missing or even that there was anything missing. This basic unhappiness has to come to awareness now, if you really want to proceed in inner growth. You have to reexperience the acute pain you once suffered but you pushed out of sight. Now you have to look at this pain conscious of the understanding you have gained. Only by doing this will you grasp the reality value of your current problems and see them in their true light.

Now, *how can you manage to reexperience the hurts of so long ago?* There is only one way, my friends. Take a current problem. Strip it of all the superimposed layers of your reactions. The first and most handy layer is that of rationalization, that of "proving" that others, or situations, are at fault, not your innermost conflicts that make you adopt the wrong attitude to the actual problem that confronts you. The next layer might be anger, resentment, anxiety, frustration. Behind all these reactions you will find the hurt of not being loved. When you experience the hurt of not being loved in your current dilemma, it will serve to reawaken the childhood hurt. While you face the present hurt, think back and try to reconsider the situation with your parents: what they gave you, how you really felt about them. You will become aware that in many ways you lacked a certain something you never clearly saw be-

fore—you did not want to see it. You will find that this must
have hurt you when you were a child, but you may have forgotten this hurt on a conscious level. Yet it is not forgotten at
all. The hurt of your current problem is the very same hurt.
Now, reevaluate your present hurt, comparing it with the
childhood hurt. At last you will clearly see how it is one and
the same. No matter how true and understandable your present pain is, it is nevertheless the same childhood pain. A little
later you will come to see how you contributed to bringing
about the present pain because of your desire to correct the
childhood hurt. But at first you only have to feel the similarity
of the pain. However, this requires considerable effort, for
there are many overlaying emotions that cover the present
pain as well as the past one. Before you have succeeded in
crystallizing the pain you are experiencing, you cannot understand anything further in this respect.

   Once you can synchronize these two pains and realize
that they are one and the same, the next step is much easier.
Then, by perceiving the repetitious pattern in your various
difficulties, you will learn to recognize the similarities between your parents and the people who have caused you hurt
or are causing you pain now. Experiencing these similarities
emotionally will carry you further on the particular road toward dissolving this basic conflict. Mere intellectual evaluation will not yield any benefit. To be fruitful and bring real
results, the process of giving up the recreation must go beyond
mere intellectual knowledge. You have to allow yourself to
feel the pain of certain unfulfillments now and also the pain
of the unfulfillment of your childhood, then compare the two
until, like two separate picture slides, they gradually move
into focus and become one. *Experiencing the pain of now and
the pain of then,* you will slowly come to understand how you
thought you had to choose the current situation because deep
inside you could not possibly admit "defeat." Once this happens, the insight you gain, the experience you feel exactly as I
say here, will enable you to take the next step.

   It goes without saying that many people are not even
aware of any pain, past or present. They busily push it out of

sight. Their problems do not appear as "pain." For them, the very first step is to become aware that this pain is present and that it hurts infinitely more as long as they have not become aware of it. Many people are afraid of this pain and like to believe that by ignoring it they can make it disappear. They chose such a means of relief only because their conflicts have become too great for them. How much more wonderful it is for a person to choose this path with the wisdom and conviction that a hidden conflict, in the long run, does as much damage as a manifest one. They will not fear to uncover the real emotion and will feel even in the temporary experience of acute pain, that in that moment it turns into a healthy growing pain, free of bitterness, tension, anxiety, and frustration.

There are also those who tolerate the pain, but in a negative way, always expecting it to be remedied from the outside. Such people are in a way nearer to the solution because for them it will be quite easy to see how the childish process still operates. The outside is the offending parent, or both parents, projected onto other human beings. They have only to redirect the approach to their pains. They do not have to find it.

How to Stop Recreating?

Only after experiencing all these emotions, and synchronizing the "now" and the "then," will you become aware of how you tried to correct the situation. You will further see the folly of the unconscious desire to recreate the childhood hurt, the frustrating uselessness of it. You will survey all your actions and reactions with this new understanding and insight, whereupon you will release your parents. You will leave your childhood truly behind and start a new, inner behavior pattern that will be infinitely more constructive and rewarding for you and for others. You will no longer seek to master the situation you could not master as a child. You will go on from where you are, forgetting and forgiving truly inside of you, without even thinking that you have done so. You will no longer need to be loved as you needed to be loved when you were a child. First you become aware that this is what you still wish, and then you no longer seek this kind of love. Since you are no longer a child, you will seek love in a different way, by giving it instead of expecting it. It must always be emphasized, however, that many people are not aware that they do expect it. Since the childish, unconscious expectation was so often disappointed, they made themselves give up all expectations and all desire for love. Needless to say, this is neither genuine nor healthy, for it is a wrong extreme.

To work on this inner conflict is of great importance for all of you, so that you gain a new outlook and further clarification in your self-search. At first these words may give you perhaps only an occasional glimpse, a temporary flickering emotion in you, but they should be of help and open a door toward knowing yourself better, toward evaluating your life with a more realistic and more mature outlook.

Now, are there any questions in connection with this lecture?

QUESTION: *It is very difficult for me to understand that one continually chooses a love object who has exactly the same negative trends that one or the other parent had. Is it reality that this particular person has these trends? Or is it projection and response?*

ANSWER: It can be both and it can be either. In fact, most of the time it is a combination. Certain aspects are unconsciously looked for and found and they are actually similar. But the existing similarities are enhanced by the person who is doing the recreation. They are not only projected qualities that are not really there, but are latent in some degree without being manifested. These are encouraged and strongly brought to the fore by the attitude of the person with the unrecognized inner problem. He or she fosters something in the other person by provoking the reaction that is similar to the parent's. The provocation, which of course is entirely unconscious, is a very strong factor here.

The sum total of a human personality consists of many aspects. Out of these, a few may be actually similar to some traits in the recreator's parent. The most outstanding would be a similar kind of immaturity and incapacity to love. That alone is sufficient and potent enough in essence to reproduce the same situation.

The same person would not react to others as he or she reacts to you because it is you who constantly do the provoking, thereby reproducing conditions similar to your childhood for you to correct. Your fear, your self-punishment, your frustration, your anger, your hostility, your withdrawal from giving out love and affection, all these trends of the child in you constantly provoke the other person and enhance a response coming from that part which is weak and immature. However, a more mature person will affect others differently and will bring out that in them which is mature and whole, for there is no person who does not have some mature aspects.

QUESTION: *How can I make the distinction as to whether the other person provoked me or I the other person?*

ANSWER: It is not necessary to find who started it, for this is a chain reaction, a vicious circle. It is useful to start by finding your own provocation, perhaps in response to an open or hidden provocation of the other person. Thus you will realize that because you were provoked, you provoke the other person. And because you do so, the other again responds in kind. But as you examine your real reason, not the superficial one, the reason why you were hurt in the first place and therefore provoked, according to tonight's lecture you will no longer regard this hurt as disastrous. You will have a different reaction to the hurt, and, as a consequence, the hurt will diminish automatically. Therefore, you will no longer feel the need to provoke the other person. Also, as the need to reproduce the childhood situation decreases, you will become less withdrawn and you will hurt others less and less, so that they will not have to provoke you. If they do, you will now also understand that they reacted out of the same childish blind needs as you did. Now you can see how you ascribe different motivations to the other person's provocation than to your own, even if and when you actually realize that you initiated the provocation. As you gain a different view on your own hurt, understanding its real origin, you will gain the same detachment from the reaction of the other person. You will find exactly the same reactions in yourself and in the other. As long as the child's conflict remains unresolved in you, the difference seems enormous, but when you perceive reality, you begin to break the repetitive, vicious circle.

As you truly perceive such a mutual interplay, it will relieve the feeling of isolation and guilt you all are burdened with. You are constantly fluctuating between your guilt and your accusation of injustice you direct at those around you. The child in you feels itself entirely different from others, in a world of its own. It lives in such a damaging illusion. As you solve this conflict, your awareness of other people will increase. As yet, you are so unaware of the reality of other people. On the one hand you accuse them and are inordinately hurt by them because you do not understand yourself and therefore do not understand the other person. On the other hand, and at the same time, you refuse to become aware when you are hurt. This seems paradoxical, yet is not. As you experience for yourself the interactions set forth tonight, you will find this to be true. While sometimes you may exaggerate a hurt, at other times you do not allow yourself to know that it happened at all, because it may not fit the picture you have of the situation. It may spoil your self-constructed idea, or it may not correspond to your desire at the time. If the situation seems otherwise favorable and fits into your preconceived idea, you leave out all that jars you, allowing it to fester underneath and create unconscious hostility. This entire reaction inhibits your intuitive faculties, at least in this particular respect.

The constant provocation that goes on among human beings, while it is hidden from your awareness now, is a reality you will come to perceive very clearly. This will have a very liberating effect on you and your surroundings.

Go your way, my dearest ones, and may the blessings we bring to all of you envelop and penetrate your body, soul, and spirit, so that you open up your soul and become your real self, your own real self. Be blessed, my friends, be in peace, be in God.

4

The Real God and the God-Image

No one can avoid facing the question of God. Does such a Being actually exist? How and where can I find God, and what is the truth behind the answers I have given myself so far, or behind the confusion I feel? And what can the Pathwork Guide—an entity of higher consciousness, an entity with an angel's-eye view—teach us that we have not read or heard before?

∽

Greetings. I bring you blessings in the name of God. Blessed is this hour, my dearest friends.

That the existence of God is so often questioned and that Divine Presence is so rarely experienced within the human soul is the result of the distorted God-image most human beings harbor.

The False Concept of God

Children experience their first *conflict with authority* at an early age. They also learn that *God is the highest authority.* Therefore it is not surprising that children project their subjective experiences with authority onto their imaginings

46

about God. Hence a wrong conclusion is formed about God, which is unconsciously carried into adulthood.

Children experience all kinds of authority. When they are prohibited from doing what they enjoy most, they experience authority as hostile. When parental authority indulges a child, authority will be felt as benign. When there is a predominance of one kind of authority in childhood, the reaction to that will become the unconscious attitude toward God. In many instances, however, children experience a mixture of both. Then the combination of these two kinds of authority will form their image of God. In the measure that a child experiences fear and frustration, to that measure will fear and frustration unconsciously be felt toward God. God is then believed to be a punishing, severe, and often even an unfair and unjust force that one has to contend with. I know, my friends, that you do not think so consciously. But in the pathwork you are asked to find the emotional reactions that do not at all correspond to your conscious concepts on whatever subject. The less the unconscious concept coincides with the conscious one, the greater is the shock when one realizes the discrepancy.

Practically everything the child enjoys most is forbidden. Whatever gives most pleasure is prohibited, usually for the child's own welfare; this the child cannot understand. It happens that parents also do this out of their own ignorance and fear. Thus it is impressed on the child's mind that for everything most pleasurable in the world one is subject to punishment from God, the highest and sternest authority.

In addition, *you are bound to encounter human injustice* in the course of your life, in childhood as well as in adulthood. Particularly if these injustices are perpetrated by people who stand for authority and are therefore unconsciously associated with God, your unconscious belief in God's severe injustice is strengthened. Such experiences also intensify your fear of God.

All this forms an image that makes, if properly analyzed, a monster out of God. *This god, living in your unconscious mind, is really more of a satan.*

You yourself have to find out in your work on yourself

how much of this holds true for you personally. Is your soul impregnated with similar wrong concepts? If and when the realization of such an impression becomes conscious within a growing human being, it is often not understood that this concept of God is false. Then the person turns away from God altogether and wants no part of the monster discovered hovering in his or her mind. This, by the way, is often the true reason for someone's atheism. The turning away is just as erroneous as the opposite extreme, which consists of fearing a god who is severe, unjust, pious, self-righteous, and cruel. The person who unconsciously maintains the distorted God-image rightly fears this deity and resorts to cajoling for favors. Here you have a good example of two opposite extremes, both of which lack truth to an equal extent.

Now let us examine the case in which a child experiences benign authority to a greater degree than fear and frustration with a negative authority. Let us assume that overindulging and doting parents fulfill the child's every whim. They do not instill a sense of responsibility in the child so that he or she can get away with practically anything. The God-image resulting from such a condition is, at first and superficial sight, closer to a true concept of God—forgiving, "good," loving, indulgent. This causes the personality to unconsciously think he or she can get away with anything in the eyes of God, can cheat life, and avoid self-responsibility. To begin with, such a child will know much less fear. But since life cannot be cheated, this wrong attitude will produce conflicts, and therefore fear will be generated by a chain reaction of wrong thinking, feeling, and action. An inner confusion will arise, since life as it is in reality does not correspond to the indulgent, unconscious God-image and concept.

Many subdivisions and combinations of these two main categories can exist in the same soul, and the development achieved in former incarnations in this particular respect also influences the psyche. It is very important, therefore, my friends, to find out what your God-image is. This image is basic and determines all other attitudes, images, and patterns throughout your life. Do not be deceived by your conscious convictions. Rather try to examine and analyze your emotional reactions to authority, to your parents, to your fears and expectations. Out of these you will gradually discover what you *feel* about God rather than what you *think*. The whole scale between the two opposite poles of monster and doting parent is reflected in your God-image, from hopelessness and despair to self-indulgence, rejection of self-responsibility, and the expectation of a god who pampers you.

Dissolving the God-Image

Now the question of how to dissolve such an image arises. How do you dissolve any image, that is, any wrong conclusion? First, you have to become fully conscious of the wrong concept. The second step is to set your intellectual ideas straight. It is most important to understand that the proper formation of the intellectual concept should never be superimposed on the still-lingering, emotional false concept. This would only cause suppression. Realize that the hitherto suppressed, wrong concepts have to evolve clearly into consciousness. Formulate the right concept. Then these two should be compared. You need constantly to check how much you still deviate emotionally from the right intellectual concept.

Do this quietly, without inner haste or anger at yourself that your emotions do not follow your thinking as quickly as you would like. Give them time to grow. This is best accomplished by constant observation and comparison of the wrong and the right concept. Realize that your emotions need time to adjust, and also observe your resistance to change and growth. The lower self of the human personality is very shrewd. Be wise to it.

The injustices in the world are so often ascribed to God, my friends. If you are convinced of injustice, the best attitude is to examine your own life and find in it how you have contributed to and even caused happenings that seemed entirely unjust. The better you understand the magnetic force of images and the powerful strength of all psychological and unconscious currents, the better will you understand and experience the truth of these teachings, and the more deeply will you be convinced that *there is no injustice*. Find the *cause and effect* of your inner and outer actions.

God Is Not Unjust

If you make half the effort you usually make when finding others' faults to find your own, you will *see the connection with your own law of cause and effect and this alone will set you free*, will show you that there is no injustice. This alone will show you that it is not God, nor the fates, nor any unjust world order wherein you have to suffer the consequences of other people's shortcomings, but your ignorance, your fear, your pride, your egotism that directly or indirectly caused that which seemed, so far, to come your way without your attracting it. Find that hidden link and you will come to see truth. You will realize that *you are not a prey to circumstances* or other people's imperfections, but really the creator of your life. Emotions are very powerful creative forces, because your unconscious affects the unconscious of the other person. This truth is perhaps most relevant to the discovery of how you call forth happenings in your life, good or bad, favorable or unfavorable.

Once you experience this, you can dissolve your God-image, whether you fear God because you believe that you live in a world of injustice and are afraid of being the prey of circumstances over which you have no control, or whether you reject self-responsibility and expect an indulgent, pampering God to lead your life for you, make decisions for you, take self-inflicted hardships from you. The realization of how you cause the effects of your life will dissolve either God-image. This is one of the main breaking-points.

The True Concept of God

God *is*. God's laws are made once and for all and work automatically, so to speak. Think of God as being, among so many other things, *life* and *life force*. Think of God as of an *electric current, endowed with supreme intelligence.* This "electric current" is there, in you, around you, outside of yourself. It is up to you how you use it. You can use electricity for constructive purposes, even for healing, or you can use it to kill. That does not make the electric current good or bad. You make it good or bad. This power current is an important aspect of God and is the one that touches you most.

This concept may raise the question whether God is personal or impersonal, directing intelligence or law and principle. Human beings, since they experience life with a dualistic consciousness, tend to believe that either the one or the other is true. Yet God is both. But God's personal aspect does not mean personality. God is not a person residing in a certain place, though it is possible to have a personal God-experience within the self. For *the only place God can be looked for and found is within,* not in any other place. God's existence can be deduced outside of the self from the beauty of Creation, from the manifestations of nature, from the wisdom collected by philosophers and scientists. But such observations become an experience of God only when God's presence is felt first within. The inner experience of God is the greatest of all experiences because it contains all desirable experiences.

This particular feeling experience might be called the *cosmic feeling.* The cosmic feeling is not a theoretical understanding or a feeling *about* the cosmos. It is a true physical, mental, emotional, and spiritual experience, which encompasses the entire person. I cannot describe this experience adequately within the limitations of human language.

The cosmic experience no longer splits off feeling from thinking. It is *feeling and thinking in one.* This is very hard to imagine when you have never had such an experience. But some of you may have occasionally had a glimpse of it. The oneness is total. It is an experience of bliss; the comprehension of life and its mysteries; all-encompassing love; a knowledge that all is well and there is nothing to fear.

In the state of cosmic feeling you experience the immediacy of the *presence of God within.* The immediacy of this incredibly powerful presence is at first shocking. The good feeling is shocking. It is as if literally an electric shock went through your entire system. Therefore the ego-personality has to grow sufficiently strong and healthy so that it can acclimatize itself to the high vibrations of the inner presence of God. This manifestation is then experienced as your eternal reality and state, as your true identity.

The moment you find yourself in this state you know in a most profound way that what you now discover you have always known, that you had only temporarily cut yourself off from the state of feeling and knowing, of experiencing and perceiving life *as it really is.*

This description is, of course, extremely limited, for words cannot convey the experience. What you can do at this very moment to gain an inkling of the reality is to pray to be able to perceive a taste of it. Open your inner faculties, your higher self, to an understanding on the deepest level, my friends.

The Eternal, Divine Laws

God's love is not only personal in God-manifest within the human soul, but also in the *divine laws,* in the *being* of the laws. The apparently impersonal love in the laws that *are*—understand what is implied in the words *"that are"*—shows clearly in the fact that they are made in such a way as to lead you ultimately into light and bliss, no matter how much you deviate from them. The more you deviate from them, the more you approach them by the misery that the deviation inflicts. This misery will cause you to turn around at one point or another. Some sooner, some later, but all must finally come to the point where they realize that they themselves determine their misery or bliss. This is the love in the law—this is the "Plan of Salvation." Deviation from the law is the very medicine to cure the pain caused by the deviation and therefore it brings you closer to the goal: union with God.

God lets you deviate from the universal laws if you so wish. You are made in God's likeness, meaning that you are completely free to choose. You are not forced to live in bliss and light, though you can if you wish. All this expresses the love of God.

When you have difficulty in understanding the justice of the universe and the self-responsibility in your own life, do not think of God as "He" or "She." Rather think of God as the Great Creative Power at your disposal. It is not God who is unjust; the injustice is caused by the wrong use of the powerful current at your disposal. If you start from this premise and meditate on it, and if from now on you seek to find where and how you have ignorantly abused the power current in you, God will answer you. This I can promise.

If you find the cause and effect in your life, you have no idea what this discovery will mean to you. The greater the resistance to it at first, the greater the victory. You have no inkling how free it will make you, how safe and secure. You will understand the marvel of the creation of these laws that let you, with the power current of life, do as you please in creating your own life. This will give you confidence and the deep, absolute knowledge that you have nothing to fear.

The universe is a whole of which humanity is an organic part. To experience God is to realize oneself as an integral part of this oneness. Yet in their present inner state of development, most human beings can only experience God under the dual aspects of spontaneously active consciousness and automatic law. In actuality these two aspects form an interacting unity.

The aspect of spontaneous consciousness is the active principle, which in human terms is called the masculine aspect. It is the life force which creates; it is potent energy. This life force permeates the entire creation and all creatures. It can be used by all conscious living beings.

The aspect of automatic law is the passive, receptive principle, the life substance or feminine aspect, which the creative principle molds, forms, and plays upon. These two aspects, together, are necessary to create anything. They are the conditions of creation and are present in every form of creation, whether it be a galaxy or a simple gadget.

When speaking of God, it is important to understand that all divine aspects are duplicated in the human being, who lives and whose being rests upon the same conditions, principles, and laws as those pertaining to Cosmic Intelligence. They are both the same in essence, differentiated only by degree. Self-realization, then, means activating the maximum potential of God in oneself.

God Is in You and Creates Through You

God, as deliberate, spontaneous, directing intelligence, does not act *for* you but *through* you, being *in* you. It is very important that you understand this subtle, but decisive, difference. When you have an erroneous approach to God in this respect, you vaguely expect God to act for you, and you resent the inevitable disappointments; hence you conclude that there is no Creator. If one could contact an outer deity, one could logically expect it to act for one. But waiting for responses outside the self means focusing into the wrong direction. When you contact God within the self, responses must come and, what is more, you will notice and understand them. Such manifestations of God's presence within the self demonstrate God's personal aspect. They demonstrate active, deliberate, directing intelligence, forever changing and fresh, adapted in infinite wisdom to any situation. They express the Spirit of God manifesting through the spirit of the human being.

When you discover yourself and, consequently, the role you play in creating your fate, you truly come into your own. You are no longer driven but are master of your life. No longer bound by forces you do not understand, you can deliberately use these powers in the most constructive way, express more of the best of you, expand to ever greater potentials, add more to life, and therefore derive more from it.

You must discover this power and the freedom to master your life by yourself. If life forced you into your true birthright in order to save you from suffering, you would never be a free creature. The very meaning of freedom implies that no force or constraint can be used, not even for good or desirable results. Not even the greatest of all discoveries on the road of your evolution would have any meaning if you were compelled to experience it. The choice to turn in the direction that will finally yield true freedom and power must be left to each individual. Self-discovery—first on the mundane, so-called psychological level—when followed through, must lead to the realization that you are master over the universe to the exact degree that you master yourself. This self-mastery depends on a thorough knowledge of yourself and on the depth and width of the concepts your mind is capable of embracing.

Since you *are* created in the image of God, *you, too, must create.* You constantly do so, whether you know it or not. You create your life, your fate, your experiences. Every thought, every reaction, every emotion, every response, every intent, every action, every opinion, every motivation is a creative process. When one is torn in contradictions and conflicts between mutually exclusive motivations, when one fluctuates between automatic blind reflexes and deliberate action, the result of all this is one's own creation. Ideas, intent, thoughts, will, feelings, attitudes as expressed by conscious beings are the greatest forces in the universe. This means that the power of spirit is superior to all other energies. If this power is understood and used according to its inherent law, it supersedes all other manifestations of power. No physical power can be as strong as the power of the spirit. Since the human being is spirit and intelligence, he or she is inherently capable of directing all automatic, blind law. It is through this capacity that God is truly experienced.

When you deliberately contact and request your higher self, which contains all divine aspects, for guidance and inspiration, and when you experience the result of this inner act, you will know that God is present within you. So, my dearest friends, find out what distorted image you have of God that stands in the way of your God-experience as the total, blissful cosmic feeling it is in reality. Make yourself open to it. May the words I am giving you bring light into your soul, into your life. Let them fill your heart. Let them be an instrument to liberate you from illusions. I bless each one of you, individually and as a whole. God's world is a wonderful world and there is only reason to rejoice on whatever plane you live,

whatever illusions or hardships you temporarily endure. Let
them be a medicine for you, and grow strong and happy with
whatever comes your way. Be blessed. Be in peace. Be in God!

5

Unity and Duality

We live on a plane of duality. All our experiences are filtered through a dualistic consciousness. The dualistic state is painful, because we are fluctuating between opposing alternatives; we perceive life as a series of events which we call good or bad. The most threatening of dualities is that between life and death. Yet we know that a higher consciousness exists on a unified plane and that to be in contact with it is blissful. We strive toward unification, but how can we attain it without denying parts of our present being?

This lecture explains our dualistic condition and shows how we can transform those parts in ourselves which prohibit unification.

❧

Greetings, my dearest friends. May this evening be a blessing and an enrichment for every one of you here and for all who read these words. May you open your minds and hearts so you can deeply understand yourselves. And even if you cannot understand my words immediately, some of them may take root in your psyche and come to fruition later. Full understanding of this lecture may reach you only as you work your way through the deep layers of your unconscious where what I say here will apply.

There are two basic ways to approach life and the self. Or, to put it differently, there are two fundamental possibilities for human consciousness: the dualistic and the unified plane. The majority of human beings live predominantly on the dualistic plane, where you perceive and experience everything in opposites: either/or; good or bad; right or wrong; life or death. In other words, practically everything you encounter, every human problem, is shaped by this dualism. The unified principle combines the opposites of dualism. By transcending dualism you will also transcend the pain it causes. Few human beings transcend the dualistic plane, so most people experience only an occasional taste of the limitless outlook, the wisdom and freedom of the unified plane.

On the unified plane of consciousness there are no opposites. There is no good *or* bad, no right *or* wrong, no life *or* death. There is only good, only right, only life. Yet it is not the kind of good, or right, or life that comprises only one pole of the dualistic opposites. It transcends them both and is completely different from either one. The good, the right, the life that exist on the unified plane of consciousness combine both dualistic poles, so no conflict exists. This is why living in a unified state, in absolute reality, creates bliss, unlimited freedom, fulfillment, and that unlimited realization of potentials which religion calls heaven. Heaven is usually thought to be a place in time and space. This, of course, is not so. Heaven is a state of consciousness that can be realized at any time by any entity, whether a human being in the flesh, or one who does not live in a material body.

Understanding Is the Way to the Unified Plane

The unified state of consciousness is attained through understanding or knowingness. Life on the dualistic plane is a continuous problem. You have to struggle with the arbitrary, illusory division of the unified principle, through which things become opposites that impose conflicts. This creation of irreconcilable opposites generates a tension within and therefore with the outside world.

Let us understand this particular struggle, and therefore the human predicament, a little better. *You already have, in your real self, a unified state of mind, regardless of how unconscious and ignorant you may be of it.* This real self embodies the unified principle. Now, even those who have never heard of such a thing have a deep longing and a mostly unconscious sense of a different state of mind and life experience than the one they know. They yearn for the freedom, blissfulness, and mastery of life that the unified state of consciousness affords.

This longing is misinterpreted by the personality, partly because it is an unconscious yearning for happiness and fulfillment. But let us understand precisely what is really meant by these words. They mean the unification of the dualistic opposites, so that there is no longer any tension, conflict, or fear. Consequently, the world becomes alive and the self is master, not in a tight, tense, hostile way, but in the sense that life can be exactly what the individual determines it to be. The freedom, mastery, and bliss of this liberation are sought after consciously and unconsciously.

The misinterpretation of this longing occurs partly because it is unconscious—only a vague feeling deep within the soul. But even when the theoretical knowledge of such a state exists, it is still misinterpreted for yet another reason. When freedom, mastery, unification, and the resulting bliss of the unified state of consciousness are pursued on the dualistic plane, a tremendous conflict must ensue because they are absolutely impossible to accomplish on that plane. You strive for the fulfillment of your deep longing to transcend and find, deep within yourself, a new state of consciousness where all is one. When you seek this on a plane where all is divided, you cannot ever find what you seek. You will despair and split yourself further apart in conflicts, for illusion creates duality.

This happens overwhelmingly among people who are ignorant of these possibilities, but it also happens among people who are more spiritually enlightened, yet are nevertheless ignorant both of the difference between these two planes and of how they can learn to transcend the dualistic plane in their practical daily existence.

When the vague longing for, or the precise theoretical knowledge of, the unified plane of consciousness is misread and therefore sought on the dualistic plane, here is what happens: You sense that there is only good, freedom, right, beauty, love, truth, life, without a threatening opposite, but when you apply this on the dualistic plane, you will immediately be plunged into the very conflict you seek to avoid. You then fight for one of the dualistic aspects and against the other. Such a fight makes transcendence impossible.

Let me demonstrate this in a familiar, everyday human problem, so that you can understand these words more concretely. Let us assume that you are quarreling with a friend. You are convinced, from where you sit, that you are right; therefore, immediately, the friend becomes wrong. With dualistic understanding issues can only be either/or. The outcome seems to matter more than the issue itself, for when the intensity of emotions is truly tested, it often has no relationship to the issue at stake. It would rather be commensurate with a life-or-death issue. Although you may think this irrational on a conscious level, on an unconscious level being wrong truly means being dead, for being wrong means being denied by the other. On the dualistic plane, your sense of identity is associated with the other person, not with your real self. *As long as you experience yourself only as the outer ego-self, you will depend on others*. Hence, a slight quarrel truly becomes a matter of life or death, which explains the intensity of emotions when it comes to proving your right and the other's wrong. Only when you have realized the center of your being, which embodies unification, does your life cease to depend on others.

On the dualistic plane each issue ends with either life or death. Life becomes terribly important in order to avoid death. Often people fear death so much that they run into it head on. Such individuals do not escape fear of death. Quite the contrary. Their constant struggle with life, which results from their fear and struggle against death, renders them so unhappy that they believe they don't fear death. This is an illusion as long as life is experienced on the dualistic plane, as long as one side is viewed as important and is fought for, and the other side is seen as a threat and is fought against. As long as you feel that you must win because your side is true, while the other's is false, you are deeply involved in the world of duality, and therefore in illusion, conflict, and confusion. The more you fight in this way, the greater the confusion becomes.

Human beings are habitually trained by upbringing, and everything they learn from their surroundings agrees that one must fight for one and against the other of any number of opposites. This applies not only to material issues but even more to concepts. Every truth can thus be divided into two opposites, one being adhered to as the "right" and the opposite aspect being declared the "wrong" idea. In reality, however, the two complement one another. On the unified plane, neither aspect is thinkable without the other. There the complements are not "enemies" or negations of each other; only on the dualistic plane of consciousness are they so opposed. There every conflict multiplies into intricate subdivisions of the primary dualistic split. Since all this is a product of illusion, the longer the conflict continues, the less it can be solved and the more hopelessly enmeshed you become in it.

Let us now return to our example and demonstrate how this is so. The more you prove your friend wrong, the more friction exists and the less you obtain what you thought you would by proving yourself right and your friend wrong. You believe that by proving yourself right and your friend wrong, your friend will finally accept and love you again and all will be well. When you do not succeed, you misinterpret that and try harder, for you think you have not sufficiently proven that you are right and the other is wrong. The rift widens, your anxiety increases, and the more weapons you use to win the fight, the deeper your difficulties, until you actually damage yourself and the other and act against your own best interest. You are then faced with a further conflict, which arises out of the first dualistic split. In order to avoid a total rift, with all its real and imagined threats—for real damage has begun to be wrought—you are now faced with the alternatives of having to give in, in order to appease your friend and avoid further damage to yourself, or to continue fighting. Since you are still convinced that there is a right versus a wrong, such appeasement robs you of self-respect and you fight against that. Whether you use this "solution" or not, you will be torn between fighting or submitting. Both create tension, anxiety, and inner and outer disadvantages.

Thus, a second duality develops out of the first. The first is: "Who is right and who is wrong? Only I can be right. Otherwise all is bad." The second is either giving in to a wrong that you cannot admit, for it is a total wrong, or continuing the fight. Admitting a wrong means death, in a sense. So you are faced with the alternatives of either admitting a wrong, which means death in the deep psyche, in order to avoid dreaded consequences and the possibility of a real risk, putting your life at a grave disadvantage, again death, in the deepest sense, or insisting on your total rightness. Any way you turn you find death, loss, annihilation. The harder you fight for and against, the less there is to fight for and the more all alternatives turn against you. The illusion that one side was good and the other was bad has brought you to the inevitable next step on this road of illusion, which is that all alternatives are bad. All dualistic struggle is fated to lead you into further traps, which are all products of illusion.

When the road to the unified principle is chosen, soon what at first appeared as one certain good and one obvious bad ceases to be so, and you inevitably encounter good and bad on both ends. When this road is pursued still further, no longer is there any bad, but only good. The road leads deep inside the real self, into truth that goes way beyond the fearful little ego's interests. When this truth is sought deep inside the self, one approaches the unified state of consciousness. Our example is a banal one and can be translated into many everyday issues, big or small. It can take shape as a small squabble between mates or as a conflict between countries at war. It exists in all difficulties humanity encounters, individually and collectively. As long as you find yourself in this illusory dualistic conflict, you will experience hopelessness, for there is no way out on the dualistic plane of thinking. As long as your very existence is identified with the ego-self and therefore with the dualistic approach to life, you cannot help but despair, no matter how much this despair is covered up or momentarily alleviated by occasional success with the desirable alternative of the two opposites. The helplessness and hopelessness, the wasted energy of the dualistic struggle, rob you of your birthright. *You can find your birthright only on the plane of unification.*

Since everything you learn from your education and environment is geared to dualistic standards, it is not surprising that you are totally attached and adapted to this state of consciousness. And even when you learn about the other possibility, you are frightened of it. You cannot believe in it and you cling to what you know. This creates a vicious circle, in that the dualistic rules and precepts, which condition you to this way of life, are themselves a result of your fear of giving up the egotistical state that alone seems to guarantee life. It appears that giving up this ego state means annihilation of your individuality, which, of course, is utterly erroneous. So, you have these dualistic rules because of your erroneous fears, and you cling to the false fears because of your indoctrination.

Before we discuss in greater detail why you cling to the painful dualistic state, despite the immediate accessibility of the unified plane of consciousness, I would like to say more about *how to realize unification within yourself.* The real self, the divine principle, the infinite intelligence, or whatever you wish to call that deep inner center existing in every human being, contains all wisdom and truth you can possibly envisage. The truth is so far-reaching and so directly accessible that no further conflict exists when this truth is allowed to take effect. The ifs and buts of the dualistic state cease to exist. The knowledge of this inborn intelligence far surpasses the ego intelligence. It is completely objective; it disregards the small, vain self-interest—and this is one of the reasons you fear and avoid contact with it. The truth that flows out of it equalizes the self with others. Far from being the annihilation that the ego fears, that truth opens up the storehouse of vibrant life force and energy that you usually use to only a minor degree and that you misuse in directing your attention and hopes to the dualistic plane, with its tightly held opinions, false ideas, vanity, pride, self-will, and fear. When this live center activates you, you begin your limitless unfoldment, a process whose accomplishments become possible precisely because the little ego no longer wants to misuse them in order to find life, as it did, on the dualistic plane.

The unified real self can always be contacted. Let us again return to our example in order to see how. The hardest act to perform, which, in reality, is the easiest act possible, is to ask, "What is the truth of the matter?" The moment you are more intent on the truth than on proving that you are right, you contact the divine principle of transcendent, unified truth. If the desire to be in truth is genuine, the inspiration must come forth. No matter how strongly circumstances seem to point in one direction, you must be willing to relinquish and to question whether what you see is all there is to the issue. This generous act of *integrity* opens the way to the real self.

It will be easier to follow through when you consider that it is not necessarily a question of either/or, but that there may be aspects of right in the other person's view and of wrong in yours, aspects that, so far, you have not seen because your attention was not even directed to this eventuality. This approach to a problem immediately opens the way to rise to the unified plane of existence and to be moved by the real self. It immediately releases an energy that is distinctly felt when this act is done with a deep and sincere commitment. It brings release from tension.

What you then find out is always totally different both from what you hoped for and feared on the dualistic plane. You find that you are not as right and innocent as you thought, nor as wrong as you feared. Neither is your opponent. You soon discover aspects of the matter you never saw before, although they were not necessarily concealed. You understand exactly how the quarrel came into existence in the first place, what led to it, what its history was long before its actual manifestation. With such discoveries you gain insight into the very nature of the relationship. You learn about yourself and the other, you increase your understanding of the laws of communication. The more vision you gain, the freer, stronger, and more secure you feel. This vision not only eliminates this particular conflict and shows the right way to straighten it out, but it also reveals important aspects of your general difficulties and makes their elimination easier through this understanding. The vibrant peace that comes from this extended understanding is of lasting value. It affects your self-realization and your daily life. What I described is a typical example of unified, intuitive understanding: of knowing the truth. After the initial apparent need for courage and the momentary resistance to seeing a wider truth than the egotistic one, your path becomes so much easier than the struggle that ensues on the either/or plane of the dualistic life.

Before you can bring yourself to the unified way of thinking and being, the tension will mount, for as long as you remain on the dualistic plane, you struggle against unification because you falsely believe that the moment you admit and see where you are wrong and the other is right, you submit and enslave yourself. You become nothing, worthless, pitiful—and from there it is only a step to annihilation in your fantasy life. Hence, you feel that leaving your dualistic plane is the greatest danger. The tension will mount as your conflicts escalate. But the moment you are willing to be in truth, the moment you are eager and prepared, not merely to see your way, your little truth, not to give in to the other's little truth in fear of the consequences if you do not, but when you wish to possess the *larger, more encompassing truth,* which transcends both of your little truths, a specific tension will be removed in your psyche. The way toward the manifestation of the real self will have been prepared.

Obstructions to Finding the Real Self

Let me recapitulate here: The two most significant obstructions to the real self are ignorance of its existence and the possibility of connecting with it; and a tight, cramped psychic state with tight, cramped soul movements. These two factors make contact impossible with the real self, and therefore with a unified state of existence. As long as you are on a dualistic plane, you must be in a constant soul cramp. When you fight against one dualistic aspect and press for the other, *observe your soul movements*. Superficially, you may lean on the apparent justification of the position you press for. You may say, "Am I not perfectly justified in combating this wrong in the world?" On the dualistic plane this may indeed be so. But with this limited outlook you ignore that this very wrong exists only because of your dualistic approach to the problem and your prevalent ignorance that there is another approach. The resulting tension blurs the view that other aspects exist which both unify what you deem right and what you deem wrong, regardless of what the wrong actually is.

This simple act of wanting the truth requires several conditions, the most important being the willingness to relinquish what one holds on to, whether this be a belief, a fear, or a cherished way of being. When I say relinquish, I merely mean questioning it and being willing to see that there is something else beyond this outlook. This brings us back to why you are terrified to relinquish the ego state, hence the dualistic, painful way of life. Why do you resist so much committing yourself to this deep inner center, which unifies all good and is instantly accessible? It is, however, beyond the personal, little considerations of the ego.

Your Ego Versus Your Divine Center

The dualistic plane is the plane of the ego. The unified plane is the world of the divine center, the larger self. The ego finds its whole existence on the plane in which it is at home.

To relinquish this plane means to give up the claims of the little ego. This does not mean annihilation, but to the ego it seems to mean just this. Actually, the ego is a particle, an isolated aspect of the master intelligence, the real, inner self. It is not different from it; there is simply less of the real self in it. Since it is separate and limited, it is less reliable than what it stems from. But this does not mean that the ego has to be annihilated. In fact, the ego will eventually integrate with the real self so that there is one self, which will be fuller, better equipped, wiser. It will have more and better assets than you can imagine.

But the separated ego thinks this development means annihilation. In its ignorant, limited way, the ego exists only as a separated being; hence, it pursues further separateness. Since the limited consciousness ignores the existence of the real self—even if it is accepted as a theory, its living reality will be doubted as long as personal misconceptions are not eliminated—it fears letting go and relaxing its tight hold, the very soul movement that leads to the real self. This is the constant struggle of the ego until it ceases fighting against an opposite through repeated recognitions of a wider truth in every small personal issue.

The real self cannot manifest as long as personal problems are not straightened out. But the process of doing this and the first inklings of self-realization often overlap; the one furthers the other. This way of looking at your basic human struggle may help you considerably. As long as you are totally identified with your ego, you will continue to cultivate more separation, and self-idealization must be the consequence. Self-glorification and idealization seem, from this point of view, the apparent salvation and guarantee to assuage your existential fears. The ego thinks, "If everyone around me considers me special, better than others, smart, beautiful, talented, happy, unhappy, or even bad"—or whatever specialty you have chosen for your idealized self-glorification—"then I will receive the necessary approval, love, admiration, agreement that I need in order to live." This argument means that somewhere deep down you believe that you can exist only through being noticed, affirmed, and confirmed by others. You feel that if you go by unnoticed, you cease to live. This may sound exaggerated, but it is not. It explains why your idealized self-image is so destructive. *You feel more confident when you make yourself noticed than when you make positive efforts.*

So your salvation seems to lie in others who would acknowledge your existence only if you are special. At the same time, the misinterpreted message from the real self wants you to master life, but you master it on the wrong plane and believe that you must vanquish every resistance that is in your way. Each personal *pseudo-solution* is a way you have to eliminate your obstructions on the way to specialness. Which pseudo-solution you have chosen depends on individual character traits, on circumstances and early influences. Whatever they are—and there are three basic ones: the *aggressive*, the *submissive*, and the *withdrawal solutions*—they are destined to triumph over others and establish your freedom and fulfillment.

Your existence seems to be guaranteed when you are totally loved, accepted, and served by others, and you hope to attain this by triumphing over them. You can now see that you are governed by a succession of wrong conclusions, which are all completely different in reality.

Of course, all your reactions and beliefs can be ascertained only when you have learned to admit them. You also need to question the meaning of a particular reaction and look behind the facade, beyond what it pretends to mean. Once you admit this, it is easy to verify that all these misconceptions govern you and rob you of the beauty of reality. You will further come to see—not as a theory, but as a reality—that your life does not depend on other people's affirmation of your existence; that you do not need to be special and separate from others; that this very claim traps you in loneliness and confusion; that others will give you love and acceptance only when you do not wish to be better than they are, or special or different from them. Also this love will come when your very life no longer depends on it.

When you have truly attained knowledge, your accomplishment, in whatever field this may be, cannot have the effect on others that it has when accomplishment serves to set you apart. In the one case your accomplishment will be a bridge to others, because it is not a weapon against them. In the other instance it will create antagonism because you wish to be accomplished in order to be better than others, which always means that others should be less. When you need to be better through your accomplishments, what you give to the world must turn against you because you offer it in a *spirit of war*. When you give of your accomplishments in order to enrich life and others, you and your life will be enhanced by it because what you offer is given in a *spirit of peace*. In the latter case, you become a part of life. In taking from life—and the live center within yourself—and in giving back to life as an integral part of it, you act according to the unified principle.

Whenever you believe that "in order to live I must be better than others, I must be separate," disappointment is inevitable. This belief cannot bring the desired result because it is based on illusion. The dualistic concept is "me versus the other." The more you fight others, the less they will comply with your demand to affirm your self and the more you will experience this as a danger equal to giving up the fight itself. So every way you turn seems to be blocked. You make yourself utterly dependent on others with your illusory concept that unless they approve of you, you are lost, while, at the same time, trying to overrun them and triumph. You will resent the former and feel guilty about the latter. Both create intense frustrations and anxiety; both yield no salvation whatever.

Notice the initial disinclination to question your assumptions concerning any problematic issue in your life. This is your very stumbling block, because your shying away from what appears so painful and frightening makes it impossible to uncover the fallacy of your hidden belief. When you look at your problems in as objective and detached a way as you can muster, expressing the wider outlook of the real self, as you turn your best intent and will to the matter that disturbs you with a genuine wish for impartiality, you will first notice a shrinking back from such a desire and a more or less overt or subtle way of covering up your desire for flight. Catch yourself in this act and courageously forge on, questioning yourself further and deeper. You will then come to see that, finally, the outer difficulty is a symbolic representation of your inner quarrel where you fight for life against death, for existence against annihilation. You will see what you evidently believe is required from others in order for you to exist.

The Transition from Dualistic Error to Unified Truth

When you have arrived at this level of your being, you will be able to question your precepts that lay the foundation for this. And this is the first step to make possible the transition from dualistic error to unified truth. You will further notice that relinquishing ideals and convictions also feels like annihilation, for being wrong means dying, and being right means living. The moment you go through this movement of opening up and have the courage to want the truth, a more complete truth than you can see at the moment in whatever issue, you will come to a new peace and a new intuitive knowledge about the way things are. Something in your hardened psychic substance will have loosened up and will further prepare the way for total self-realization.

Each time you loosen up, the climate in your psyche will be more auspicious for the final, total awakening to your inner center, which contains all life, all truth, all the unified goodness of creation. Every step in this direction abandons another misconception; and each misconception represents another burden. The giving up of what first seemed like protection from annihilation will now be disclosed as what it really is: the giving up of a burden, suffering, imprisonment. You then comprehend the preposterous fact that you are actually opposed to leaving the dualistic life, with all its hardship and hopelessness.

Perhaps you can now understand some of this, and it will help you in your personal path. When you apply this to your everyday life, you will see that the abstract-sounding words I use here are not something far away, but accessible for every one of you. You will see that these words are practical and concrete, if only you are willing to see yourself in relationship to life in a wider truth than you are as yet willing even to contemplate.

The message coming from the real self says, "Your birthright is perfect happiness, freedom, and mastery over life." When you fight for this birthright according to dualistic principles, you remove yourself further and further from self-realization, in which you could truly have mastery, freedom, and total fulfillment. You seek all this with false means. They are as varied as each individual's character.

See how you personally try to set up the false fight leading into more confusion and pain. In whatever way you try to win, you are dependent on others and on circumstances often way beyond your actual control and therefore doomed to failure. This futile struggle hardens your psychic material. The more brittle it becomes the less you are able to contact the center of your inner being where everything you could possibly need is found: vital well-being and productivity and inner peace, which are byproducts of finding the real self.

The only way you can enter the unitive state where you can truly achieve mastery is by letting go of the false need to win, to be separate, to be special, to be right, to have it your way. Discover the good in all situations, whether you deem them good or bad, right or wrong. Needless to say, this does not mean resignation, nor does it mean fearful giving in or weakness. It means going with the stream of life and coping with what is as yet beyond your immediate control, whether or not it is according to your liking. It means accepting where you are and what life is for you at this moment. It means being in harmony with your own inner rhythm. This procedure will open the channel to your Godself, so that finally total self-realization takes place. All your expressions in life will be motivated and lived through by the divine principle operating in you and expressing itself through your individuality, integrating your ego faculties with the universal self. Such integration enhances your individuality; it does not diminish it. It enhances every one of your pleasures; it takes nothing away from you whatever.

May every one of you comprehend that the truth is in you. Everything you need is in you. May you find that you actually do not have to struggle, as you constantly do. All you have to do is recognize the truth, wherever you stand now. All you have to do, at this time, is acknowledge that there may be more in you than you see; call upon this inner center, and allow yourself to be open to its intuitive messages to you. May you find this possible exactly where you need it most at this particular moment. *Your gauge is always what feels most uncomfortable, what you are most tempted to look away from.*

Be blessed, continue on your wonderful path, which will bring you to the realization that you already have what you need and are where you need to be. You merely look away because you are geared in the opposite direction. Be in peace. Be in God.

6

The Forces of Love, Eros, and Sex

Since the dualistic state expresses itself on the level of our bodies as the two sexes, we might just as well continue with the lecture on love, eros, and sex, a particular favorite. No one is exempt from the touch, or sometimes even the onslaught, of these forces. This lecture sheds light on the confusion that exists in all of us whenever we love or desire and helps to sort out the contradictory feelings. How to keep eros? That is the question!

ᴧ

Greetings in the Name of the Lord. I bring you blessings, my dearest friends. Blessed is this hour.

Tonight I would like to discuss three particular forces in the universe: the love force as it manifests between the sexes, the erotic force, and the sex force. These are three distinctly different principles or forces that manifest differently on every plane, from the highest to the lowest. Humanity has always confused these three principles. In fact, it is little known that three separate forces exist and what the differences between them are. There is so much confusion about this that it will be quite useful to clear them up.

The Spiritual Meaning of the Erotic Force

The erotic force is one of the most potent forces in existence and has tremendous momentum and impact. It is supposed to serve as the bridge between sex and love, yet it rarely does. In a spiritually highly developed person, the erotic force carries the entity from the erotic experience, which in itself is of short duration, into the permanent state of pure love. However, even the strong momentum of the erotic force carries the soul just so far and no farther. It is bound to dissolve if the personality does not learn to love by cultivating all the qualities and requirements necessary for true love. Only when love has been learned does the spark of the erotic force remain alive. By itself, without love, the erotic force burns itself out. This of course is the trouble with marriage. Since most people are incapable of pure love, they are also incapable of attaining ideal marriage.

Eros seems in many ways similar to love. It brings forth impulses a human being would not have otherwise: impulses of unselfishness and affection he or she might have been incapable of before. This is why eros is so very often confused with love. But eros is just as often confused with the sex instinct which, like eros, also manifests as a great urge.

Now, my friends, I would like to show you what the spiritual meaning and purpose of the erotic force is, particularly as far as humanity is concerned. Without eros, many people would never experience the great feeling and beauty that is contained in real love. They would never get the taste of it and the yearning for love would remain deeply submerged in their souls. Their fear of love would remain stronger than their desire.

Eros is the nearest thing to love the undeveloped spirit can experience. It lifts the soul out of sluggishness, out of mere contentment and vegetation. It causes the soul to surge, to go out of itself. When this force comes upon even the most undeveloped people they become able to surpass themselves. Even a criminal will temporarily feel, at least toward one person, a goodness he has never known. The utterly selfish person will, while this feeling lasts, have unselfish impulses. Lazy people will get out of their inertia. The routine-bound person will naturally and without effort get rid of static habits. The erotic force will lift a person out of separateness, be it only for a short time. Eros gives the soul a foretaste of unity and teaches the fearful psyche the longing for it. The more strongly one has experienced eros, the less contentment will the soul find in the pseudo-security of separateness. Even an otherwise thoroughly self-centered person may be able to make a sacrifice during the experience of eros. So you see, my friends, eros enables people to do things they are disinclined to do otherwise; things that are closely linked with love. It is easy to see why eros is so often confused with love.

The Difference Between Eros and Love

How then is eros different from love? Love is a permanent state in the soul; eros is not. Love can only exist if the foundation for it is prepared through development and purification. Love does not come and go at random; eros does. Eros hits with sudden force, often taking a person unawares and even finding him or her unwilling to go through the experience. Only if the soul is prepared to love and has built the foundation for it will eros be the bridge to the love that is manifest between a man and a woman.

Thus you can see how important the erotic force is. Without the erotic force hitting them and getting them out of their rut, many human beings would never be ready for a more conscious search for the breaking down of their own walls of separation. The erotic experience puts the seed into the soul and makes it long for unity, which is the great aim in the plan of salvation. As long as the soul is separate, loneliness and unhappiness must be its lot. The erotic experience enables the personality to long for union with at least one other being. In the heights of the spirit world, union exists among all beings—and thus with God. In the earth sphere, the erotic force is a propelling power regardless of whether or not its real meaning is understood. This is so even though it is often misused and en-joyed for its own sake, while it lasts. It is not utilized to cul-tivate love in the soul, so it peters out. Nevertheless, its effect will inevitably remain in the soul.

The Fear of Eros and the Fear of Love

Eros comes to people suddenly in certain stages of their lives, even to those who are afraid of the apparent risk of ad-venturing away from separateness. People who are afraid of their emotions and afraid of life as such will often do anything in their power to avoid—subconsciously and ignorantly—the great experience of unity. Although this fear exists in many hu-man beings, there are few indeed who have not experienced some opening in the soul where eros could touch them. For the fear-ridden soul that resists the experience, this is good medi-cine regardless of the fact that sorrow and loss may follow due to other psychological factors. However, there are also those who are overemotional, and although they may know other fears of life, they are not afraid of this particular experience. In fact, the beauty of it is a great temptation to them and therefore they hunt greedily for it. They look for one subject after another, emotionally too ignorant to understand the deep meaning of eros. They are unwilling to learn pure love, and simply use the erotic force for their pleasure and when it is worn out they hunt elsewhere. This is an abuse and cannot continue without ill effects. Such a personality will have to make amends for the abuse—even if it was done in ignorance. In the same vein, the too-fearful coward will have to make up for trying to cheat life by hiding from eros and thus withhold-ing from the soul a medicine, valuable if used properly. Most people in this category have a vulnerable point somewhere in their soul through which eros can enter. There are also a few who have built such a tight wall of fear and pride around their souls that they avoid this part of life-experience entirely and so shortchange their own development. This fear might exist be-cause in a former life they had an unhappy experience with eros, or perhaps because the soul has greedily abused the beauty of the erotic force without building it into love. In either case, the personality may have chosen to be more careful. If this decision is too rigid and stringent, the opposite extreme will follow. In the next incarnation circumstances will be chosen in such a way that a balance is established until the soul reaches a harmonious state wherein there are no more extremes. This balancing in future incarnations always applies to all aspects of the personality. In order to approach this harmony to some extent at least, the proper balance between reason, emotion, and will has to be achieved.

The erotic experience often mingles with the sexual urge, but it does not always have to be that way. These three forces—love, eros, and sex—often appear completely separately, while sometimes two mingle, such as *eros and sex*, or *eros and love* to the extent the soul is capable of love, or *sex and a semblance of love*. Only in the ideal case do all three forces mingle harmoniously.

The Sex Force

The sex force is the creative force on any level of existence. In the highest spheres, the same sex force creates spiritual life, spiritual ideas, and spiritual concepts and principles. On the lower planes, the pure and unspiritualized sex force creates life as it manifests in that particular sphere; it creates the outer shell or vehicle of the entity destined to live in that sphere.

The pure sex force is utterly selfish. *Sex without eros and without love* is referred to as animalistic. Pure sex as the reproductive force exists in all living creatures: animals, plants, and minerals. Eros begins with the stage of development where the soul is incarnated as a human being. And pure love is to be found in the higher spiritual realms. This does not mean that eros and sex no longer exist in beings of higher development, but rather that all three blend in harmoniously, are refined, and become less and less selfish. Nor do I mean that a human being should not try to achieve a harmonious blend of all three forces.

In rare cases, *eros alone, without sex and love,* exists for a limited time. This is usually referred to as platonic love. But sooner or later with the somewhat healthy person, eros and sex will mingle. The sex force, instead of being suppressed, is taken up by the erotic force and both flow in one current. The more the three forces remain separate, the unhealthier the personality is.

Another frequent combination, particularly in relationships of long standing, is the coexistence of genuine *love with sex, but without eros.* Although love cannot be perfect unless all three forces blend together, there is a certain amount of affection, companionship, fondness, mutual respect, and a sex relationship that is crudely sexual without the erotic spark, which evaporated some time ago. When eros is missing, the sexual relationship must eventually suffer. Now this is the problem with most marriages, my friends. There is hardly a human being who is not puzzled by the question of what to do in a relationship to maintain the spark that seems to evaporate the more habit and familiarity with one another set in. You may not have posed the question in terms of three distinct forces, yet you know and sense that something goes out of a marriage that was present at the beginning; that spark is actually eros. You find yourself in a vicious circle and think that marriage is a hopeless proposition. No, my friends, it is not, even if you cannot as yet attain the ideal.

The Ideal Partnership of Love

In the ideal partnership of love between two people, all three forces have to be represented. With love you do not seem to have much difficulty, for in most cases one would not marry if there did not exist at least the willingness to love. I will not discuss at this point the extreme cases where this is not so. I am focusing on a relationship where the choice is a mature one and yet the partners cannot get around the pitfall of becoming bound by time and habit, because *elusive eros has disappeared.* With sex it is very much the same. The sex force is present in most healthy human beings and may only begin to fade—particularly with women—when eros has left. Men may then seek eros elsewhere. For the sexual relationship must eventually suffer unless eros is maintained.

How can you keep eros? That is the big question, my dear ones. Eros can be maintained only if it is used as a bridge to true partnership in love in the highest sense. How is this done?

The Search for the Other Soul

Let us first look for the main element in the erotic force. When you analyze it, you will find that it is the adventure, the search for the knowledge of the other soul. This desire lives in every created spirit. The inherent life-force must finally bring the entity out of its separation. Eros strengthens the curiosity to know the other being. As long as there is something new to find in the other soul and as long as you reveal yourself, eros will live. The moment you believe you have found all there is to find, and have revealed all there is to reveal, eros will leave. It is as simple as that with eros. But *where your great error comes in is that you believe there is a limit to the revealing of any soul, yours or another's.* When a certain point of usually quite superficial revelation is reached, you are under the impression that this is all there is, and you settle down to a placid life without further searching.

Eros has carried you this far with its strong impact. But after this point, your will to further search the unlimited depths of the other person and voluntarily reveal and share your own inward search determines whether you have used *eros as a bridge* to love. This, in turn, is always determined by your will to learn how to love. Only in this way will you maintain the spark of eros in your love. Only in this way will you continue to find the other and let yourself be found. There is no limit, for the soul is endless and eternal: A whole lifetime would not suffice to know it. There can never be a point when you know the other soul entirely, nor when you are known entirely. The soul is alive, and nothing that is alive remains static. It has the capacity to reveal even deeper layers that already exist. The soul is also in constant change and movement as anything spiritual is by its very nature. Spirit means life and life means change. Since soul is spirit, the soul can never be known utterly. If people had the wisdom, they would realize that and make of marriage the marvelous journey of adventure it is supposed to be, instead of simply being carried as far as you are taken by the first momentum of eros. You should use this potent momentum of eros as the initial thrust it is, and then find through it the urge to go on further under your own steam. Then you will have brought eros into true love in marriage.

The Pitfalls of Marriage

Marriage is intended by God for human beings, and its divine purpose is not merely procreation. That is only one aspect. The spiritual idea of marriage is to enable the soul to reveal itself and to be constantly on the search for the other to discover forever new vistas of the other being. The more this happens, the happier the marriage will be, the more firmly and safely it will be rooted, and the less it will be in danger of an unhappy ending. Then it will fulfill its spiritual purpose.

In practice, however, marriage hardly ever works that way. You reach a certain state of familiarity and habit and you think you know the other. It does not even occur to you that the other does not know you by any means. He or she may know certain facets of your being, but that is all. This search for the other being, as well as for self-revelation, requires inner activity and alertness. But since people are often tempted into inner inactivity, while outer activity may be all the stronger as an overcompensation, they are being lured to sink into a state of restfulness, cherishing the delusion of already knowing each other fully. This is the pitfall. It is the beginning of the end at worst, or at best a compromise leaving you with a gnawing, unfulfilled longing. At this point the relationship turns static. It is no longer alive even though it may have some very pleasant features. Habit is a great temptress, pulling one toward sluggishness and inertia, so that one does not have to try and work or be alert any more.

Two people may arrange an apparently satisfactory relationship, and as the years go by they face two possibilities. The first is that either one or both partners become openly and consciously dissatisfied. For the soul needs to surge ahead, to find and to be found, so as to dissolve separateness, regardless of how much the other side of the personality fears union and is tempted by inertia. This dissatisfaction is either conscious—although in most instances the *real* reason for it is ignored—or it is unconscious. In either case, the dissatisfaction is stronger than the temptation of the comfort of inertia and sluggishness. Then the marriage will be disrupted and one or both partners will delude themselves into thinking that with a new partner it will be different, particularly after eros has perhaps struck again. As long as this principle is not understood, a person may go from one partnership to another, sustaining feelings only as long as eros is at work.

The second possibility is that the temptation of a semblance of peace is stronger. Then the partners may remain together and may certainly fulfill something together, but a great unfulfilled need will always lurk in their souls. Since men by nature embody more of the active and adventurous principle, they tend to be polygamous and are therefore more tempted by infidelity than women. Thus you can also understand what the underlying motive for men's inclination to be unfaithful is. Women tend much more to be passive because they carry more of the receptive principle and are therefore better prepared to compromise. This is why they tend to be monogamous. Of course, there are exceptions, in both sexes. Such infidelity is often as puzzling to the active partner as to the "victim." They do not understand themselves. The unfaithful one may suffer just as much as the one whose trust has been betrayed.

In the situation where *compromise* is chosen, both people stagnate, at least in one very important aspect of their soul development. They find refuge in the steady comfort of their relationship. They may even believe that they are happy in

it, and this may be true to some degree. The advantages of
friendship, companionship, mutual respect, and a pleasant
life together with a well-established routine outweigh the unrest of the soul, and the partners may have enough discipline
to remain faithful to one another. Yet an important element of
their relationship is missing: the revealing of soul to soul as
much as possible.

True Marriage

Only when two people do this can they be *purified to-*
gether and thus help each other. Two developed souls can fulfill one another by revealing themselves, by searching the
depths of each other's soul. Thus what is in each soul will
emerge into their conscious minds, and purification will take
place. Then the life-spark is maintained so that the relationship can never stagnate and degenerate into a dead end. For
you who are on this path and follow the various steps of these
teachings, it will be easier to overcome the pitfalls and dangers of the marital relationship and to repair damage that has
occurred unwittingly.

In this way, my dear friends, you not only maintain eros,
that vibrating life-force, but you also transform it into true
love. Only in a true partnership of love and eros can you discover in your partner new levels of being you have not hereto-
fore perceived. And you yourself will be purified also by
putting away your pride and revealing yourself as you really
are. Your relationship will always be new, regardless of how
well you think you know each other already. All masks must
fall, not only those on the surface, but even those deeper down
that you may not even have been aware of. Then your love will
remain alive. It will never be static; it will never stagnate. You
will never have to search elsewhere. There is so much to see
and discover in this land of the other soul you have chosen,
whom you continue to respect, but in whom you seem to miss
the life-spark that once brought you together. You will never
have to be afraid of losing the love of your beloved; this fear
will be justified only if you refrain from risking the journey of

self-revelation together. *This*, my friends, *is marriage in its true sense*, and this is the only way it can be the glory it is supposed to be.

Separateness

Each of you should think deeply about whether you are afraid to leave the four walls of your own separateness. Some of my friends are unaware that to stay separate is almost a conscious wish. With many of you it is this way: You desire marriage because one part of you yearns for it—and also because you do not want to be alone. Quite superficial and vain reasons may be added to explain the deep yearning within your soul. But aside from this yearning and aside from the superficial and selfish motives of your unfulfilled desire for partnership, there must also be an unwillingness to risk the journey and adventure of revealing yourself. An integral part of life remains to be fulfilled by you—if not in this life, then in future lives.

Should you find yourself alone, you may, with this knowledge and this truth, repair the damage that you have done to your own soul by harboring wrong concepts in your unconscious. You may discover your fear of the great adventurous journey with another, which will explain why you are alone. This understanding should prove helpful and may even enable your emotions to change sufficiently so that your outer life may change too. This depends on you. Whoever is unwilling to take the risk of this great adventure cannot succeed in the greatest venture humanity knows—marriage.

Choice of Partner

Only when you meet love, life, and the other being in such readiness will you be able to bestow the greatest gift on your beloved, namely your true self. And then you must inevitably receive the same gift from your beloved. But to do that, a certain emotional and *spiritual maturity* has to exist. If this maturity is present, you will intuitively choose the right partner, one who has, in essence, the same maturity and readiness to embark on this journey. The choice of a partner who is unwilling comes out of the hidden fear of undertaking the journey yourself. *You magnetically draw people and situations toward you that correspond to your subconscious desires and fears.* You know that.

Humanity, on the whole, is very far away from this ideal of the marriage of true selves, but that does not change the idea or the ideal. In the meantime you have to learn to make the best of it. And you who are fortunate enough to be on this path can learn much wherever you stand, be it only in understanding why you cannot realize the happiness that a part of your soul yearns for. To discover that is already a great deal and will enable you in this life or in future lives to get nearer to the realization of what you yearn for. Whatever your situation is, whether you have a partner or are alone, search your heart and it will furnish you the answer to your conflict. The answer must come from within yourself, and in all probability it will relate to your own fear, unwillingness, and ignorance of the facts. Search and you will know. Understand that God's purpose in the partnership of love is the *complete* mutual revelation of one soul to another—not just a partial revelation.

Physical revelation is easy for many. Emotionally you share to a certain degree—usually as far as eros carries you. But then you lock the door, and that is the moment when your troubles begin.

There are many who are not willing to reveal anything. They want to remain alone and aloof. They will not touch the experience of revealing themselves and of finding the soul of the other person. They avoid this in every way they can.

Eros as a Bridge

My dear ones, once again: Understand how important the erotic principle is in your sphere. It helps many who may be unwilling and unprepared for the love-experience. It is what you call "falling in love," or "romance." Through eros the personality gets a taste of what the ideal love could be.

As I said before, many use this feeling of happiness carelessly and greedily, never passing the threshold into true love. True love demands much more of people in a spiritual sense. If they do not meet this demand, they forfeit the goal for which their soul strives. This extreme of hunting for romance is as wrong as the other, where not even the potent force of eros can enter the tightly locked door. But in most cases, when the door is not too tightly bolted, eros does come to you at certain stages of your life. Whether you can then use eros as a bridge to love depends on you. It depends on your development, your willingness, your courage, your humility, and your ability to reveal yourself.

Are there any questions in connection with this subject, my dear friends?

QUESTION: *When you talk about the revelation of a soul to another, do you mean that, on a higher level, this is the way the soul reveals itself to God?*

ANSWER: It is the same thing. But before you can truly reveal yourself to God, you have to learn to reveal yourself to another beloved human being. And when you do that, you reveal yourself to God too. Many people want to start with revealing themselves to the personal God. But actually, deep in their hearts, such revelation to God is only a subterfuge because it is abstract and remote. No other human being can see or hear what they reveal. They are still alone. One does not have to do the one thing that seems so risky, requires so much humility, and thus threatens to be humiliating. By revealing yourself to another human being, you accomplish so much that cannot be accomplished by revelation to God who knows you anyway, and who really does not need your revelation.

When you find the other soul and meet it, you fulfill your destiny. When you find another soul, you also find another particle of God, and if you reveal your own soul, you reveal a particle of God and give something divine to another person. When eros comes to you, it will lift you up far enough so that you will sense and know what it is in you that longs for this experience and what is your true self, which is longing to reveal itself. Without eros, you are merely aware of the lazy outer layers.

Do not avoid eros when it wants to come to you. If you understand the spiritual idea behind it, you will use it wisely. God will then be able to lead you and enable you to make the best of helping another being and yourself on the way to true love, of which purification must be an integral part. Although your purification work through a deeply committed relationship manifests differently than it does in the work on this path, it will help you toward a purification of the same order.

QUESTION: *Is it possible for a soul to be so rich that it can reveal itself to more than one soul?*

ANSWER: My dear friend, do you say that facetiously?

QUESTION: *No, I do not. I am asking whether polygamy is within the scheme of spiritual law.*

ANSWER: No, it certainly is not. And when someone thinks it may be within the scheme of spiritual development, that is a subterfuge. The personality is looking for the right partner. Either the person is too immature to have found the right partner, or the right partner is there and the polygamous person is simply carried away by eros' momentum, never lifting this force up into the volitional love that demands overcoming and working in order to pass the threshold I mentioned before.

In cases like this, the one with an adventurous personality is looking and looking, always finding another part of a being, always revealing himself or herself only so far and no further, or perhaps each time revealing another facet of his or her personality. However, when it comes to the inner nucleus, the door is shut. Eros then departs and a new search is started. Each time it is a disappointment that can only be understood when you grasp these truths.

Raw sexual instinct also enters into the longing for this

great journey, but sexual satisfaction begins to suffer if the relationship is not kept on the level I show you here. It is, in fact, inevitably of short duration. There is no richness in revealing oneself to many. In such cases, one either reveals the same wares all over again to new partners, or, as I said before, one displays different facets of one's personality. The more partners you try to share yourself with, the less you give to each. That is inevitably so. It cannot be different.

QUESTION: *Certain people believe that they can cut out sex and eros and the desire for a partner and live completely for love of humanity. Do you think it is possible that a man or woman can swear off this part of life?*

ANSWER: It is possible, but it is certainly not healthy or honest. I might say that there is perhaps one person in ten million who may have such a task. That may be possible. It may be in the karma for a particular soul who is already developed this far, has gone through the true partnership experience, and comes for a specific mission. There may also be certain karmic debts that have to be paid off. In most cases—and here I can safely generalize—avoidance of partnership is unhealthy. It is an escape. The real reason is fear of love, fear of the life-experience, but the fearful renunciation is rationalized as a sacrifice. To anyone who would come to me with such a problem, I would say, "Examine yourself. Go below the surface layers of your conscious reasoning and explanations for your attitude in this respect. Try to find out whether you fear love and disappointment. Isn't it more comfortable to just live for yourself and have no difficulties? Isn't really this what you feel deep inside and what you want to cover up with other reasons? The great humanitarian work you want to do may be for a worthy cause indeed, but do you really think one excludes the other? Wouldn't it be much more likely that the great task you have taken upon yourself would be better fulfilled if you learned personal love too?"

If all these questions were truthfully answered, the person would be bound to see that he or she is escaping. Personal love and fulfillment is man's and woman's destiny in most cases, for so much can be learned in personal love that cannot be attained in any other way. And to form a durable and solid relationship in a marriage is the greatest victory a human being can achieve, for it is one of the most difficult things there is, as you can well see in your world. This life experience will bring the soul closer to God than lukewarm good deeds.

QUESTION: *I was going to ask a question in connection with my previous one: Celibacy is supposed to be a highly spiritualized form of development in certain religious sects. On the other hand, polygamy is also recognized in some religions—the Mormons, for instance. I understand what you said, but how do you justify these attitudes on the part of people who are supposed to look for unity with God?*

ANSWER: There is human error in every religion. In one religion it may be one kind of error, in other religions another. Here you simply have two extremes. When such dogmas or rules come into existence in the various religions, whether at one extreme or another, it is always a rationalization and subterfuge to which the individual soul constantly resorts. This is an attempt to explain away the countercurrents of the fearful or greedy soul with good motives.

There is a common belief that anything pertaining to sexuality is sinful. The sex instinct arises already in the infant. The more immature the creature, the more sexuality is separated from love, and therefore the more selfish it is. Anything without love is "sinful," if you want to use this word. Nothing that is coupled with love is wrong—or sinful.

In the growing child who is naturally immature, the sex drive will first manifest selfishly. Only if and when the whole personality grows and matures harmoniously will sex become integrated with love. Out of ignorance, humanity has long believed that sex as such is sinful. Therefore it was kept hidden and this part of the personality could not grow up. Nothing that remains in hiding can grow; you know that. Therefore, even in many grownups, sex remains childish and separate from love. And this, in turn, has led humanity to believe that sexuality is a sin and that the truly spiritual person must abstain from it. Thus one of those oft-mentioned vicious circles came into existence.

Because of the belief that sex was sinful, the instinct could not grow and meld with the love force. Consequently, sex in fact often is selfish and loveless, raw and animalistic. If people would realize—and they are beginning to do so increasingly—that the sex instinct is as natural and God-given as any other universal force and in itself not more sinful than any other existing force, they would break this vicious circle, and more human beings would let their sex drives mature and mingle with love—and with eros, for that matter.

How many people exist for whom sex is completely separate from love! They not only suffer from bad conscience when the sex urge manifests, but they also find themselves in the position of being unable to handle sexual feelings with the person they really love. Because of the distorted conditions and the vicious circle just described, humanity came to believe that you cannot find God when you respond to your sex urges. This is all wrong; you cannot kill off something that is alive. You can only hide it so that it will come out in other ways which may be much more harmful. Only in the very rarest cases does the sex force really become constructively sublimated and make this creative force manifest in other realms. Real sublimation can never occur when it is motivated by fear and used as an escape. Does that answer your question?

QUESTION: *Perfectly, thank you. How does friendship between two people fit into this picture?*

ANSWER: Friendship is brotherly love. Such friendship can also exist between man and woman. Eros may want to sneak in, but reason and will can still direct the way in which the feelings take their course. Discretion and a healthy balance between reason, emotion, and will are necessary to prevent the feelings from going into an improper channel.

QUESTION: *Is divorce against spiritual law?*

ANSWER: Not necessarily. We do not have fixed rules like that. There are cases when divorce is an easy way out, a mere escape. There are other cases when divorce is reasonable because the choice to marry was made in immaturity and both partners lack the desire to fulfill the responsibility of marriage in its true sense. If only one—or neither—is willing, divorce is better than staying together and making a farce out of marriage. Unless both are willing to take this journey together, it is better to break clean than to let one prevent the growth of the other. That, of course, happens. It is better to terminate a mistake than to remain indefinitely in it without finding an effective remedy.

To generalize that divorce is always wrong is just as incorrect as to say that it is always right. One should not, however, leave a marriage lightly. Even though it was a mistake and does not work, one should try to find the reasons and do one's very best to search out and perhaps get over the hurdles that are in the way, if both are in any way willing. One should certainly do one's best, even if the marriage is not the ideal experience that I discussed tonight. Few people are ready and mature enough for it. You can make yourself ready by trying to make the best of your past mistakes and learn from them.

My dearest friends, think carefully about what I have said. There is much food for thought in what I told you for each of you here, and for all those who will read my words. There is not a single person who cannot learn something from them.

I want to close this lecture with the assurance to all of you that we in the spirit world are deeply grateful to God for your good efforts, for your growth. It is our greatest joy and our greatest happiness. And so, my dear ones, receive the blessings of the Lord again; may your hearts be filled by this wonderful strength coming to you from the world of light and truth. Go in peace and in happiness, my dear ones, each one of you. Be in God!

7

The Spiritual Significance of Relationship

"Life is relationship," says the Guide. Of all relationships, that between man and woman is the greatest challenge and opportunity for spiritual growth and mutuality. "But how can I relate harmoniously with another person when I am still split within myself?" This is the question the Guide wants us to ask of ourselves. He teaches us to establish intimate relationship with our own true inner being and, through this newly acquired inner honesty, to handle the various problems that arise in our relationships in a truthful and constructive way.

∽

Greetings, my dearest, dearest friends. Blessings for every one of you. Blessed be your very life, your every breath, your thoughts and your feelings.

This lecture deals with relationships and their tremendous significance from the spiritual point of view—that of individual growth and unification. First, I would like to point out that on the human level of manifestation individual units of consciousness do exist, which sometimes harmonize, but very often conflict, with one another, creating friction and crisis. Yet beyond this level of manifestation there are no other fragmented units of consciousness. Above the human level there is only one consciousness, through which every single created entity is expressed differently. When one comes into one's own, one experiences this truth, without, however, losing a sense of individuality. This can be felt very distinctly when you deal with your own inner disharmonies, my friends. For there, too, exactly the same principle applies.

Unequal Development of Parts of Consciousness

In your present state, a part of your innermost being is developed and governs your thinking, feeling, willing, and acting. There are other parts, still in a lower state of development, that also govern and influence your thinking, feeling, willing, and acting. Thus you find yourself divided, and this always creates tension, pain, anxiety, as well as inner and outer difficulties. Some aspects of your personality are in truth; others, in error and distortion. The resulting confusion causes grave disturbances. What you usually do is push one side out of the way and identify with the other. Yet this denial of a part of you cannot bring unification. On the contrary, it widens the split. What must be done is to bring out the deviating, conflicting side and face it—face the entire ambivalence. Only then do you find the ultimate reality of your unified self. As you know, unification and peace emerge to the degree you recognize, accept, and understand the nature of the inner conflict.

Exactly the same law applies to the unity or dissension between outwardly separate and different entities. They, too, are one, beyond the level of appearance. The dissension is caused not by actual differences among units of consciousness, but, just as in the individual, by differences in the development of the manifesting universal consciousness.

Even though the principle of unification is exactly the same within and among individuals, it cannot be applied to another human being unless it has first been applied to one's inner self. If the divergent parts of your self are not approached according to this truth, and your ambivalence is not faced, accepted, and understood, the process of unification cannot be put into practice with another person. This is a very important fact, which explains the great emphasis of this pathwork on *first approaching the self*. Only then can relationship be cultivated in a meaningful and effective way.

Elements of Dissension and Unification

Relationship represents the greatest challenge for the individual, for it is only in relationship to others that unresolved problems still existing within the individual psyche are affected and activated. Many individuals withdraw from interaction with others, so they can maintain the illusion that the problems arise from the other person because one feels disturbance only in his or her presence, and not when by oneself.

However, the less contact is cultivated, the more acute the longing for contact becomes. This, then, is a different kind of pain—*the pain of loneliness and frustration*. But contact makes it difficult to maintain for any length of time the illusion that the inner self is faultless and harmonious. It requires mental aberration to claim for too long that one's problems in relationship are caused only by others and not by oneself. This is why relationships are simultaneously a fulfillment, a challenge, and a gauge to one's inner state. *The friction that arises out of relating with others can be a sharp instrument of purification and self-recognition* if one is inclined to use it.

By withdrawing from this challenge and sacrificing the fulfillment of intimate contact, many inner problems are never called into play. The illusion of inner peace and unity that comes from avoidance of relating has even led to concepts that spiritual growth is being furthered by isolation. Nothing could be farther from the truth. This statement must not be confused with the notion that intervals of seclusion are necessary for inner concentration and self-confrontation. But these periods should always alternate with contact—and the more intimate such contact is, the more it expresses spiritual maturity.

Contact and lack of contact with others can be observed in various stages. There are many degrees of contact between the crass extremes of total outer and inner isolation, at one end, and the deepest, most intimate relatedness at the other. There are those who have obtained a certain superficial ability to relate but who still withdraw from a more meaningful, open, unmasked mutual revealing. I might say that the average present-day human being fluctuates somewhere between the two extremes.

Fulfillment as a Yardstick for Personal Development

It is also possible to measure one's personal sense of fulfillment by the depth of relatedness and intimate contact, by the strength of the feelings one permits oneself to experience, and by the willingness to give and receive. Frustration indicates an absence of contact, which, in turn, is a precise indicator that the self withdraws from the challenge of relationship, thereby sacrificing personal fulfillment, pleasure, love, and joy. When you want to share only on the basis of receiving according to your own terms, and you are in fact secretly unwilling to share, your longings must remain unfulfilled. People would be well advised to consider their unfulfilled longings from this point of view, rather than indulging in the usual assumption that one is unlucky and unfairly put upon by life.

One's contentment and fulfillment in relationship is a much neglected yardstick for one's own development. Relationship with others is a mirror of one's own state and thus a direct help to one's self-purification. Conversely, only by thorough self-honesty and self-facing can relationships be sustained, can feelings expand, and contact blossom in long-term relationships. So you can see, my friends, that relationships represent a tremendously important aspect of human growth.

The power and significance of relationship often pose severe problems for those who are still in the throes of their own inner conflicts. The unfulfilled longing becomes unbearably painful when isolation is chosen due to the difficulty of contact. This can be resolved only when you seriously settle down to *seek the cause for this conflict within your self*, without using the defense of annihilating guilt and self-blame, which of course eliminates any possibility of really getting at the core of the conflict. This search, together with the inner willingness to change, must be cultivated in order to escape the painful dilemma in which both available alternatives—isolation and contact—are unbearable.

It is important to remember that withdrawal can be very subtle and may be outwardly unnoticeable, manifesting only in a certain guardedness and distorted self-protection. Outer good fellowship does not necessarily imply a capacity and willingness for inner closeness. For many, closeness is too taxing. On the surface this seems related to how difficult others are, but actually the difficulty lies in the self, regardless of how imperfect others may also be.

Who Is Responsible for the Relationship?

When people whose spiritual development is on different levels are involved with one another, *it is always the more highly developed person who is responsible for the relationship*. Specifically, that person is responsible for searching the depths of the interaction which create any friction and disharmony between the parties.

The less developed person is not as capable of such a search, being still in a state of blaming the other and depending on the other's doing "right" in order to avoid unpleasantness or frustration. Also, the less developed person is always caught up in *the fundamental error of duality*. From this perspective any friction is seen in terms of "only one of us is right." When caught up in dualistic thinking, such a person, when noticing a defect in the other party, will automatically assume innocence, although in reality his or her own negative involvement may be infinitely more weighty than the other person's.

The spiritually more developed person is capable of realistic, *non-dualistic perception*. That person may see that one of the two may have a deeper problem, but that does not eliminate the importance of the possibly much lesser problem of the other one. The more developed one will always be willing and able to search for his or her own involvement whenever he or she is negatively affected, no matter how blatantly at fault the other may be. A person of spiritual and emotional immaturity and crudeness will always put the bulk of the blame on the other. All this applies to any kind of relationship: mates, parents and children, friendships, or business contacts.

The tendency to make yourself emotionally dependent on others, the overcoming of which is such an important aspect of the growth process, largely comes from wanting to absolve yourself from blame or extract yourself from difficulty when establishing and maintaining a relationship. It seems so much easier to shift most of this burden to others. But what a price to pay! Doing this renders you helpless indeed and brings about isolation, or unending pain and friction with others. It is only when you begin truly to assume self-responsibility by looking at your own problem in the relationship, and by a willingness to change, that freedom is established and relationships become fruitful and joyous.

If the more highly developed person refuses to undertake the appropriate spiritual duty to assume responsibility for the relationship and look for the core of dissension within, he or she will never really understand the mutual interaction, how one problem affects the other. The relationship must then deteriorate, leaving both parties confused and less able to cope with the self and others. On the other hand, if the spiritually developed person accepts this responsibility, he or she will also help the other in a subtle way. If he or she can desist from the temptation to constantly belabor the obvious defects of the other and look within, he or she will raise his or her own development considerably and spread peace and joy. The poison of friction will soon be eliminated. It will also become possible to find other partners for a truly mutual growth process.

When two equals relate, both carry the full responsibility for the relationship. This is indeed a beautiful venture, a deeply satisfying state of mutuality. The slightest flaw in a mood will be recognized for its inner meaning and thus the growth process is kept up. Both will recognize their co-creation of this momentary flaw—whether it be an actual friction or a momentary deadness of feelings. The inner reality of the interaction will become increasingly more significant. This will largely prevent injury to the relationship.

Let me emphasize here that when I speak of being responsible for the less developed person, I do not mean that another human being can ever carry the burden for the actual difficulties of others. This can never be. What I mean is that difficulties of interaction in a relationship are usually not explored in depth by the individual whose spiritual development is more primitive. He or she will render others responsible for his or her unhappiness and disharmony in a given interaction and is not able, or willing, to see the whole issue. Thus that person is not in a position to eliminate the disharmony. Only those who assume responsibility for finding the inner disturbance and mutual effect can do so. Hence the spiritually more primitive person always depends on the spiritually more evolved one.

A relationship between individuals in which the destructiveness of the less developed one makes growth, harmony, and good feelings impossible, or in which the contact is overwhelmingly negative, should be severed. As a rule, the more highly developed person should assume the initiative. If he or she does not, this indicates some unrecognized weakness and fear that needs to be faced. If a relationship is dissolved on this ground, namely, that it is more destructive and pain-producing than constructive and harmonious, it should be done when the inner problems and mutual interactions are fully recognized by the one who takes the initiative to dissolve an old tie. This will prevent him or her from forming a new relationship with similar underlying currents and interactions. It also means that the decision to sever the connection has been made because of growth, rather than as a result of spite, fear, or escape.

Destructive Interactions

To explore the underlying interaction and the various effects of a relationship in which both people's difficulties are laid bare and accepted is by no means easy. But nothing can be more beautiful and rewarding. Anyone who comes into the state of enlightenment where this is possible will no longer fear any kind of interaction. *Difficulties and fears arise to the exact degree that you still project on others your own problems* in relating and still render others responsible for anything that goes against your liking. This can take many subtle forms. You may constantly concentrate on the faults of others, because at first glance such concentration appears justified to you. You may subtly overemphasize one side of an interaction, or exclude another. Such distortions indicate projection and denial of self-responsibility for the difficulties in relating. This denial fosters *dependency on the perfection of the other party*, which in turn creates fear and hostility for feeling let down when the other does not measure up to the perfect standard.

My dear friends, no matter what wrong the other person does, if you are disturbed, there must be something in you that you overlook. When I say disturbed, I mean this in a particular sense. I do not speak of clear-cut anger that expresses itself guiltlessly and does not leave a trace of inner confusion and pain. I mean the kind of disturbance that comes out of conflict and breeds further conflict. A favorite tendency among people is to say, "You are doing it to me." The game of making others guilty is so pervasive that you hardly even notice it. One human being blames the other, one country blames the other, one group blames the other. This is a constant process at humanity's present level of development. It is indeed one of the most harmful and illusory processes imaginable.

People derive pleasure from doing this, although the pain that ensues and the insoluble conflicts that follow are infinitely disproportionate to the puny, momentary pleasure.

Those who play this game truly harm themselves and others, and I strongly recommend that you begin to be aware of your blind involvement in this guilt-shifting game.

But how about the "victim"? How is that person to cope? As a victim, your first problem is that *you are not even aware of what is happening*. Most of the time, the victimization happens in a subtle, emotional, and unarticulated fashion. The silent, covert blame is being launched without a spoken word. It is expressed indirectly in many ways. Now, obviously, the first necessity is concise, articulate awareness, for otherwise you will unconsciously respond in equally destructive, falsely self-defensive ways. Then neither person really knows the intricate levels of action, reaction, and interaction until the threads become so enmeshed that it seems impossible to disentangle them. Many a relationship has faltered due to such unconscious interaction.

The *launching of blame spreads poison*, fear, and at least as much guilt as one tries to project. The recipients of this blame and guilt may react in many different ways, according to their own problems and unresolved conflicts. As long as the reaction is blind and the projection of guilt unconscious, the counter-reaction must also be neurotic and destructive. Only conscious perception can prohibit this. Only then will you be able to refuse a burden that is being placed on you. Only then can you articulate and pinpoint it.

How to Reach for Fulfillment and Pleasure

In a relationship that is about to blossom, one must be on the lookout for this pitfall, which is all the more difficult to detect because guilt projection is so widespread. Also, the recipients should look for it in themselves as well as in the other. And I do not mean here a straightforward confrontation about something the other person did wrong. I mean the subtle blame for personal unhappiness. This is what must be challenged.

The only way you can avoid becoming a victim of blame and guilt projection is to avoid doing it yourself. To the degree you indulge yourself in this subtly negative attitude—and you may do it in a different way than the one who does it to you— you will be unaware of it being done to you and will therefore become victimized by it. The mere awareness will make all the difference—whether or not you verbally express your perception and confront the other person. Only to the degree that you undefensively explore and accept your own problematic reactions and distortions, negativities and destructiveness, can you defuse someone else's guilt projection. Only then will you not be drawn into a maze of falseness and confusion in which uncertainty, defensiveness, and weakness may make you either retreat or become overaggressive. Only then will you no longer confuse self-assertion with hostility, or flexible compromise with unhealthy submission.

These are the aspects that determine the ability to cope with relationships. The more profoundly understood and lived these new attitudes are, the more intimate, fulfilling, and beautiful human interaction will become.

How can you assert your rights and reach into the universe for fulfillment and pleasure? How can you love without fear unless you approach relating to others the way I have outlined above? Unless by learning to do this you purify yourself, there must always be a threat when it comes to intimacy: that one or both will resort to using the whip of loading guilt upon the other. Loving, sharing, and profound and satisfying closeness to others could be a purely positive power without any threat if these snares were looked at, discovered, and dissolved. It is of utmost importance that you look for them in yourselves, my friends.

The most challenging, beautiful, spiritually important, and growth-producing kind of relationship is the one between man and woman. The power that brings two people together in love and attraction and the pleasure involved are a small aspect of cosmic reality. It is as though each created entity knew unconsciously about the bliss of this state and sought to realize it in the most potent way open to humanity: in love and sexuality between man and woman. The power that draws them together is the purest spiritual energy, leading to an inkling of the purest spiritual state.

However, when a man and a woman stay together in a more enduring and committed relationship, maintaining and even increasing bliss depends entirely on how the two relate to each other. Are they aware of the direct relationship between enduring pleasure and inner growth? Do they use the inevitable difficulties in the relationship as yardsticks for their own inner difficulties? Do they communicate in the deepest, most truthful, self-revealing way, sharing their inner problems, helping each other? The answers to these questions will determine whether the relationship falters, dissolves, stagnates—or blossoms.

When you look at the world around you, you will undoubtedly see that very few human beings grow and reveal themselves in such an open way. Equally few realize that *growing together and through each other* determines the solidity of feelings, of pleasure, of enduring love and respect. It is therefore not surprising that long-lasting relationships are almost invariably more or less dead in feelings.

Difficulties that arise in a relationship are always signals for something unattended to. They are a loud message for those who can hear it. The sooner it is heeded, the more spiritual energy will be released, so that the state of bliss can expand along with the inner being of both partners. There is a mechanism in a relationship between a man and a woman that can be likened to a very finely calibrated instrument that shows the finest and most subtle aspects of the relationship and the individual state of the two people involved. This is not sufficiently recognized by even the most aware and sophisticated people who are otherwise familiar with spiritual and psychological truth. Every day and every hour one's inner state and feelings are a testimony to one's state of growth. To the degree they are heeded, the interaction, the feelings, the freedom of flow within and toward each other will blossom.

The perfectly mature and spiritually valid relationship must always be deeply connected with personal growth. The moment a relationship is experienced as irrelevant to inner growth, left on its own, as it were, it will falter. Only when both grow to their ultimate, inherent potential can the relationship become more and more dynamic and alive. This work has to be done individually and mutually. When relationship is approached in that way, it will be built on rock, not sand. No fear will ever find room under such circumstances. Feelings will expand, and security about the self and each other will grow. At any given moment, each partner will serve as a mirror to the inner state of the other and therefore to the relationship.

Whenever there is friction or deadness, it is an indication that something must be stuck. Some interaction between the two people remains unclear and it needs to be looked at. If it is understood and brought out into the open, growth will proceed at maximum speed, and, in the dimension of feeling, happiness, bliss, profound experience, and ecstasy will become forever deeper and more beautiful, and life will acquire more meaning.

Conversely, fear of intimacy implies rigidity and the denial of one's own share in the relationship's difficulties. Anyone who ignores these principles, or who pays only lip service to them, is emotionally not ready to assume the responsibility for his or her inner suffering—either within a relationship or in its absence.

So you see, my friends, it is of the greatest importance to recognize that *bliss and beauty, which are eternal spiritual realities, are available to all* those who seek the key to the problems of human interaction, as well as to loneliness, within their own hearts. True growth is as much a spiritual reality as are *profound fulfillment,* vibrant aliveness, and blissful, *joyous relating.* When you are inwardly ready to relate to another human being in such a fashion, *you will find the appropriate partner* with whom this manner of sharing is possible. It will no longer frighten you, will no longer beset you with conscious or unconscious fears when you use this all-important key. You cannot ever feel helpless or victimized when the significant transition has taken place in your life and you no longer render others responsible for what you experience or fail to experience. Thus growth and fulfilled, beautiful living become one and the same.

May you all carry with you this new material and an inner energy awakened by your goodwill. May these words be the beginning of a new inner modality to meet life, to finally decide, "I want to risk my good feelings. I want to seek the cause in me, rather than in the other person, so that I become free to love." This kind of meditation will indeed bear fruit. If you carry away a germ, a particle, of this lecture, it has truly been fruitful. Be blessed, all of you, my dearest friends, so that you become the gods that you potentially are.

8

Emotional Growth and Its Function

"If I didn't feel anything, I wouldn't suffer." Most people are trying very hard not to feel in the mistaken belief that then they could avoid being unhappy. Haven't you had such a thought? We think it is only a thought, but this wish has its consequence: the numbing of our feeling capacity. Yet, the repression of feelings does not alleviate suffering; on the contrary, it increases the pain. Feelings need room to grow, just as our minds and bodies do, so that we achieve a higher emotional state in which we can dare to love.

∽

Greetings, my dearest friends. God bless each one of you, blessed is this hour.

In order to know yourself on a deeper level, it becomes increasingly necessary to allow all emotions to reach surface awareness, so as to understand these emotions and to enable them to mature. Most of you have a great resistance to letting this happen. You are unaware of the obstructions you put in the way of your own growth. Hence it is necessary that I discuss the mechanism of your resistance.

Let us first be clear about the unity of the human personality. Human beings who function harmoniously have developed the physical, mental, and emotional sides of their nature. These three spheres are supposed to function harmoniously with one another, each helping the other, rather than one faculty subduing another. If one function is under-developed, it causes a disharmony in the human structure, and also cripples the entire personality.

Now let us understand what causes human beings to particularly neglect, repress, and cripple the growth of their emotional nature. This neglect is universal. Most human beings look mainly after the physical self. They do more or less what is necessary to make it grow and remain healthy. A good portion of humanity cultivates the mental side. In order to do so you learn, you use your brain, your thinking capacity; you absorb, you train your memory and your logical reasoning. All this furthers mental growth.

But why is the emotional nature generally neglected? There are good reasons for that, my friends. To gain more clarity, let us first understand the function of the emotional nature in human beings. It includes, first of all, *the capacity to feel*. The capacity to experience feeling is synonymous with the capacity to give and receive happiness. To the degree you shy away from any kind of emotional experience, to that extent you also close the door to the experience of happiness. Moreover, the emotional side of your nature, when functioning, possesses creative ability. *To the degree you close yourself off from emotional experience, to that very degree the full potential of your creative ability is hindered in manifesting itself.* Contrary to what many of you may believe, the unfolding of creative ability is not a mere mental process. In fact, the intellect has much less to do with it than may appear at first glance, in spite of the fact that technical skill also becomes a necessity in order to give the creative outflow full expression. Creative unfoldment is an intuitive process. Needless to say, intuition can function only to the degree that your emotional life is strong, healthy, and mature.

Therefore, your intuitive powers will be hindered if you have neglected emotional growth and discouraged yourself from experiencing the world of feeling. Why is there such a predominant emphasis in your world today on physical and mental growth and a conspicuous neglect of emotional growth? Several general explanations could be advanced, but I would like to go immediately to the root of the problem.

Numbing of Feelings to Avoid Unhappiness

In the world of feeling you experience the good and the bad, the happy and the unhappy, pleasure and pain. Contrary to just registering such impressions mentally, emotional experience really touches you. Since your struggle is primarily for happiness, and since immature emotions lead to unhappiness, your secondary aim becomes the avoidance of unhappiness. Unhappy circumstances exist in every child's life; pain and disappointment are common. This creates the early, mostly unconscious, conclusion: *"If I do not feel, then I will not be unhappy."* In other words, instead of taking the courageous and appropriate step of living through negative, immature emotions in order to afford them the opportunity to grow and thus become mature and constructive, the childish emotions are suppressed, put out of awareness and buried, so that they remain inadequate and destructive, even though the person is unaware of their existence.

Although it may be true that you can anesthetize your capacity for emotional experience, and therefore cannot feel immediate pain, it is also true that you dull your capacity for happiness and pleasure while not really avoiding the dreaded unhappiness in the long run. The unhappiness you seem to avoid will come to you in a different and much more painful, but indirect, way. The bitter hurt of isolation, of loneliness, of the gnawing feeling of having passed through life without experiencing its heights and depths, without developing yourself to the most and best you can be, is the result of such a wrong solution.

Using such evasive tactics you do not experience life at its fullest. By withdrawing from pain, you withdraw from happiness and, most of all, you withdraw from experience. At one time or another—and you may never remember the conscious declaration of intent—you withdrew from living, loving, and experiencing—from everything that makes life rich and rewarding. The result is that your intuitive powers are dulled together with your creative faculties. You only function to a fraction of your potential. The damage you have inflicted upon yourself with this pseudo-solution, and go on inflicting upon yourself as long as you adhere to it, is one that eludes your comprehension and evaluation at the present time.

Isolation

Since this was your defense against unhappiness to begin with, it is understandable that unconsciously you fight tooth and nail against giving up what seems to you a vital protection. You do not realize that not only do you miss out on life's richness, life's rewards, your own full potential, but you do not really avoid unhappiness. This painful isolation was not willingly chosen by you and therefore it is not accepted as a price to be paid. Rather, it came as a necessary byproduct of your pseudo-solution, and with this defense mechanism at work the child in you hopes and fights for receiving what you cannot possibly receive. In other words, somewhere deep inside, you hope and believe that it is possible to belong and to be loved while you dull your world of feeling into a state of numbness and thereby prohibit yourself from truly loving others. Yes, you may need others and this need may appear as love to you, but now you know that it is not the same. Inside, you hope and believe it possible to unite with others, to communicate in a rewarding and satisfying way with the world around you, while you put up a wall of false protection against the impact of emotional experience. If and when you cannot help but feel, you are busy hiding such feelings from yourself and others. How can you receive what you yearn for—love, belonging, communication—if you neither feel nor express the occasional glimpses of feelings that the still healthy part in you strives for? You cannot have it both ways, though the child in you never wants to accept that.

Since you "protect" yourself in this foolish manner, you isolate yourself, which means exposing yourself much more to that which you strive to avoid. Hence you miss out doubly: You do not avoid that which you fear—not really and not in the long run—and you miss out on all you could have if you would not run away from living. For living and feeling are one. The love and fulfillment you must increasingly crave for makes you blame others, circumstances, the fates, or bad luck, instead of seeing how you are responsible for it. You resist such insight because you sense that the moment you see it fully, *you will have to change,* and you can no longer cling to the comfortable but unrealizable hope that you can have what you want without meeting the necessary conditions to get it. If you want happiness you must be willing to give it. How can you give it, if you are unwilling and unable to feel as much as you are capable of feeling? Realize that it is you who caused this state of unfulfillment, and it is you who can still change it, regardless of your physical age.

The Need to Exercise the Emotions

Another reason for resorting to this unsuccessful pseudo-solution is the following: As in everything else, feeling and emotional expression can be mature and constructive or immature and destructive. As a child you possessed an immature body and mind and therefore, quite naturally, an immature emotional structure. Most of you gave your body and mind a chance to grow out of the immaturity and to reach a certain physical and mental maturity. Let me give you an example on the physical level: An infant will feel the strong urge to use its vocal cords. It has an instinct with the function of promoting the growth of certain organic matter through strong use of the vocal cords. It is not pleasant to hear a baby screaming, but this period of transition leads to strong healthy organs in this particular aspect. For the baby, not going through this unpleasant time by suppressing the instinctual urge to scream would eventually damage and weaken the respective organs. The urge to indulge in strong physical exercise has the same

function. All this is part of the growing process. To stop the
growing process with the excuse that there is a danger in over-
exertion would be foolish and damaging.

Yet this is done with your emotional self. You stop its
functioning because you consider the growing transitional period so dangerous that you proceed to stop growth altogether.
You not only hinder excesses as a result of this reasoning, but
you also hinder all the transitory functioning that alone can
lead to constructive, mature emotions. Since this is more or
less the case with every one of you, the growth period of experiencing and maturing has to happen now.

When your mental processes mature, you have to go
through transition periods too. You not only learn, you are
also bound to make mistakes. In your younger years you often
hold opinions which you later grow out of. While later you
perceive that these opinions are not as "right" as they seemed
to you during your youth and see another side that earlier
eluded you, it was nevertheless beneficial for you to go
through those times of error. How could you appreciate truth
if you had not gone through error? You can never gain truth
by avoiding error. It strengthens your mental faculties, your
logic, as well as your range and power of deduction. Without
being allowed to make mistakes in your thinking or your opinions, your mental faculties could not grow.

Strangely enough, there is much less resistance in human
nature to the necessary growing pains of the physical and
mental sides of the personality than to the growth of the emotional nature. Hardly anyone recognizes that *emotional growing pains* are necessary too, and that they are constructive and
beneficial. Without consciously thinking about it in these
terms, you believe that the emotional growth process should
come about without growing pains. Most of the time it is completely ignored that this area exists at all, let alone that it
needs growth; neither do you know how such growth is to be
accomplished. You who are on this path ought to begin to understand this. If you do, your insistence on remaining dead-
ened and dulled will finally give way and you will no longer
object to going through a period of growth now.

Allowing Immature Feelings to Surface

In this growing period, *immature emotions have to express themselves*. Only as they are allowed expression for the purpose of understanding their significance will you finally reach a point when you no longer need such immature emotions. This will not happen through a process of will, an outer mental decision which represses what is still a part of your emotional being, but through an organic process of emotional growth wherein feelings will naturally change their direction, their aim, their intensity, their nature. But this can only be done if you experience your emotions as they exist in you now.

When you were hurt as a child, your reactions were anger, resentment, hate—sometimes to a very strong degree. If you prevent yourself now from consciously experiencing these emotions, you will not get rid of them; you will not enable healthy mature emotions to follow in their place, but you will simply repress existing feelings. You will bury them and deceive yourself that you do not feel what you actually still feel. Since you dull your capacity to feel, you become unaware of what exists underneath. Then you superimpose feelings that you think you ought to have but that you do not really and truly have.

You all operate—some more, some less—with feelings that are not genuinely yours, with feelings you think you ought to have but do not have. Underneath, something entirely different is taking place. Only in times of extreme crisis do these actual feelings reach the surface. Then you believe it is the crisis that has caused these reactions in you. No: the crisis reactivated the still immature emotions. It is the effect of the hidden emotional immaturity, as well as of the existing self-deception.

The fact that you put raw, destructive, immature emotions out of sight instead of growing out of them and then deceive yourself, believing you are a much more integrated and mature person than you actually are, is not only a self-deception, but it also leads you more deeply into isolation, unhappiness, alienation from yourself, and unsuccessful, un-rewarding patterns that you repeat over and over again. The result of all this seems to confirm your pseudo-solution, your defense mechanism, but this is a very misleading conclusion.

Immature emotions earned you punishment as a child; either they caused you actual pain, or produced an undesired result when you expressed them. You lost something you wanted, such as the affection of certain people, or a desired goal became unattainable when you expressed what you really felt. This then became an additional reason for you to hinder self-expression. Consequently, as you perceived such emotions to be undesirable, you proceeded to whisk them also out of your own sight. You found it necessary to do so because you did not want to be hurt, you did not wish to experience the pain of feeling unhappy. You also found it necessary to re-press existing emotions because the expression of the negative produced an undesirable result.

You might say that because the latter is true, your proce-dure is therefore valid, necessary, and self-preserving. You will rightly say that if you live out your negative emotions, the world will punish you in one form or another. Yes, my friends, this is true. Immature emotions are indeed destructive and will indeed bring you disadvantages. But *your error lies in the conscious or unconscious thought that to be aware of what you feel and to give vent to it in action are one and the same*. You cannot discriminate between the two courses. Neither can you discriminate between a constructive aim—for which it is necessary to express and talk about what you feel, at the right place, with the right people—and the destructiveness of heed-lessly letting go all control, of not choosing the right aim, the right place, and the right people, of not wanting to use such expression as would yield you insight into yourself. If you merely let go because you lack discipline, or an aim, and ex-pose your negative emotions, that is indeed destructive.

Try to distinguish between constructive and destructive aims, try to realize the purpose of exposing your emotions, and then develop the courage and humility to allow yourself to be aware of what you really feel, and to express it when it is meaningful. If you do this, you will see the tremendous difference between merely allowing immature and destructive emotions to come to the fore in order to relieve yourself of pressure and give them an outlet without aim or meaning, and the purposeful activity of reexperiencing all the feelings that once existed in you and that still exist in you. What has not been properly assimilated in emotional experience but has instead been repressed will constantly be reactivated by present situations. These remind you in one way or another of the original "solution" that brought on such unassimilated experience in the first place. Such a reminder may not be factual. It can be an emotional climate, a symbolic association that lodges exclusively in the subconscious. As you learn to become aware of what is really going on in you, you will also notice such reminders. With this may come the realization that you often actually feel very much the opposite of what you force yourself to feel.

How to Activate the Growth Process

As the first few tentative steps are taken in the direction of becoming aware of what you feel and expressing it in a direct way without finding reasons and excuses, you will gain an understanding about yourself such as you never had before. You will feel the growing process at work, because you are actively engaged in it with your innermost self, not merely with outer gestures. You will not only come to understand what brought on many unwelcome results, but how it is in your power to change them. Understanding the interaction between yourself and others will show you how your unconscious, distorted pattern has affected others in exactly the opposite way to what you originally wanted. This will give you an inner understanding about the process of communication.

This is the only way emotions can mature. By going through the period that was missed in childhood and adolescence, the emotions will finally mature and you will no longer need to fear the power of those emotions that you cannot con-

trol by merely putting them out of awareness. You will be able
to trust them, and to be guided by them—for that is the final
aim of the mature and well-functioning person. I might say
that this has happened to all of you to some degree. There are
times when you allow yourself to be guided by your power of
intuition. But it happens more as an exception than as a rule.
It cannot happen as a rule as long as your emotions remain destructive and childish; they are unreliable in this state. Since
you discourage their growth, you live by your mental faculties
only—and they are secondary in efficiency. When healthy
emotions make your intuition reliable, there will be a mutual
harmony between the mental and emotional faculties. One
will not contradict the other. As long as you cannot rely on
your intuitive processes, you must be insecure and lacking in
self-confidence. You try to make up for this by relying on others, or on false religion. This makes you weak and helpless.
But if you have mature, strong emotions, you will trust yourself and therein find a security you never dreamed existed.

After the first painful release of negative emotions, you
will find a certain relief in the realization that poisonous matter has left your system in a manner that was not destructive
for you or for others. After thus having gained insight and understanding, new warm, good emotions will come out of you
that could not express themselves as long as the negative emotions were held in check. You will also learn to discriminate
between genuine good feelings and the false good feelings that
you superimpose out of the need to maintain your idealized
self-image: "This is the way I should be." Because you cling to
this idealized self-image, you cannot find your real self, and
do not have the courage to accept that a comparatively large
area of your personality is still childish, incomplete, and imperfect.

What Is True Security?

To acknowledge this is the first necessary step to destroy
your destructive processes and *to build a real solid self* that
will stand on firm ground. For only in the mature emotions, in

the courage to make this maturity and growth possible, will you gain the security within yourself you so ardently hunt for elsewhere.

So, build your true security. You have nothing to fear from becoming aware of what is already in you. Looking away from what is does not cause it to cease to exist. Therefore, it is wise on your part to want to look at, to face, and to acknowledge what is in you—no more and no less! To believe that it harms you more to know what you feel and are than not to know is extremely foolish. Yet to some degree that is exactly what you all do. That is the nature of your resistance to accepting and facing yourself. Only after you face what is in you will your much more mature intellect be able to make the decision as to whether these inner behavior patterns are worth keeping or not. You are not forced to give up what seems a protection to you, but look at it with the clear and lucid eyes of truth. That is all I ask you to do. You have nothing to fear from it.

And now, my friends, let us consider this subject in the light of spirituality. You all have come originally with the idea of growing spiritually. I might say that more or less all of you hope to accomplish this without tending to your emotional growth. You want to believe that the one is possible without the other. Needless to say, this is a complete impossibility. Sooner or later all of you will reach the point where you have to make up your mind as to whether you really want emotional growth or you still want to cling to the childish hope that spiritual growth is possible while you neglect the world of feeling and allow it to lie dormant without giving it the opportunity to grow. Let us examine this for a moment, my friends.

If the Feelings Are Stunted, Love Cannot Grow

You all know, regardless of what religion or spiritual philosophy or teaching you follow, that *love is the first and the greatest power.* In the last analysis, *it is the only power.* Most of you have used this maxim many times, but I wonder, my friends, if you ever knew that you were using empty words, always veering away from feeling, reacting, and experiencing. Now, *how can you love if you do not let yourself feel?* How can you love and at the same time remain what you choose to call "detached"? That means remaining personally uninvolved, not risking pain, disappointment, personal involvement. Can you love in such a comfortable way? If you numb your faculty of feeling, how can you truly experience love? Is love an intellectual process? Is love a lukewarm matter of laws, words, letters, regulations, and rules you talk about? Or is love a feeling that comes from deep within the soul, a warmth of flowing impact that cannot leave you indifferent and untouched? Is it not foremost a feeling, and only after the feeling is fully experienced and expressed, will wisdom, and perhaps even intellectual insight—as a byproduct, so to speak—result from it?

How can you hope to gain spirituality—and spirituality and love are one—by neglecting your emotional processes? Think about this, my friends. Begin to see how you all sit back, hoping for a comfortable spirituality that leaves out your personal involvement in the world of feelings. After you see this clearly, you will comprehend how preposterous this attitude is. Your conscious or unconscious rationalizations in still denying the awareness and expression of your emotions, even though they are at the moment still destructive to quite a degree, will take on a different light in your own eyes. You will look upon your resistance to doing what is so necessary with a little more understanding and truth. Any spiritual development is a farce if you deny this part of your being. If you do not have the courage to allow the negative in you to reach your surface awareness, how can healthy, strong emotions fill your being? If you cannot deal with the negative because it is out of your awareness, this very same negative element will stand in the way of the positive.

Those of you who now follow this path and do what is so necessary will first experience a host of negative feelings. But after these are dealt with and properly understood, mature, constructive feelings will evolve. You will feel warmth, compassion, and good involvement such as you never thought possible. You will no longer feel yourself isolated. You will begin to relate to others in truth and reality, not in falsehood and self-deception. When this happens, a new security and respect for yourself will become part of you. You will begin to trust and like yourself.

QUESTION: *Is a faith in God and love without emotional maturity possible?*

ANSWER: That is impossible, if we speak about real love, the willingness to be personally involved, and not about the childish need to be loved and cherished that is so often confused with love. For real love and real, genuine faith to exist, emotional maturity is a necessary basis. Love and faith and emotional immaturity are mutually exclusive, my child. The ability to love is a direct outcome of emotional maturity and growth. True faith in God, in the sense of true religion as opposed to false religion, is again a matter of emotional maturity because true religion is self-dependent. It does not cling to a father-authority out of the need to be protected. False faith and false love always have the strong emotional connotation of need. True love and true faith come out of strength, self-reliance, and self-responsibility. All these are attributes of emotional maturity. And only with strength, self-reliance, and self-responsibility are true love, involvement, and faith possible. Anyone who ever attained spiritual growth, known or unknown in history, had to have emotional maturity.

QUESTION: *If someone doing this work finds wild emotions going back to childhood, how is it possible to handle them and substitute for them and let them disintegrate without the person who helps in this work right there? At the time, let us say twice a month, when we have the opportunity to express them with a helper present, we may not feel such emotions, while we strongly feel them at other times. If one is on one's own, what is the right way to handle these emotions at the moment they come up?*

ANSWER: In the first place, it is significant if emotions only come out when one is not actively doing this work with the so-called helper. This in itself points to a strong resistance. It is the long, drawn-out result of consistent repression. Due to such repression, the emotions that come out first will appear at inopportune moments and will be so strong as to confuse the person. But after a comparatively short time, with the inner will truly determined to face the self in its entirety, destructive emotions will not only appear at the proper time and in the proper place, but you will be able to handle them with a meaningful result. The state of resistance points to the fact that inward struggle and hate still exist along with the child's desire that manifest conflicts should be resolved while the basic defense-mechanism is left untouched. If destructive emotions govern you, instead of your being able to govern them without repression, it is a form of temper tantrum in which the psyche says, "You see, you have forced me to do this, and now see where this leads to." If such subtle hidden emotions can be detected, it will alleviate any danger of negative emotions taking on a power that the personality cannot handle.

In the second place, it is important that you do not feel guilty about the existence of such emotions, which are probably incompatible with the image you have of yourself. If you learn to accept the reality of yourself instead of your mistaken self-image, the strength of negative emotions will abate. Yes, you will, of course, experience negative emotions, but you will never fear that they can lead you into losing self-control. Let me put it this way: The strong impact of negative emotions, to the point where you fear that you are unable to handle them, is due not so much to their existence *per se* but due to the lack of acceptance on your part of the fact that you are not your idealized self. The negative emotions in themselves would be much less disturbing if you did not cling to the idealized self while struggling to give it up. Once you have accepted yourself as you now happen to be, and have made the inner decision to part with the illusion of yourself, you will feel much more at ease. You will become capable of experiencing negative emotions in a way that promotes growth. You will derive insight from them, even if you are alone at the moment. More-over, emotions will come up during working sessions and will yield even greater insight if they are expressed and worked with.

So, I cannot give you rules to observe. I can only point to the reason behind this manifestation. If you truly absorb it, wish to understand it, and go on from there, this will help you a great deal. Of course, this is addressed to all of my friends.

QUESTION: *That means that the emotions as such are not dangerous, but it is our disappointment in ourselves that makes them so powerful or dangerous?*

ANSWER: Yes, that is right. But they need not be danger-ous, if you do not want them to be. If inner anger is not prop-erly understood and released in a constructive way, such as you learn on this path, a so-called temper tantrum takes place and the child in you lashes out, destroying others and the self. Find the child who wants to strike out and you will be in control of evolving negative emotions without repressing them, but expressing them constructively and learning from them. Find the area in which you resent not being taken care of, not being given all you want. Once you are aware of the reason for all this anger, you will be able to humor yourself be-cause you will see the preposterous demands of the child in you. This is the work you have to do in this particular phase. It is a crucial and decisive milestone on your road. When you get over this particular hump, the work will proceed much more easily. Whenever you are afraid of losing control, I ad-vise you to think of the image you have of yourself, of what you think you should be, as opposed to the emotions that actually come to the fore. The moment you see this discrep-ancy, you will no longer feel threatened by the negative emotions. You will be able to handle them. This is the best ad-vice for you in this respect. Find in yourself where you are an-gry at the world for not allowing you to be your idealized self-image, where you feel it prevents you from being what you could be without its interference. Once you are aware of such emotional reactions, you will again come a great step forward.

You see, my friends, your misunderstanding is that you think the harm comes from the existence of the negative emotions as such. It does not. It comes from your non-acceptance of your real self, from the blame you throw into the world for not allowing you to be what you feel you could be if the world would let you. This is the nature of such strong, powerful emotions, and they can endanger you only as long as you are unaware of their nature. Therefore, seek their meaning. Seek their true message and you will never have to fear.

With this, my dearest, dearest friends, I go from you. Blessings for each one of you. May you all gain further strength, further wisdom to conduct your life and your inner growth so that you do not stand still. For this is the only thing that gives meaning to life—continuous growth. The better you accomplish this, the more you will be at peace with yourself. Blessings with all strength, love, and warmth are given unto you. Be blessed, be in peace, be in God.

9

Real and False Needs

Most of us are convinced that our troubles are caused by other people who do not respond to our needs. Not so, says the Guide. Many of the specific fulfillments we strive for are based on false needs and can therefore never be fulfilled. How the false needs came to substitute for unfulfilled real needs; how to distinguish them from the real ones and let them go; and, finally, how to recognize and fulfill our present real needs is the content of this lecture.

༄

Greetings to all of you, my friends. Blessings and strength are pouring forth. If you open your hearts as well as your minds, you can receive them.

Most human beings are not yet aware of the immense spiritual potentials and powers they have. Now, what do I mean when I say spiritual potentials and powers? I mean that these powers transcend by far the human capacities considered normal in your sphere of being.

Awakening the Dormant Spiritual Potentials

These powers remain inaccessible or may even be dangerous if the human being is not purified to a certain degree, or if the consciousness is still in a state of half-sleep, which is always connected with destructive attitudes such as selfwill, pride, fear, greed, envy, malice, cruelty, spite, and selfishness. The majority of human beings find themselves in a state of being approximately ninety percent asleep and only ten percent awake to what exists in the world around them, and within themselves. The process of reawakening the self requires a great deal of effort, commitment, work, and also the willingness to sacrifice destructive patterns with their short-lived, expensive satisfactions. Only then can awareness gradually grow, perception sharpen, and new inner knowledge become available as a manifestation of the awakening real self.

This growing intuitive perception, this inner knowledge—first about the self, then about the innermost being of others, and eventually also about cosmic truth and creation—extends into an experience of eternal life. The certainty of it! Awakening the spiritual potentials also involves access to the ever-present forces of life, all of which exist within and around you. These powers can be utilized for healing, for helping, and for increasing fulfillment and consciousness in the self and others. Needless to say that if the little ego still predominates over the spiritual real self, abuse of these powers will be inevitable. *Love has to first be awakened in the soul of a person so that the new powers will be safe to use*. If the energy force field of a human being is geared to low frequencies due to the soul's undeveloped state, the much higher frequencies of spiritual powers can destroy health and life and create tremendous hazards. This is why it is so important for development to proceed in certain rhythms. The safest way is always to emphasize, above all else, *purification*.

When purification precedes the development of spiritual and psychic potential and power, bliss grows. Fearlessness increases. Solutions to all problems become increasingly more accessible: They present themselves because the problems are faced and dealt with. Healing of all the ills of the mind, the soul, and the body will then be possible.

But this utopian state cannot be obtained unless you deal with your needs, both real and false, both conscious and unconscious. Any person not bringing his or her unconscious feeling experiences into consciousness must carry all the re-pressed material into the next incarnation. The embedded material seeks out circumstances and people for the next in-carnation that will give an opportunity to bring this dormant, unassimilated material to the fore again. Thus a set of parents or a certain environment will seem to be responsible for pain-ful experience in childhood. Actually, the undeveloped state of the parents functions as a means to bring out images that would otherwise remain dormant and inaccessible to con-sciousness, thereby blocking total purification. Of course, it is possible to treat painful experience in the old ways of avoid-ance and prolong the cycle. But the day comes for every entity when it is no longer possible to avoid confronting this experi-ence openly.

You can follow this chain of events even within the pres-ent life span. To the degree you have not experienced fully your past as a child, you must attract similar experiences later in life. If you have avoided your childhood and are unaware of what truly went on in you, you tend to not recognize what you feel and experience now as you repeat the experience. Con-versely, as you become conscious of your past feelings, you also become aware of how past experience repeats itself. Your state of numbness about your past feelings numbs you to similar present experiences, unless and until you make a real commit-ment and a real effort to awaken yourself, no matter how painful this may seem at first.

The Unfulfillment of the Child's Legitimate Needs

You can only be alert to and have full knowledge of what happens to you now when the similar experiences of the past are out in the open and fully dealt with. Then not only will the residual soul matter of this life be cleared up, but also si-multaneously the legacy of previous existences. When in your pathwork you experience more of this residual matter, you en-counter the fact that the most painful element in it is the un-fulfillment of your legitimate needs as a child. The negation of your real needs creates your false needs. This is tremendously important to observe.

What are real needs and what are false needs? In the first place, whatever is real at one period of a person's life may be utterly false and unreal at a later period. What is a real need for a child is not at all a real need for an adult. When the growing person denies the pain of an unfulfilled real need, this need does not disappear. On the contrary, the denial of the pain of its unfulfillment perpetuates the need and projects it into a later time and onto other people, so that it becomes a false need. Take the specific example of a child needing solely to receive care, nursing, good feelings, attention, and appreciation of his or her own uniqueness. If these needs are not fulfilled, the child must suffer. If this suffering is accepted and worked through on the conscious level, the person does not remain crippled, in spite of what many would want to believe. What does create a crippled state is the *belief* that this pain can only be eliminated when the person is finally given all that was lacking, even years later. This can never happen, of course. For even if it were possible for an adult to finally find substitute parents, ideal and perfect according to the notions of the deprived child, for the adult all this giving, coming from outside the self, could never bring real fulfillment.

The fulfillment so painfully longed for can be attained only when you, as an adult, proceed to search within yourself for all that you still look for outside of yourself. This must begin with self-responsibility. If you remain stuck by making your parents and life responsible, you deprive yourself of the vital center of all good within you. Only when you search to alter your own attitude and discover that your suffering is induced by your attitude *now*, can you begin to find security—the security you once looked for in the sustenance given you by others. Anxiety will disappear to the exact degree you search within yourself for the cause of your present suffering. And this suffering is the *denial of the original pain* and the consequent negative and destructive patterns of feeling and thinking.

When people begin to assume true self-responsibility,

they will gradually also cease to wait for the good feelings to come from outside. They will be less dependent on being praised and loved because they will be able to give themselves the self-esteem they could not feel when remaining demanding, resentful children. This is yet another step toward being centered within the real self. This, in turn, increases the ability to have a strong flow of good, warm feelings, and nourishes the desire to share them rather than spitefully withhold them. The ability to experience pleasure from within the body and soul, and offer it to others, becomes a real alternative to greedily insisting on receiving. All these increased abilities will fill the emptiness created by the child's unfulfilled need.

How to Dissolve the Pain of the Unfulfilled Legitimate Needs

The more the pain of the unfulfilled legitimate need remains unfelt or only half experienced, the more *false needs* will fill the personality, which then is bound to make demands on others. When these demands are not being fulfilled, the resentments—and often the venom with which cases are being built against life and others—increase one's sense of deprivation, so that a continuous vicious circle seems to entrap the person in a state of hopelessness. It is not too difficult to rationalize a case and produce a blaming accusation. One can always find actual, imagined, or exaggerated and distorted reasons for focusing the weight of responsibility outside of the self. Since all this is subtle and concealed, it requires specific attention in self-observation and self-honesty to see this process at work. Only when you are capable of admitting your irrational demands and of seeing how you want to deal out punishment to those you blame can you truly understand the connections I make here.

What are the real needs of an adult? They are self-expression, growth, development, reaching one's spiritual potential, and everything that accrues from that. This means pleasure, love, fulfillment, good relationships, and a meaningful contribution to the great plan in which everyone has his or her task. When a certain amount of growth has taken place, this task begins to be felt and inwardly experienced until it becomes a reality. It is a real need to perceive one's inner growth; the lack of it brings unhappiness. You must then proceed to search for the obstructions within your own soul and remove them. They are always, in one way or another, connected with a perpetuation of needs once real, which have now become false needs.

Overcoming the Resistance to Exposing False Needs

The perpetuation of false needs creates any number of destructive conditions within the soul of a person. Since these needs can never be fulfilled, continuous frustration and emptiness wipe out hope, blacken vision, and induce resentment, hate, blame, and often spite. A venomous, passive resistance and self-punishment are used to punish others who appear to cause the negative state. The worse these inner traits are, the greater the guilt and the self-evasion, which make it impossible to get down to the roots of the problem, change direction and focus. Only when resistance to recognizing the false needs is vigorously overcome can all this be reversed.

Real needs never require others to comply and "give it to you." Only to the little self does that appear necessary. The real need for love, companionship, and sharing can only begin to be fulfilled when the soul is ready to love and give, which must never be confused with the *neurotic* need to be loved. But this confusion between the two needs is quite frequent. As long as you believe that you are really willing to love, but fate is slighting you and withholding from you the person who loves you and whom you can love, you are really still ardently engaged in trying to fulfill the childhood need with a substitute parent. Once you are truly ready to give up the old case, start to live in the now, and look within yourself, real love will come to you and your present real need will be fulfilled.

Legitimate needs can be fulfilled only to the degree you experience your original feelings and your residual feelings of the past. This means that you discover and give up the false needs that have accrued from denying the pain of the original unfulfillment. Let yourself regress into the child state, and allow the irrational child in you to be expressed.

If you give voice to this irrational side, you will find that it invariably says: "I need to be always loved and approved by everyone. If I am not, it is a catastrophe." The self then talks itself into believing this, as a means to force others to comply, and the non-fulfillment of these insatiable demands for total, unconditional gratification of selfwill and pride will seem indeed a catastrophic fact of life. No matter how mature you may be in many respects of your being, look for these hidden reactions in you whenever you feel consistently anxious and uncomfortable in your environment.

Just to think all this through clearly will make it impossible for you to believe in catastrophe quite as much. So it is necessary to discover the concept, or rather the misconception, entrapped in your strong reaction to an unfulfillment, to a hurt, a criticism, or a frustration. It is then possible to *recognize the unreal need* and the vengeance with which it is perpetuated, pursued, and justified. *Unreal needs are demands made upon others.* Unreal needs can never be fulfilled.

Often the dualistic misunderstanding that either you depend on yourself and therefore must be all alone, or that you are in a fulfilling relationship and then utterly depend on the other, prevents you from even wanting to assume self-responsibility. Doing so seems to require giving up all hope for a loving partner. Exactly the opposite is true. Only as you bring your feelings back to yourself, tap the resources within yourself, and open the wells of your giving and loving feelings, will fulfillment become an inevitable reality. Conversely, to the degree you cling to and insist on the other's fulfilling you, to that degree you must remain lonely and unfulfilled in your real needs now—thereby perpetuating the old wounds of your childhood. Your present state can thus be used as a gauge that is more reliable than anything else.

When the real need to remove the blocks to awareness, self-fulfillment, to intimacy and closeness with others, is expressed by the spiritual self by discarding the false needs, a wonderful force is awakened. This is the all-important aim, out of which everything else follows. This plea is never answered with a stone. Even if you feel as yet too weak to make the necessary total commitment, you can ask to be helped to be able to do so. The help will come.

Present Suffering Is the Result of Pursuing False Needs

As you see how you now avoid the long-forgotten pain of the past still festering within you, you also discover how you have remained hooked on blaming. For no matter how much your parents failed—for they themselves are failing human beings—they cannot be held responsible for your suffering now. Even less can others whom you expect to be able to make up for all the injuries you have endured. Your suffering now is a result of this very distortion of pursuing false needs and insisting on their fulfillment. This mechanism seems at first extremely subtle, but once you have trained yourself to observe it, it will become only too obvious. As long as you choose to stay unaware, you may be very adept in rationally explaining your case, but this will only make your condition worse, not better. You may indeed deceive others about how legitimate your case is. You may even deceive your outer conscious self. But you can never deceive your real inner self nor life. Life plays out its laws and rules very squarely, fairly, and impartially. It waits until you find the truth where your nonrecognized, legitimate needs as a child created fear and pain that you were unwilling and unable to experience fully. That cup has to be emptied. Your unwillingness, in turn, created false needs whose nature and meaning also became concealed. When all this is out in the open, you can deal with it.

The pursuit of false needs causes unbearable pain. It is tight, locked, and bitter, with the added connotation of hopelessness. It is very different from the pain of a real unfulfillment, a hurt, or a deprivation. The moment these difficulties are not channeled into unreal needs, the pain can be dissolved and can transform itself back into its original, flowing, life-bringing energy current. *Hard pain is a result of fighting against what is. Soft pain is a result of acceptance.*

Letting Go of the Demand for Fulfillment of Unreal Needs

When you specifically let go one by one of your insatiable demands and unreal needs, you will find out that they are indeed illusory. You started off with the premise, for example, that you could not live without total approval, unconditional acceptance and love, uncritical admiration, or whatever else it may be. As you consider the possibility that you might even gain fulfillment, contentment, pleasure, and happiness without these demands being fulfilled—a novel idea at first—you will be surprised to find that it is quite possible to do so. New ways will make themselves known, new possibilities you could never even have sensed before, because you were so bent on the one way it had to be.

Wherever there is obstruction, unfulfillment, or an unyielding wall in your life, an unreal need has to be looked for. You must find your own insistence that says, "It must be this way, not that way. Life must give me this; I must have it." When you find and express this voice and recognize it for its fallacy, something will loosen up instantly. The very fact that you question the validity of these unreal needs, which you had taken for granted as being real until now, will liberate your creative energies. Deep from your innermost being, *from the center of your solar plexus, the voice of wisdom will guide you.*

The energies that are being released by following through the process described here are not merely physical energies that bring well-being, flow, and pleasure. They release the voice of truth and wisdom that is your own, innermost spiritual self.

When you go deep into your innermost feelings, my friends, there will be no danger of losing yourself in unendurable pain. For no matter how difficult your childhood was, and no matter how much negative experience you had, and no matter how cruel a parent may have been, the real cause of pain is not that. The cause is your persistence and insistence on staying hooked on needs that are by now false needs, on demanding that conditions be different, and that life now make up for it all and give to you gratuitously, leaving you as a recipient, leaving you out of the magnificent game of life. This is what really hurts and pains you now. You must start with yourself, at all junctures. If you proceed in this way, you will be able to allow the positive feelings to become as deep and as real experiences as the negative and painful feelings.

May you all, each one of you, find in tonight's lecture something that will bring a little more light and help to your work; a little further incentive, hope, strength, and inner pride, so as to free yourself from your own enslavement, to make yourself whole instead of divided. Go all in peace, my dearest ones, on this glorious road of self-realization and freedom. Be blessed, be in God!

10

Infinite Possibilities of Experience Hindered by Emotional Dependency

It is a universal law that you cannot bring into existence that which you cannot first conceive of. From this metaphysical concept, the Guide leads us right into our childish self that keeps us, through our continued dependency on outside approval, within the narrow confines of our limitations. Happiness, fulfillment, is our birthright. But how can we bring it into manifestation? This is a truly mind-expanding lecture.

∽

Greetings, my dearest friends. Again, I shall try to help you to move on from where you may be stuck.

It is being said by all great spiritual teachings that creation is infinite in its possibilities and that humanity's potential for realizing these infinite possibilities of happiness exists in the inner depths of each person's being. Almost all of you have heard these words. Some of you may believe them, at least in principle; others may have their doubts about accepting them even in theory. Let us now try to overcome some of the difficulties in understanding these principles.

Everything in the World Exists
in a State of Potentiality

First of all, it is necessary to understand that no one person creates anything new. It is also impossible for anything new to come into existence. However, it is possible for a person to make manifest something that already exists. It is a fact that everything, absolutely everything, exists already on another level of consciousness. The word everything cannot convey the scope of this concept. When one speaks about God's infinity or about Creation's infinity, this is part of the meaning. There is no state of being, no experience, no situation, no concept, no feeling, no object that does not already exist. Everything in the world exists in a state of potentiality which already contains the finished product within it. I can see that this idea is not easy for human beings to embrace, for it is so contrary to your way of thinking, being, and experiencing on your average level of consciousness. But the more you can deepen your thoughts on this subject, the easier will it become for you to perceive, to sense, and to grasp it. Knowing and understanding this principle of creation—that all exists already and that human beings can make these existing possibilities manifest—is one of the necessary prerequisites to experiencing the fullness of life's infinite potential.

Before you can create new possibilities of unfoldment and entirely new ranges of experience in your personal life, you must first learn to apply these laws of creation to the problem areas of your life where you feel troubled, limited, handicapped, or trapped. Healthy unfoldment of the real self follows the creation of a healthy personality. This can happen once you learn and comprehend that the laws of creation can work only if you apply them first to the troubled areas of the personality.

Whatever possibility you can conceive of, you can realize. Suppose you are immersed in a conflict from which you cannot see a way out. As long as you do not conceive of a way out, you truly cannot realize the already existing possibility of a resolution. If your concepts about the way out are hazy or unrealistic, so will be the temporary solutions that will appear to you as the only possibilities. The same applies to your life as a whole. If you truly comprehend that an infinite number of possibilities exist in any given situation, you can find solutions where it was hitherto impossible to do so.

It is your prerogative as human beings to make use of these laws of creation and to reach out so that these infinite possibilities can unfold, enabling you to partake fully of life's offerings. If your life seems limited, it is only because you are convinced your life must be limited. You cannot conceive of anything more than what you have experienced up until now and are experiencing in the present. This is precisely the first handicap. Therefore, in order to expand your own possibilities of happiness, your mind must grasp the principle that *you cannot bring something to life if you cannot first conceive of it*. This sentence should be truly meditated on, for understanding this concept will open new doors for you. You should also understand that there is a vast difference between conceiving of further possibilities of expansion or happiness on the one hand, and daydreaming on the other. Wistful, resigned daydreaming that grabs fantasy as a substitute for drab reality is not at all what is meant here, and is in fact a hindrance to the proper conceiving of life's potentials. You need to have a vigorous, active, dynamic concept of what is possible in reality. When you know that something you wish to bring about exists in principle, you have made the first step toward realizing it.

Avoidance Motivation Closes Out New Vistas

Therefore, I invite every one of you to contemplate what you truly conceive of as possibilities for your life. If you examine yourself closely, you will find primarily that you conceive of negative possibilities which you naturally fear, wish to avoid, and defend yourself against. When you use most of your psychic energies to defend yourself against possible negative experience, your motivation is negative.

Negative motivation does not necessarily imply a destructive intent. For that matter, a positive motivation in this context could also mean a very destructive intent or aim. The avoidance of a feared possibility implies negative motivation. Upon close examination of your mental and emotional processes you will find that you are negatively motivated to a considerable extent. This is one of the first obstructions which enclose you in an imaginary and unnecessary prison. This applies, of course, to all levels of your personality. It applies to the mental level, where you cannot really envisage the infinite vistas of experience, of expansion, of stimulation, of all sorts of wondrous and happy possibilities you have a prerogative to achieve in this life. It exists on the emotional level, where you do not allow the spontaneous and natural flow of your feelings, where you fearfully, anxiously, and suspiciously hold back. It also exists on the physical level, in that you do not permit your body to experience the pleasure it is destined to experience. All these are limitations that you artificially and needlessly inflict upon yourself.

A Cluster of Popular Misconceptions

The next obstruction to expanding your life and creating the best of all possible lives for yourself is the following cluster of misconceptions that are widespread in the world: "It is not possible to be really happy! Human life is very limited. Happiness, pleasure, and ecstasy are frivolous, selfish aims that truly spiritual people must abandon for the sake of their spiritual development. Sacrifice and renunciation are the keys to spiritual development." We do not have to further elucidate these deeply lodged misconceptions, which are often more unconscious than conscious. But it is necessary for you to discover the subtle way in which you abide by such general concepts, no matter what you consciously believe. You may discover these subtle reactions by observing your reluctance to take steps to realize a perfectly harmless and normal fulfillment of a genuine need or a truly constructive aim. You feel as though something were holding you back, paralyzing your efforts. Although there are often a number of other reasons for this reluctance as well—some of which we shall discuss shortly—it is also often true that you have simply accepted a negative idea that really makes no sense and has no good purpose.

Fear of happiness, of pleasure, of wide expansion into one's life experiences is based on ignorance that such fulfillment could exist or that you possess all the powers, faculties, and resources to create and bring about what you wish. It is also based on misconceptions such as, "pleasure is wrong," or "it is selfish to want personal fulfillment." Fear of happiness is also based on the fear of being annihilated and dissolved if you ever trusted the flow of the universal forces and went with them. Such trust necessitates letting go of the ego-will and the ego-forces, and then surrendering to the beneficial forces of your deep nature.

Devices to Hide Weakness and Dependency on Others

Every single human being in this world harbors an attitude of fear and weakness. Because this corner of the personality usually induces a strong shame, it is kept secret, often even from the conscious mind. Many a different device is invented in order to hide this weakness and dependency that make you feel utterly helpless, unable to assert yourself, and even unable to protect your truth and integrity. When it comes to this area of the soul one is constantly compelled to sell out and betray oneself in order to ward off disapproval, censure, and rejection. The need to be accepted by others is usually less shameful than the means to which the personality resorts to placate and appease others. The ways of defending yourselves are psychologically so fundamental that you cannot get far in your self-purification work unless you work on seeing how they function in your life. All the defense mechanisms you have discovered and perhaps even begun to remove are either your ways of obtaining what you consider to be the apparently vital acceptance of others, or your ways of hiding your shameful submission, often by an apparently opposite attitude of indifference, hostility, or compulsive and blind rebellion and over-aggressiveness.

The Child Within You Still Wants Validation from Others

Few things give human beings as much pain and shame as this inner, fearful, weak spot that makes them feel impotent and compelled to sell out. You already know, my friends, that *this area of the personality has remained a child*. The child does not yet know that the whole of the personality has grown up and is indeed no longer helpless and dependent. Infants and young children truly are helpless and dependent on the parents. But in the childish corner of your being you either do not know or do not want to know that this is no longer true.

The young child is dependent on parents for all the basics of life: shelter, food, affection, protection, and, last but not least, for the very necessary supply of pleasure. A human being cannot live without pleasure. To deny this truth is one of the most harmful errors. Body, soul, mind, and spirit wither without pleasure. As an adult you are able to find through your own efforts and resources your own shelter, food, affection, and safety, so you are also able to do the same with pleasure. In all these areas you must have contact, cooperation, and communication with others in varying degrees. You cannot provide yourself with any of these necessities without interacting with other people. But this interaction is entirely different from the passive, weak dependency of the small child. The thoroughly adult person uses his or her own best forces, intelligence, intuition, talents, observation, and flexibility to get along with others in giving and taking. Your adult sense of fairness makes you sufficiently pliable to give in. And your sense of self makes you sufficiently assertive not to be stepped on and abused. The often fine balance in these forces of communication cannot be taught. It can only come through personal growth.

Children are incapable of achieving this balance. They are rigidly one-sided in their insistence to receive, for this is their need. The same applies to pleasure. Children must have the parents' permission to establish and utilize the source of all pleasure deep within themselves. Through the parents' permission the child will develop the strength and security to make meaningful contact. When you still need another person to permit you to experience pleasure, you are still in the position of the child or infant. I repeat, this never implies that anyone can do without others, but for adults the emphasis is shifted. Mature adults find within themselves an inexhaustible well of wonderful feelings. Insecurity and weakness cannot exist when these feelings are activated.

When part of your development is arrested, you wait for another person, a parent-substitute, to make it possible for you to draw on the deep source of your own rich feelings. You know of and yearn for these pleasurable feelings, but you do not know that you are no longer a child dependent on others for being allowed to activate and express them. This is your human tragedy, for you thus move into a vicious circle. Whenever a misconception is accepted as truth, immediately a vicious circle comes into being, paralyzing the pleasure forces, which are a good part of the energy available to you. Your life thus becomes dull and lusterless.

To deny the intense pleasure of being, the pleasure of feeling the energy flow of your body, soul, and spirit, is to deny life. When a child suffers such denial, his or her psyche receives a shock from the repeated absence of pleasure and therefore the repeated presence of unfulfilled yearning. The shock prevents growth in this one area so that the whole personality grows lopsidedly. Your adult conscious mind ignores the fact that a crying, demanding, angry, and helpless child still exists within you. You do not know that you are free to move toward pleasure, toward your own fulfillment, toward the realization of your own powers to obtain whatever you want and need. This is one of the most fundamental splits in the human personality.

Vicious Circle and Forcing-Current

Let us now look a bit closer at this hidden corner of your psyche where all of you have remained children. Where do you ignore this fact and where does your inner child ignore the rights and powers of your adult state? The particular vicious circle I mentioned before is this: When you do not know that everything in the universe already exists, and that you can manifest whatever you need in your own life, you feel dependent on an outside force or authority for all your wants and needs. Because of this distortion of the facts, you wait for fulfillment from the wrong source. Such waiting keeps your need perpetually unfulfilled. *The more unfulfilled it is, the more urgent the need becomes. The more urgent the need, the greater your dependency,* your hope, and the more frantic your attempts to please the other who is supposed to fill your need. You then become desperate; the more you try, the less you fulfill your need precisely because your attempts are unrealistic. Consciously you know none of this; you do not know what forces drive you nor even in what direction you are driven. You become desperate because in your urgency to have the need fulfilled you betray yourself, your truth, and the best in you. Your frustrated striving and your self-betrayal create a *forcing-current.*

The forcing-current may manifest in a very subtle way and may not be overt at all, but the emotions are all cramped up with it. This must inevitably affect others and have its lawful and appropriate consequences. *Any forcing-current is bound to make others resist and shrink back*, even if what they are forced to do is for their own benefit and delight. Thus the vicious circle continues. The continued frustration, which you believe to be caused by the other person's mean refusal to cooperate and to give, brings into your soul rage, fury, perhaps even vindictiveness and varying degrees of cruel impulses. This, in turn, weakens the personality even more as guilt comes up. You conclude that your destructive feelings must be hidden so as not to antagonize this other person whom you perceive as the source of life. The net of entanglement becomes tighter and tighter; the individual is completely ensnarled in this trap of misconceptions, distortions, and illusions with all the destructive emotions that follow suit. You find yourself in the preposterous position of craving the love and acceptance of a person whom you hate and resent for having left you unfulfilled for so long. This one-sided insistence on being loved by a person one deeply resents and wishes to punish increases the guilt, for the ever-wakeful presence of your real self flashes its reaction into a mind that is unable to interpret and sort out the messages of the real self from those that come from the child inside.

The fact that your need is not fulfilled by the other also weakens your conviction that you have a right to the pleasure you so much desire. You vaguely suspect that you may be wrong to even want this pleasure. Thus you begin to displace the original, natural need and desire for pleasure into other channels where they are sublimated. Other, more or less compulsive, needs come into existence. All the while you are torn between the force of the deeply hidden original need and the doubt that you have a right to its fulfillment. The more you doubt, the more dependent you become on reconfirmation by an outside authority—a parent-substitute, public opinion, or certain groups of people who represent the last word of truth to you.

The more this vicious circle goes on, the less pleasure remains in the psyche, while unpleasure accumulates. Such a person must increasingly despair about life and doubt that fulfillment is possible. There comes a point when a person inwardly gives up.

There is not a single human being who does not harbor within such a weak area, at least to some degree. In this secret corner, you feel not only helpless and dependent, but also deeply ashamed. The shame is due to the methods you employ to placate the person who at any given period is supposed to fulfill the role of the authority and grant you what you need in the way of pleasure, safety, and self-respect.

The forcing-current says, "you must," and you make demands on others to be, feel, and do what you need and desire. These demands may not manifest outwardly at all. In fact, on the surface you may totally lack self-assertion. Your inability or difficulty to healthily assert yourself is a direct result of having to hide the underlying shameful and threatening forcing-current. It is threatening because you know quite well that if it shows openly, it will evoke great censure and disapproval and possibly even overt rejection.

I invite all of you to vigorously face this area in yourselves. All of you must tackle it if you wish to realize life's and your own best potentials, and if you wish to discover your own infinite powers to create infinite goodness in your life.

The stronger the "you must" is secretly thrown at others, the more you inactivate your own powers. The result is that you become paralyzed and inactive in body, soul, and mind. This inactivity keeps you from moving into your own nucleus, the place where all realistic promise and all potential for every kind of fulfillment and delight exist. You inadvertently make yourself hang on to others, which must elicit hate in you. Finding the treasure of your own nucleus, on the contrary, makes you free. Then contact with others becomes a delightful luxury that elicits love.

By continually using inner, covert pressure on others because you believe you are dependent on them, you diminish your available energy supply. If energy is used in its natural, correct, and meaningful way, it never exhausts itself. You know this, my friends. Energy only exhausts itself when it is wrongly used. There are innumerable methods that human beings use in order to switch on this forcing-current. They include compliance in varying degrees, passive resistance, spite, withdrawal, refusal to cooperate, forceful outer aggression, intimidation, and persuasion through false strength and assumption of an authority role. Deep down they all mean, "You must love me and give me what I need." The more blindly you are involved in this way of being, the more you weaken and then further alienate yourself from the center of your true inner life, where you find all that you can ever need and want.

Let Go—Let Out

In order to *reorient the soul forces* toward health and re-
store their true nature, the following has to happen: *Let go* of
the particular person or persons from whom you expect your
life fulfillment and whom you simultaneously resent for this
very fact. You must all recognize that you place expectations
and make demands on others that no one else but you yourself
can fulfill. All you need and long for, including real love, can
only come when your soul is fearless, and you know that the
strength of your feelings with which you can give and receive
love is located within you. For as long as you hang onto another person in the way of a child, denying the adult you are,
you enslave yourself in the true sense of the word. The more
you do this, the less you can either receive or give, and the less
real feelings of any sort about any vital experience can find
their home within you.

Because *fear and anger* take up most of the room in your
psyche, it is essential to let out these negative emotions in the
way you learn to do in the Pathwork where no one is harmed.
Letting out fear and anger makes room for the good feelings.
So many of you are still locked and paralyzed. Expressing fear
and anger is the last thing you want to do. Even if you admit
to such negative emotions in principle, you still prefer to act
them out in unconsciousness rather than expressing them directly and taking the responsibility for them. You still claim a
false perfection—even though you do not really believe that it
exists in you any longer—in order to favorably dispose others
toward you. Also, you cling for dear life to negative emotions
because you fear positive feelings. This is yet another aspect of
the same vicious circle.

The less you see yourself as responsible for the negative
feelings you still possess as well as for your right and ability to
create happiness, the more you must live in fear. Consequently, the more you must do something to eliminate that
fear. Thus negative motivation comes about. You live a make-
shift life of avoidance rather than create an expansive, unfold-

ing life filled with positive experience and pleasure. You aim
to avoid the threat of expressing your own negative feelings
because they would spoil your obtaining from others everything that you must in fact obtain from within yourself. You
stake your salvation on others from whom it can never come.

Your reorientation to life—apart from the fundamental
necessity of recognizing all these negative aspects—must always begin with the willingness to let go. This cannot be
forced upon one who has not been made aware of the dependency itself in very exact ways. But once this is the case, it becomes possible to give up what one has been so tightly holding
on to. This loosening up must occur to bring about a change
in the balance structure of soul forces so that benign circles
can begin to perpetuate themselves.

You also need to be willing to dispense with your rationalization that appears to make your case seem justified. For
you can always succeed in presenting your life to yourself and
to others as though your wishes, needs, and demands on others are not only justified, since there is nothing wrong with
them, but are also beneficial for the other person. This may
even be quite true, as far as it goes. What you want, in principle, may indeed be good and within your right. But when
using a hidden, emotional forcing-current, you go about seeking satisfaction in the wrong way and not granting the other
person the same freedom you wish for yourself. You do not
give the other person the right to freely choose whom to love
and accept or the right not to be rejected and hated for as-
serting this freedom. You do not even give the other *the right
to be wrong* without being hated and totally denied. *This is a
freedom which you very much wish for yourself,* and you
deeply resent others when they do not grant it to you. You are
unable to defend yourself in an adequate way in such cases
only because on certain emotional levels you do not grant this
same freedom to others. When you look very closely you will
find this to be true. And when you do so, your sense of fairness
and objectivity will help you to give up what you so desperately hold on to, even while you emotionally still believe that

your life depends on getting the other to feel and do as you wish.

Take Off the Leash Around Your Neck

Once you have learned this initial condition, allowing for the number of inevitable relapses that must forever be newly observed, you will make a huge step toward that source of your inner being where you are not chained in weakness and anxiety, or in fear and anger. You all chafe at some leash around your neck that keeps you dependent and anxious in a situation in which you cannot find the strength to assert yourself, in which you find yourself absolutely caught and unable to see a way out because each possibility seems wrong. You know that none of the visible alternatives give you that good feeling about yourself, that resilient strength and well-being in which even difficult steps become feasible because you know they are right for you. Most of you have at least occasionally experienced this state of *inner knowingness* when your real self was freely operative within you. *It is our aim to bring out that real self completely.*

In order to liberate the real self, you must *find that area of your life where you are most bound and most anxious.* Ask yourself what it is you want from the other when you are so bound, so resentful, so afraid, so weak, so unable to be yourself. Experience this leash which can be given up only when you stop wanting from others what you must supply for yourself. *Verbalize concisely* to yourself whatever you find you need from others. This will bring you nearer to letting go. You will then know that this is precisely the compulsive need with which you enslave, weaken, and paralyze yourself. When you let go, you will experience a new, resilient strength coming out of you that suddenly conciliates apparently insoluble problems. You will become free as you let free. Only when you can lose on the ego-level can you win on the level of the real self, where the power is to create a good life.

Conversely, your inability to give up, to be fair, to let others free, your insistence to win and have your way, and your refusal to lose on the ego-level make it impossible for you to win where it counts and where you would find your real strength. Jesus Christ meant this when he said that he who wants to live must be willing to lose his life. In one of my very first lectures, I spoke of this when I said, "You must give up what you want to gain."

Here we are dealing with levels of consciousness. I hope it is quite clear that *no sacrifice or renunciation is required*. What is meant is that you cannot obtain what you want, and what you indeed should have, by pressuring an outer source with all your efforts. *The emphasis must shift*. If you insist that you must win on the wrong level, you cannot truly win. *If you can lose on that ego level, you will win*. You will then inevitably come into that nucleus of yourself where every conceivable power exists. As you grant others the right to be, whether it is convenient to you or not, to that extent you will truly find your own rights.

It is a steady growing process to find these rights. The process will first manifest by your no longer selling out or downgrading yourself. You will find genuine, good defenses against abuse and you will feel good about them. Later you will discover your ever-increasing right for pleasure and happiness. You will find that you move toward visions of what your life could be, toward possibilities you never dreamed could exist. You will suddenly permit yourself pleasure. You will no longer cramp up against it, as you inadvertently continue to do now. You will stop undermining the spontaneous processes, and you will learn to trust them. This will open a richness of life and a security that truly are heavenly. By letting go and giving up your inner forcing-current, you will experience the beauty of free, unforced relationships. When you live in the old dependency pattern, you force others to make them do what you want. Thus you have mutual forcing-currents. This weakens you and creates a host of negative emotions that cause you to lose contact with the nucleus of your real being, as well as with your good feelings. When you can lose gracefully, you will find a treasure within, a new way of life that is an entirely new venture on which you are just embarking. The areas in your life where you feel so weak and so trapped will cease to exist.

Reach into your inner being and communicate with it for the purpose of eliminating this weakness in you that binds you and that wastefully and needlessly holds you back in your life. No matter how much you may glorify this holding back, it serves no good purpose. All of you do hold back in one way or another, just as humankind has done for millennia, by saying that pleasure is wrong and frivolous and unspiritual. You may have your own private excuse to beautify your weakness and apparently make an asset out of it. Yet in following this reasoning you cannot really come face to face with yourself. Only by coming face to face with your weakness and dependency, with your forcing-current that says to others "you must," can you also come face to face with your strength and beauty, and with all the potentials that exist in you in a way you cannot even fathom yet.

Be blessed by the great strength that is here now, but even more so by the great strength that dwells in you. Be in peace. Be in God!

11

The Spiritual Meaning
of Crisis

*There are moments—and even protracted peri-
ods—in our lives when suddenly everything seems
to have come to an end. We are shaken to the very
depths of our being by events that compel us to
make difficult decisions, while our feelings are in
such turmoil that we don't know what to do. Why
such crises arise and how we can handle the over-
whelming problems that confront us at such times in
a constructive way is the topic of this soul-
penetrating lecture.*

⌇

Greetings and blessings to every one of my friends.

What is the real, spiritual meaning of crisis? Crisis is an
attempt of nature to effect change through the cosmic lawful-
ness of the universe. If change is obstructed by the ego, the
part of the consciousness that directs the will, crisis will occur
to make structural change possible.

Without such structural change in the entity, no balance
can be attained. Every crisis ultimately means such a readjustment, whether it appears in the form of pain, difficulties,
upheaval, uncertainty, or merely the insecurity that comes
from starting out on unaccustomed ways of living after giving

up a familiar one. Crisis in any form attempts to break down old structures based on false conclusions and therefore on negativity. Crisis shakes loose ingrained, frozen habits so that new growth becomes possible. It tears down and breaks up, which is momentarily painful, but transformation is unthinkable without it.

The more painful a crisis is, the more the will-directing part of consciousness is attempting to obstruct the change. Crisis is necessary because human negativity is a stagnant mass that needs to be shaken up in order to be let go of. *Change is an integral characteristic of life;* where there is life there is unending change. Only those who still live in fear and negativity, who resist change, perceive change as something that ought to be resisted. They resist life itself, and suffering closes in on them more tightly. This happens in people's overall development as well as in specific instances.

Human beings can be free and healthy in areas where they do not resist change. There they are in harmony with the universal movement. They constantly grow and experience life as deeply satisfying. Yet these same individuals react entirely differently in areas where they have blocks. They fearfully cling to unchanging conditions inside and outside themselves. Where they don't resist, their lives will be relatively free from crises; in the areas where they do resist change, crises are unavoidable.

The function of human growth is to free one's inherent potentials, which are truly infinite. However, where negative attitudes stagnate, realizing these potentials is impossible. Only crisis can tear down a structure that is built on premises that contradict the laws of cosmic truth, love, and bliss. *Crisis shakes up the frozen state, which is always negative.*

On the path to emotional and spiritual fulfillment you need to work intensively in order to free yourself from your negativities. What are they? The misconceptions; the destructive emotions, attitudes, and behavior patterns that arise from them; the pretenses and the defenses. But none of these would present too much difficulty in themselves if it were not for the self-perpetuating force that compounds each negative aspect in an ever-increasing momentum within the human psyche.

All thoughts and feelings are energy currents. Energy is a force that increases with its own momentum, always based on the nature of the consciousness that nourishes and directs the energy current in question. Hence, if the underlying concepts and feelings accord with truth and are therefore positive, the self-perpetuating momentum of the energy current will increase *ad infinitum* the expressions and attitudes implicit in the underlying thoughts. If the underlying concepts and feelings are founded on error and are therefore negative, the self-perpetuating momentum of the energy current will compound, though *not ad infinitum*.

The Self-Perpetuating Force of Negative Emotions

You know that misconceptions create behavior patterns that inevitably seem to prove the correctness of the assumption, so that the destructive, defensive behavior will become more firmly entrenched in the soul substance. The same principle applies to feelings. For example, fear could easily be overcome if it were challenged and its underlying misunderstanding and mishandling exposed. Many times manifest emotions are not direct primary emotions: Fear may disguise rage; depression may disguise fear. The problem is that fear creates more fear of facing and of transcending itself. Then one fears this fear of fear and so on. The fear compounds.

Let us take *depression*. If the underlying causes of the original feeling of depression are not courageously exposed, you become depressed about being depressed. You may then feel that you should be able to face your depression rather than being depressed about it, but you are not really willing or able to do so, and that depresses you even more. This becomes a vicious circle.

The first depression—or fear, or another emotion—is the first crisis that is not heeded nor is its true meaning understood. It is evaded, so that depression about being depressed will be set off in the self-perpetuating vicious circle. The consciousness of the person becomes more and more removed from the original feeling and therefore removed from itself, making it more difficult to find the original feeling. The increased negative momentum finally leads to a breakdown of the negative self-perpetuation.

Contrary to truth, love, and beauty, which are infinite divine attributes, distortion and negativity are never infinite. They come to an end when the pressure bursts. This is a painful crisis, and people usually resist it with all their might. But imagine if the universe were created differently and negative self-perpetuation continued *ad infinitum*. It could mean eternal hell.

The negative self-perpetuating principle is most obvious in the case of frustration and anger. Many people can see relatively easily that the frustration itself is less difficult to bear than their frustration at being frustrated. The same is true of anger at oneself for being angry or being impatient with one's impatience, wishing that one could react differently and not being able to do so because the underlying causes are not exposed and faced up to. Thus the "crises" of emotions such as anger, frustration, impatience, and depression are not recognized for what they are. This makes the negative self-perpetuation stronger and stronger, until the inflamed boil bursts. Then we have an obvious crisis.

Crisis Can Put an End to Negative Self-Perpetuation

Crisis can mean, if one's consciousness so chooses, the end of continually swelling negative self-perpetuation. When eruption comes, the choices of recognizing the meaning or continuing to escape become more clearly defined. Even if this eruption does not lead to recognition and an inner change of direction, a final crisis is bound to come where the entity can no longer take refuge from its message. The personality must see eventually that all eruptions, breakdowns, crises, mean to tear down the old structure so as to reerect a new and better functioning one.

The "dark night" of the mystics is such a time of the breakdown of old structures. Most human beings still fail to understand the meaning of crisis. They continually look in the wrong direction. If nothing would break down, the negativity would continue. Yet it is possible after a certain amount of awakening has taken place in the consciousness that the person does not allow the negativity to become too firmly entrenched. Thus the negativity is prevented from starting the self-perpetuating cycle. It is confronted right at the start.

Crisis can be avoided by looking at the inner truth when the first inklings of disturbance and negativity manifest on the surface. But a tremendous amount of honesty is required to challenge one's tightly cherished convictions. Such challenge cuts out the negative self-perpetuation, the motor force that compounds the destructive, erroneous psychic matter until it finds a breaking point. It avoids the many vicious circles within the human psyche and in relationships that are painful and problematic.

Growth Is Possible Without "Dark Nights"

If difficulties, upheavals, and pain in the individual's life, as well as in the life of humanity as a whole, were viewed from this point of view, the real meaning of crisis would be understood and much pain could be avoided. I say to you now: Do not wait for crisis to come in an eruption as the natural, balance-establishing event that takes place as inexorably as a thunderstorm must take place when certain atmospheric conditions have to be altered and clarity in the atmosphere is to be reestablished. This is exactly what happens within the human consciousness. Growth is indeed possible without intense painful "dark nights," if honesty with the self becomes predominant in the personality. True inner looking and deep concern with the inner being as well as giving up pet attitudes and ideas must be cultivated. Then the painful, disruptive crisis can be avoided, because no inflamed boil will form.

The process of death itself is such a crisis. I have discussed various deeper meanings of death. This is yet another. Superficial death—that is, death of the human body—takes place because the consciousness says, "I cannot go on any longer," or "I am at my wit's end." Any crisis contains this thought. Consciousness always expresses to itself, "I can no longer deal with the situation." If the situation is specific, a specific crisis occurs in life. If it is a question of one's present incarnation as a whole, then physical death will occur. In the latter case, the eruption takes the form of the spirit's breaking out of the body, until it finds new life circumstances in which to deal with the same inner distortions all over again. Since eruption, breakdown, and crisis always aim at discontinuing old ways of operating and creating new ones, the process of death and rebirth signifies the identical principle.

People tend to oppose going on to other ways of operating and reacting, however. This obstruction is so unnecessary. It is actually this opposition that creates the tension and strain of crisis, not the giving up of the old structure itself. When necessary change is not accepted willingly, you automatically put yourself into a state of crisis. The intensity of the crisis indicates the intensity of the opposition, as well as the urgency of the need for change. The greater the need for change, and the greater the obstruction to change, the more painful the crisis is going to be. The more openness and willingness there is, on any level, to change, and the less necessary the change is at any given moment of the evolutionary path of an individual, the less severe and painful the crisis is going to be.

Outer Crisis and Inner Crisis

The severity and pain of a crisis is by no means determined by the objective event. I think most of you, my friends, can readily verify this. Most of you have gone through severe changes outwardly. You have lost a loved one, you may have coped with the most drastic changes and objectively traumatic events—wars, revolution, loss of fortune and home, illness. Yet you may inwardly have been much less agitated and in pain than in situations that are outwardly incommensurate with the agitation of your inner feelings. Thus we can say that an outer crisis may leave you inwardly in greater peace than an inner one. The objectively more traumatic event hurts sometimes less than the objectively less traumatic one. In the former instance the necessary change takes place on an outer level, which your inner being accepts more, adjusts to better, and finds a new way of dealing with. In the latter instance, the need for inner change meets with greater resistance. Your subjective interpretation of the event makes the crisis disproportionately painful. Sometimes one tries to find rational explanations for such a peculiar emotional intensity—explanations that can be called rationalizations. Sometimes both inner and outer changes and crises meet the same inner attitude.

When the process of the crisis is accepted and no longer obstructed, when one goes with it, instead of fighting it, relief will come comparatively quickly. Once the pus runs out of the boil and the attitudes are adjusted, self-revelation brings peace; understanding brings new energy and aliveness. The healing process is at work, even while the boil erupts.

The negation of this process, the inner attitude that says, "I should not have to go through this. Do I have to? This and that and the other is wrong with others. If it were not, I would not have to go through this now," prolongs the agony. This attitude seeks to avoid the necessary eruption of the boil, which consists of a painful entanglement of ever-increasing negative energy whose momentum makes it more and more difficult to alter the course. The ongoing negative cycle and its futile, automatic repetition that the consciousness is unable to stop generate hopelessness. The repetition and the hopelessness could stop only by your no longer avoiding the necessary change.

Every negative experience, every pain, is the result of a wrong idea. A critical aspect of this work is the articulation of these ideas. And yet, how often all of you still miss the necessary recognition by not keeping these incontrovertible facts in mind when you meet with an unhappy situation?

Leaving Crises Behind

Once you take on the habit of first questioning your hidden wrong assumptions and destructive reactions when anything unwelcome comes your way, and fully open to truth and change, your life will alter drastically. Pain will become proportionately less frequent, and joy will become more and more the natural state. The rhythm of growth can then proceed smoothly, without the leaps and bounds of breaking up negative structures in the soul substance.

We have discussed the *negative* aspects of self-perpetuation. Of course, it exists primarily on the *positive* side. Let us look at love. The more you love, the more you can produce genuine love feelings without impoverishing yourself and others. You realize that you do not take away anything from anyone by giving out. On the contrary, more will come to you and others from it. You will find new ways, deeper ways, more variations of experiencing love in giving and receiving it, being in tune with this universal feeling. The ability to experience and express love will grow in an ever-increasing, self-perpetuating, motion.

So it is with every other constructive feeling and attitude. The more meaningful, constructive, fulfilled, and joyous your life is, the more of these attributes it must generate. It is an ongoing, never-ending process of steady expansion and self-expression. The principle is exactly the same as that of the negative self-perpetuation. The only difference is that *the positive process is infinite*.

Once you establish the contact with your innate wisdom, beauty, and joyousness and allow them to unfold, they will increase themselves. The self-perpetuation takes over once these energies are released and admitted to consciousness. The initial actualization of these powers requires effort, but once the process is flowing, it is effortless. The more you bring forth of the universal qualities, the more there will be to bring forth.

Your own potentials to experience beauty, joy, pleasure, love, wisdom, and creative expression, my dearest friends, are indeed infinite. Again the words have been said, heard, registered. But how deeply do you know that this is a reality? How deeply do you believe in your innermost potential to be self-creating, to be in bliss, to live the infinite life? How much do you believe in your resources to solve all your problems? How much do you trust in the possibilities that are not yet manifest? How much do you believe it is real that new vistas of yourself can be discovered? How much do you truly believe that you can unfold qualities of peace coupled with excitement, of serenity coupled with adventure, through which life becomes a string of beautiful experiences even though initial difficulties are still to be overcome? *How much do you really believe in all this, my friends?*

Ask yourself this question. To the extent you pay only lip-service to this belief, you will still feel hopeless, depressed, fearful or anxious, entangled in apparently insoluble conflicts with yourself and others. This is a sign that you do not yet believe in your own infinitely expanding potential. If you do not truly believe this, my dearest ones, it is because there is something in you that you desperately hold on to. You do not wish to expose it because you do not wish to give it up or change.

This applies to every single one of you here, and of course to everyone else in the world. For who has not the "dark nights" to put up with? Some have many little "dark nights" coming and going, or their "dark night" is gray. They may not be in a great crisis at any given moment, but life is gray and fluctuates comparatively little. But then there are those who have already worked their way out of this grayness. They no longer want to content themselves with comparative safety from crisis. They are willing, deep within themselves, to chance temporary upheaval for the sake of reaching a more desirable, steady state. They want to realize their potential for deeper joy and self-expression. Then the "dark nights" will become more circumscribed, experienced either as fluctuating periods of upheaval and joy, or, in some lives, bunched up in stronger episodes. Utter darkness, loss, pain, and confusion alternate with heights of golden light, carrying justified hope for an eventual, uninterrupted state of bliss.

The Message of Crises

No matter how any one of you experiences crises, there is always a message in them for you to discover about your own life. It is up to you not to project your experiences outwardly, on others, which is always the most dangerous temptation. Or, for that matter, to project them into yourself in a self-devastating way, which avoids the issue just as much as when you project it onto others. The attitude "I am so bad, I am nothing" is always dishonest. This dishonesty has to be exposed, so that the crisis can become meaningful, whether it be small or great.

If you learn eventually to take the smallest shadow of your everyday life and explore its deepest meaning, you will handle the little crises in a way that makes the swelling of the boil impossible. Hence no painful eruption is needed to destroy rotten structures. This will reveal the stark reality to you that universal life untampered is golden joyousness of ever-increasing beauty.

Every smallest shadow is a crisis, for it need not be there. It is only there because of your turning away from the issue that creates crisis. So take those smallest shadows of your everyday life and ask yourself what they mean. What do you not wish to see and not wish to change? If you face this, and truly wish to face the real issue and make the necessary change, the crisis will have fulfilled its function. You will discover new dimensions of the issue that will make the sun rise, and the dark night will turn out to be the educator, the therapist that life always is once you try to understand it.

Your capacity *to cope with the negativity of others* grows only to the extent that you can do what I explain in this lecture. How often do you sense negative feelings from others but cannot handle them because you are anxious, uncertain, and not clear about the nature of your involvement and interaction with them? At other times, you may not even sense the actual presence of hostility in others. Their subtlety and indirectness confuse you, make you feel guilty about your instinctive responses, but you are even less able to handle the situation. This frequent occurrence is entirely due to your blindness to yourself and your resistance to change. When you project all your old negative experiences onto others, it is impossible for you to have adequate awareness of what actually goes on in the other person, and therefore you cannot deal with it. You will experience a magnificent new turn in your life as you grow in your capacity to look honestly at what disturbs you within yourself and as you become willing to change. Almost inadvertently, and as if it had nothing to do with your efforts, a new gift arises in you: You see the negativity in others in a way that leaves you free, that permits you to confront them, that is effective. It has no adverse effect on you. It must, in the long run, also be beneficial for others, whenever they want it to be.

When you resist change, fear grows because your innermost being knows that crisis, eruption, breakdown, are inevitable and are steadily drawing nearer. Yet you resist doing what could avoid the crisis. What I say here is the story of human life. This is where human nature is caught. The lesson must then be repeated until the illusory fear of change is exposed as an error. If crisis can be understood the way I show you here, and if you really meditate to understand your own crisis and to give up what you hold on to, and challenge the limitations you place on the particular issue, life will open up almost at once.

You must also realize that change cannot be executed only by the ego. The willing, conscious self alone is incapable of doing it. The difficulty of changing, and the resistance to it, come to a large extent from having forgotten that you cannot do it without *divine help*. Thus you go from one wrong extreme to the other. One extreme is that you think you are the one who must accomplish inner transformation. Since you know deep inside that you cannot do this, that you just do not have the equipment to do it, you give up. You feel it is hopeless to make yourself change, so you do not even really try, nor do you express the concisely formulated desire to do so.

You are right to believe that the capacity to change is

missing when you consider yourself exclusively as the conscious, willing, ego-self. Resistance is partly an expression of avoiding the frustration of wanting something that cannot be done and must prove a disappointment. This extreme reaction takes place in the innermost layer of the human psyche. So does the opposite extreme, in which you profess the belief in a higher power, or God, who is supposed to do it all for you. You remain in an absolutely passive state, waiting for it. Again, the conscious self does not try where it should. False hope and false resignation are only two sides of the same coin: absolute passivity. But the pushing ego, attempting to go beyond its own capacity, must inevitably end in the same passive state of either falsely waiting or falsely giving up hope. The pushing exhausts the self and renders it passive. These attitudes may exist simultaneously or alternately.

The way to go about making a positive change is to want it; you must be willing to be in truth and to change. And you have to pray to the innermost divine functioning within your soul to make the change possible. Then you wait for the change to take place, in a trusting, confident, and patient way. This is the absolute prerequisite for change. When it does not even occur to you to assume this prayerful attitude and say, "I want to change, but my ego cannot do it. God will do it through me. I will make myself a willing, receptive channel for this to happen," you are basically unwilling to change and/or are doubtful about the reality of the higher forces within you.

This confident, patient waiting, this assurance and trust that help will come when you are utterly willing to look at the truth, *can* be acquired. It is not a childish attitude that wants an authority to do it for you. Quite the contrary. This approach conciliates the attitude of adult self-responsibility that takes action by facing the self with the receptive attitude in which the ego knows its own limitations. In this receptive attitude, wanting truth and change, you let God into your soul from deep within yourself. You open up for it to happen.

When this attitude is adopted, *change becomes a living reality* for anyone and everyone. When trust and faith are lacking that the divine can actualize itself through you, it is because you have not given yourself the opportunity to experience the stark reality of these processes. You have denied yourself this experience. And since you have never experienced it, how can you trust it?

Also, since you still have some little escape hatch in reserve, which keeps you from entering into life fully and committedly, you cannot experience the marvel of the reality of the Universal Spirit within yourself. Since you are not honest with life, you cannot really believe in the power of the Universal Intelligence dwelling in you at all times, which goes to work the instant you make room for it. Total commitment to it is necessary, without reservation. This commitment is the absolute prerequisite for your discovery of its reality within you. Even if you do not know what the outcome will be, whether or not God's way will be agreeable to you, the commitment must be made. Not knowing the total answer right now is part of it. Considerations of ways that avoid full commitment keep you holding on to the old, distorted, cheating way of life, while still wanting to reach for the new, liberated, free way in which you are whole, instead of inwardly divided and racked by the pain of this division. But you cannot have it both ways. *Your commitment to the Ultimate Creator must become total, applied to the most seemingly insignificant aspect of daily living and being.* You must be totally committed to the truth, because then you are also committed to the Universal Spirit.

If you thus commit yourself, you will let go of the old accustomed shore and float momentarily in what seems uncertainty. But you will not mind this. You will feel safer than ever before, when you were holding on to the old shore, to the false structure that must be torn down. You will soon know that there is nothing to fear. You need to summon courage to do this, only to find that this is really the safest and most secure way possible to live. It actually requires no courage at all. Then, and only then, will the "dark nights" turn into instruments of light.

QUESTION: *This lecture is very close to where I am. I have just begun to discover the meaning of crisis. I feel I either have to take cover somewhere or I have to ride through the storm, which I feel I am doing now.*

ANSWER: This recognition is very good. It touches upon the age-old alternatives of taking cover or driving through. It is perhaps the most important question on the evolutionary path of each entity. You remain in the cycle of death and rebirth, of pain and struggle, of conflict and strife—physically as well as spiritually and psychologically—precisely because you cling to the illusion that going through can be avoided and escaping will do some good. Actually, taking cover does not do any good; on the contrary, it increases the critical tension. The momentary relief is illusion of the most serious nature. It is so because the crisis inevitably comes later on, but by then is no longer connected with its source and therefore it hurts more. When you make up your mind, however, saying, "I will not take cover, I will go through it," the resources within the human soul will become almost instantly available. These resources remain obscure to those who still tend to escape. They then feel weak and do not believe in their own capacities to actualize the infinite powers of the Universal Spirit. They do not know their potential, the strength that will arise, the inspiration that will come. Only when you decide to go through and ask for help in meditation do these resources become available. Then you will sense an awakened trust that the conscious ego is not alone. It is not the only faculty available to deal with the issue.

I bless you and ask you to open up your innermost being, your whole soul, all your psychic forces, to let go of the cramp that denies truth and change, therefore self-expression and light. Open up in this way, to let the blessed power constantly present within you permeate your whole being.

A blessing comes forth that will meet with the inner power of which I have spoken, thus doubly strengthening you. Continue your growth so that your wholeness, your connectedness with the universe, will grow and give you more of the joy that is inherently your birthright. Be blessed, be in peace.

12

The Meaning of Evil and Its Transcendence

It is impossible to deny that evil exists on earth. What approach can we take to deal with it so that humanity can transcend its present painful state? If we strive for a unified consciousness, we would need to integrate evil, but how can we integrate something that is so contrary to everything that we consciously strive for? If we deny evil, since we know that in the greater reality it does not exist, will it also cease to exist on our plane of manifestation? Can it be that there is evil in all of us, and, if so, what can we do about it?

∽

Greetings and blessings to all my old and new friends. Human beings are continually confronted with the deep problem of how to handle the destructive forces residing within themselves and others. This problem seems unending, for ever since the beginning of human existence, theories and philosophies have been built around it. Your search has always been concerned, directly or indirectly, with this great issue.

Does Evil Exist?

There are usually two types of answers given about the existence of evil, the religious and the philosophical. One stresses evil as a force separate from and opposed to good, the other denies that evil exists at all.

To deny evil on humanity's plane of consciousness is as unrealistic as to believe that in ultimate reality two separate forces exist: one good and one evil. Such a belief implies that the evil force must be destroyed or whisked away, as if anything could be made to disappear in the universe! Only those who search for the truth between these two alternatives can find the answers.

Most religions take a dualistic approach to the great question of evil, seeing it as a force opposed to good. The dualistic approach reinforces your fear of yourself and your guilt; therefore, it only increases the chasm within your soul. The energies of fear and guilt are used to force yourself to be good. The blindness, compulsion, and the artificial concept of life that accompany this forcing create self-perpetuating patterns, with many negative ramifications.

On the other hand, there are philosophies that postulate that evil just does not exist; it is an illusion. Such philosophy has a part of the truth, just as its religious opposite does, which recognizes the danger of evil, its life-defeating power, and the unhappiness and suffering it brings. The postulate that evil is an illusion is true in the sense that there is innately only one great creative power. There *is* union, for all is one in the consciousness of those who have transcended dualism.

As is so often true, both of these opposing teachings express great truths, but the exclusiveness with which they are conceived and perpetuated ultimately renders their truth untrue. The denial of evil as a reality leads to wishful thinking, further blindness, and the denial of the self; it decreases rather than increases awareness. Thus, a false picture is created—the manifestation of the present state of humankind.

Both views of evil lead to repression; yet acknowledging

evil also leads to the possibility of further destructiveness. It might lead to justifying and condoning truly undesirable things, such as self-righteous acting out. In such a case it is the guilt that would be repressed, creating further splitting and duality. Let us now try to find a way to avoid either of these pitfalls and to reconcile the two general approaches to evil.

Right Acceptance of Evil

All suffering comes exclusively from one's own destructiveness, negativity, or evil—whatever name you give it. You have all experienced how threatened, anxious, and uncomfortable you feel when you are confronted with some of your undesirable attitudes, traits, and characteristics. This reaction must be understood in a much deeper way. The meaning of such uncomfortable, anxious reaction is plainly an expression that says, "Such and such should not exist in me." All the defenses you have so painstakingly erected serve to protect you not only from the evil of others, but primarily from your own. If you examine the cause each time you feel anxious, you will always find that, in the last analysis, you are apprehensive of your own evil, regardless of how threatening another person or an outside event appears. If you then translate this anxiety into clear-cut words, thus verbalizing your inner thought that certain attitudes or feelings "should not exist in me," you can then confront your attitude toward evil in a much better way. For the evil itself is not half as damaging as your attitude to it. We shall come back to this later.

From now on, instead of habitually evading, which breeds emotional illness, problems, and suffering, catch your fear and the thought behind the fear: "I should not be that way." If this fear is ignored, the problem becomes worse.

Evil as Distorted Creative Power

Our aim on this path is precisely the knowing and acceptance of the evil. The word "acceptance" has been used a great deal for lack of a better one, but the meaning often gets lost behind the word, so we must pay more attention to how this acceptance comes about. For only when acceptance occurs in the right way can evil be incorporated and reformed in the truest sense of the word. You can then transform a force that has gone awry. Most human beings totally forget or ignore the fact that what is worst in them is essentially highly desirable creative power and universal flow and energy. Only when you truly realize this, my friends, will you learn to cope with every aspect of yourself.

Almost all human beings, with very, very few exceptions, accept, know, and only want to know, a relatively small part of their total personality. This limitation is, of course, a terrible loss. Not being aware of that within which is undesirable in its present manifestation shuts them off from what is already clear, liberated, purified, good. It also prevents most individuals from loving and respecting themselves because they have no real perception of their divine heritage. Their actual, already manifest goodness seems unreal, even fake, because they refuse to tackle the destructive elements in themselves. But what is even more important and fundamental is that shutting off this undesirable part causes it to remain stagnant and paralyzed so that it cannot change.

The price of recognizing and accepting the destructive, evil aspect of the self seems high, but it really is not. By contrast, the price of denying it is enormous. You may grope in confusion until you find a way to accept your destructive impulses and desires without condoning them. Because you consider something in you bad, you believe all of you is bad. What you need to do is to identify with the part of you that is observing and not the rest that you observe. Understand it without identifying with it. You must learn to evaluate negative impulses and desires realistically, without falling into the trap of projection and self-justification. Such understanding requires continual inspiration from the higher forces within and deliberate requests for help in awakening and maintaining awareness of these destructive aspects and of the proper method to handle them.

Whenever you are in an unpleasant mood, a threatening

situation, confusion and darkness, you can be sure that regardless of the outer circumstances, the problem arises from denial and fear of your own destructive attitudes, and your ignorance about how to handle them. Admitting this brings immediate relief and deactivates these negative powers almost instantly. Learn by what steps you can incorporate this power rather than shut it off.

The *first step* must be applying the theory that destructiveness, evil, is not a final separate force. You must think about this not merely in general, philosophical terms. Rather, you must take the specific aspects of yourself that make you feel guilty and afraid, and apply this knowledge to all that is most distasteful in yourself and others. No matter how ugly some of those manifestations are—whether it be cruelty, spite, arrogance, contempt, selfishness, indifference, greed, cheating, or something else—you can bring yourself to realize that *every one of these traits is an energy current, originally good and beautiful and life-affirming.*

By searching in this direction, you will come to understand and experience how this or that specific hostile impulse was originally a good force. When you understand that, you will have made a substantial inroad toward transforming the hostility and freeing the energy that has either been channeled in a truly undesirable, destructive way, or become frozen and stagnant. Articulate clearly the insight that these ugly traits are a power that can be used any way you wish. This power— the same energy that may now manifest as hostility, envy, hatred, rage, bitterness, self-pity, or blame—can become a creative power to build happiness, pleasure, love, expansion, for yourself and others around you.

In other words, you have to learn to acknowledge that the way the power manifests is undesirable, but the energy current behind this manifestation is desirable in itself, for it is made of the life-stuff itself. It contains *consciousness* and *creative energy*. It contains every possibility to manifest and express life, to create new life. It contains all the best of life, as you experience it—and much more. So, too, the best of life that has revealed itself to you contains the possibility of the very worst. If you can envisage the possibilities of all life manifestations, because *life is a continuous flowing, moving, ongoing process*, you can never become fixated on the finalities, which create error, confusion, dualism.

You will see that by denying the evil in you, you do greater harm to the whole of your personality, to your manifest spirituality, than you realize. For by denying it, you inactivate an essential part of your energies and creative forces, so they stagnate. From stagnation, putrefaction follows. Matter putrefies when it stagnates, when it can no longer move. The same is true of consciousness.

Matter is always a condensation and manifestation of consciousness and energy. The way the energy flows—or does not flow—and the form it takes when it condenses depends on the attitude of consciousness "behind," or, rather, intrinsic to, a particular aspect of creation.

Destructiveness is an erroneous form of consciousness. It must lead, either directly through acting out and giving it direct expression, or indirectly, through denial, that is, stagnation, to a negation of life. This is why some supposedly negative emotions are actually desirable. For instance, anger can further life and be directed against the negation of life. Denial of anger turns into hostility, cruelty, spite, self-hate, guilt, confusion between blame of others and blame of self, and is thus a destructive energy current.

When evil is understood to be intrinsically a divine energy flow, momentarily distorted due to specific wrong ideas, concepts, and perceptions, it is no longer rejected in its essence but assimilated. This is precisely what you find most difficult to do. In fact, you find it so difficult that you tend to forget even those aspects in you that are already free of distortion, evil, and destructiveness, that are liberated and clear, that are good and beautiful and divine.

All your striving and goodwill are beautiful. Even your pangs of conscience, notwithstanding the misplaced guilt, spring from the best and most beautiful manifestations of consciousness. You will deny, ignore, fail to experience this best in you as long as you deny, ignore, fail to experience the evil in you. You distort your concept of yourself when you deny any part of yourself, no matter how ugly it may be in its present form.

The essential key to totally integrating the evil is understanding its original nature and the indwelling possibility that it may manifest again in its original form. This must be the aim, my friends. As long as you try to become good by denying evil, by forcing yourself to be what you cannot yet be, and what you can in fact never be, you remain in a painful state of inner split, partial self-denial, and paralysis of vital forces within you. I say "what you can never be," because if your expectation is to destroy or magically whisk away a vital part of yourself and not to accept the intrinsic desirability of all the creative energy contained in even your most destructive aspects, you cannot become whole. Cultivate this altered attitude.

The new attitude of acceptance does not mean condoning, excusing, or rationalizing your undesirable aspects. Quite the contrary: It means fully acknowledging them, giving honest expression to them, without finding excuses or blaming others, but not feeling hopeless and self-rejecting about them either. This seems like a tall order, but it is certainly possible to acquire this attitude if you make a sincere effort and truly pray that guidance be given to you for this very purpose.

Liberating the Inner Beauty

When you no longer negate your ugliness, you will no longer have to negate your beauty. There is so much beauty in every one of you that is already free. You actually manifest beauty that you totally negate, ignore, fail to perceive and experience! And I do not mean only potential, as yet to be developed beauty; I mean beauty that is really present.

You can think of this and pray to see it in yourself, as you pray to see the ugliness. When you can perceive both, not just one, exclusive of the other, you will have made a substantial step toward a realistic perception of life and of yourself that will enable you to integrate what now tears you asunder.

By keeping both your beauty and your ugliness in mind at all times, *you will also see both sides in others.* You tend to completely reject and negate people whose destructiveness you perceive, and react to them exactly as you do toward yourself. Or you emotionally react to their goodness and inner beauty, while unrealistically overlooking their ugly side. You cannot yet grasp the presence of duality in yourself, and therefore neither can you see it in others. This creates continual conflicts and strife. Such distortion and lack of awareness cause you to deny and paralyze the creative process itself. Only by accepting the duality can you truly transcend it.

Transformation

The overtly destructive attitudes are never the real evil. If you truly acknowledge them, you remain in the flow. The greatest hatred, the most spiteful vindictiveness, the worst impulses of cruelty, if honestly and squarely admitted, neither acted out irresponsibly nor repressed and denied, but fully accepted, will never become harmful. To the degree they are seen, faced, and admitted, such feelings will diminish in intensity and must sooner or later convert into flowing, life-giving energy. Hate will turn into love, cruelty into healthy self-assertion, stagnation into joy and pleasure.

So this is, my friends, what you have to learn. The key is to encounter the destructive force so that you can transform it back to its original nature, thus incorporating it into your whole being and creating with the life-energy at your disposal.

Are there any questions?

QUESTION: *As this lecture says, there are things in me that I feel are wrong, evil. Yet I enjoy them; they feel pleasurable. But I feel guilty. For instance, I overspend money. I negate that aspect of myself completely. Can you help me?*

ANSWER: This is a good example. What you describe is quite typical. You are confronted with an insoluble predicament: Either you give up all pleasure connected with over-spending and irresponsibility in order to become decent, mature, realistic, self-responsible and safe, or you take some pleasure from the negative trait but at the tremendous cost of guilt, self-deprivation, insecurity, and fear of not being able to run your own life.

Once you see that behind the compulsion to overspend and be irresponsible is a legitimate yearning for pleasure, expansion, and new experience, this predicament will cease to exist. In other words, you must incorporate the *essence* of this wish without acting out the destructiveness of it. You will then have much less difficulty putting the wish into effect in a realistic way that will not defeat you in the end. You are now stuck in battling with one of these typical either/or problems. How can you really want to give up irresponsibility if responsibility implies living on a narrow margin of pleasure, and confining your self-expression? Since you do not really want to give up the irresponsibility, you feel guilty. Thus you reject that vital part of you that rightfully wishes to experience the pleasure of creation at its fullest, but does not yet know how without exploiting others and being parasitic. If, however, you can fully accept the beautiful force striving for full pleasure underneath the irresponsibility and value it as such, you will also find how to give it expression without infringing on others, without violating your own laws of balance. You will not have to pay the needless cost of worry, anxiety, guilt, and inability to manage well. You only pay that when you sacrifice peace of mind for a short-lived pleasure.

The pleasure will be deeper, more lasting, and totally free of guilt when you combine its rightfulness with self-discipline. If you can reconcile desire for pleasure with self-discipline and responsibility, you will express the inner knowledge that says, "I want to enjoy life. There is unlimited abundance in the universe for every contingency. There is no limit to what is possible. There are marvelous things to be experienced. There are many beautiful means of self-expression. I can realize them and bring them into my life if I can find another, not self-destructive, way to express and obtain them."

The discipline will be much easier to acquire, the willingness to do so will grow, when you know that you have a perfect right to use it for the purpose of increasing pleasure and self-expression.

My dearest friends, I have given you new material that requires a great deal of attention. Bring it to bear on your own specific situation. Open up your innermost being to applying this material. Do not apply it only theoretically, in general terms, but see really where you deny what is in you out of fear and guilt, thereby paralyzing the best in you.

To those of you who are discouraged and feel hopeless I can only say: You are in illusion and error when you feel that way. Realize this and ask for the truth, which is that there is no reason for hopelessness, and difficult periods need only to be understood and worked through to make them *stepping stones* for opening your lives further and bringing more light and self-expression into them.

Receive the love and blessings, my dearest friends, be in peace.

13

Self-Esteem

The Guide once said that when human beings hate and reject themselves "the angels weep." We have heard it but forget too easily that as incarnated souls we are divine manifestations; we tend to identify that part of our nature which we like least as our true, permanent selves. This assumption has dire consequences, as the Guide will explain. In this very uplifting lecture he teaches us how to find our true identity in our ever-changing live core. Discovering infinite possibilities in ourselves for making positive choices, we come to respect and love ourselves.

∽

Greetings, my dearest friends. Blessings for every one of you here. May your heart be open, may your attention be focused, so that you can absorb as much as possible in this hour.

Self-esteem, self-liking, or self-value—whatever you call it—is sorely lacking in every human being who experiences feelings of uncertainty, fear, insecurity, guilt, weakness, doubt, negativity, inadequacy, and inferiority. To the degree these feelings are present, self-esteem is inevitably lacking, only this is not directly recognized. Such ignorance is all the more damaging, for you are then less capable of tackling the problem directly. Only considerable insight into the self brings the direct awareness of "I do not like and respect myself."

The Inner Conflict Between Self-Indulgence and Self-Rejection

People are constantly confronted with an inner, and rarely conscious, conflict about this recognition. The conflict arises out of the dualistic perception characteristic of humanity. I have often shown how a misconception splits the truth into two opposing halves that confuse you and make it impossible for you to make satisfying choices. You are then torn in inner dissension and painful confusion. In this case the dilemma is: How can you accept and like yourself without falling into the danger of self-indulgence and self-justification for the destructive traits that exist in all human beings, no matter how concealed they may be? Or, on the other side, how can you confront, accept, and admit those negative, destructive traits, weaknesses, little selfishnesses, cruelties, and vanities that often make you vindictive and unloving, and nevertheless maintain your self-respect? How can you avoid falling into the danger of destructive guilt, self-rejection, and self-contempt?

This is a deep-rooted conflict, and most human beings, whether or not they know it, battle with it. It is a typical dualistic confusion that apparently makes admitting an unpleasant truth and self-acceptance into mutually exclusive opposites.

But before I discuss this in greater detail and offer you a key that will make it possible to unify this split, let me discuss the conflict itself a little more. Those of you who have recently found this raging battle within yourselves will know exactly what I am talking about. Others, who have not yet recognized their self-rejection, will have to come to this awareness gradually. Perhaps the only way you can now recognize your self-dislike and your undervaluation of yourself will be an indirect one. You can certainly sense shyness, uncertainty, insecurity, apprehension about being rejected or criticized, as well as feelings of inferiority and inadequacy. Perhaps you may perceive here or there a peculiar guilt feeling that makes no sense to you. Although this guilt usually hides behind other attitudes, it is rarely so remote that it cannot be clearly perceived at times, once you set out to detect such things. Perhaps you are aware that you are not open to the untold possibilities of blissful fulfillment in life; that you make do with much less than you could experience. Perhaps you can discern that you stand back in life and feel vaguely undeserving and perceive your own possibilities negatively at least in certain areas of your life.

All these manifestations indicate self-rejection, self-dislike. It should not be too difficult to bridge the gap in consciousness between any of these manifestations with the more profound root, namely that you do not think much of yourself. You may dislike yourself for some traits and attitudes, but this specificity may be even more hidden from your awareness. It is quite possible that you can first ascertain only the vague general feelings of self-disdain, without being able to pinpoint the specific traits you dislike in yourself.

Once you feel, however vaguely, that you do not respect yourself and lack esteem and appreciation for yourself as a human being, the next step must be to make this attitude more specific. If you really want to find it, you will do so, although the recognition of exactly what this attitude is may come quite indirectly. This is the way the path often works.

On the other hand, you may see something quite clearly in yourself that is truly regrettable and undesirable. Then you may fall into the erroneous attitude of defiance and self-justification, because you believe that admitting your undesirable traits means that you must dislike and reject your entire self. You fail to differentiate between rejecting a trait and rejecting the person, whether yourself or others. Therefore you fall into the error of justifying, denying, falsifying, and rationalizing—and often even beautifying—a very undesirable and destructive trait. Here you have the full-fledged confusion!

What Brings Self-Respect?

Here is how to find the key that will enable you to squarely confront the undesirable attitudes, without in the least losing respect for yourself or losing the sense that you are a valuable human being. First, you have to perceive and experience life in a new way. Your life—and you are life because you are alive—represents all life, all nature. One of the earmarks of life is its untold potential for change and expansion. To be more specific: Once you perceive life as it is, you will sense that even the lowliest of all destructive creatures has every possibility for change and for goodness, for greatness, and for growth. At any moment, the thinking may change and create new attitudes and behavior, new feelings, new ways of being. And if these do not happen now, that alters nothing, for one day things are bound to change and then your true nature must finally emerge. The knowledge of one's true nature having to emerge sooner or later changes everything: It changes your despair about yourself. It opens the door to knowing your potential for goodness, regardless of how malicious you now may be; for generosity, regardless of how mean you may now be; for loving, regardless of how selfish you now may be; for strength and integrity, regardless of how weak you may now be and how tempted to betray your best self; for greatness, regardless of how petty you may now be.

Look at nature, at any manifestation of life, and it is forever changing; it is forever dying and being reborn; it is forever expanding and contracting and pulsating. It is always moving and branching out. This applies particularly to life that is conscious, and even more so to life that is self-conscious. The power of thought, of will, of emotions is infinitely greater than any inanimate power. And yet, the inanimate power of, say, electricity, and even more of atomic energy, is so great that you have barely begun to gain an inkling of its possibilities both for good and constructive, as well as for destructive, ends. Wherever there is life and consciousness, both these possibilities exist.

Using the Power of the Conscious Mind

Now, if in the smallest atom—so small that it cannot even be perceived with the naked eye—a power exists to release untold energies for building or destroying, how infinitely more is this the case with the power of the mind: the power of thinking, feeling, and willing. Just dwell on this significant fact, my friends, and it will open new vistas to you. Why do you blindly assume that the power of inanimate things is greater than the power of the mind?

The powers to think, will, feel, express, act, and decide are the earmarks of consciousness. They are vastly underrated by humanity. Living consciousness therefore deserves a respect that can hardly be put into words. It does not matter how it manifests; no matter how undesirable and destructive the present manifestation may be, the life that issues from the momentary destructiveness holds all the potential for turning into constructive channels, for life's source is truly inexhaustible.

Since the very essence of life is movement, and therefore change, this is what justifiably and realistically gives hope, no matter how hopeless a situation or a state of mind may appear. People in deep depression and hopelessness must be in error, for they negate the very essence of life. And those who despair about themselves because they feel they are so bad, so unacceptable, so destructive, so negative, find themselves in the error of perceiving and experiencing life in a fixed way, as though what is now must always be. This is the error of deadness: "This is so, and that is all there is to it." Such thinking ignores and negates the flux of true life. Since you are alive, this fluidity is yours; in reality you are fluid.

The only thing that keeps you from being fluid, and therefore changing into a state of realistic hopefulness and light, into the essence of life itself, is your own enclosure, your ignorance of this truth—your momentary state of consciousness. This state of consciousness is now fixed in the conviction that life and your personality traits are static and must remain that way. Your state of consciousness remains fixed in this dark imprisonment as long as you know nothing else.

You have the possibility of applying these words to your personal situation. Where are you hopeless? Why are you hopeless? Do you feel hopeless because of life itself? Because you believe the possibilities for expansion and happiness are too limited to give you sufficient scope? Are you hopeless because you feel you do not deserve and cannot have a more meaningful, fulfilled experience of life? The latter thought may smolder secretly beneath your perception of life's limitations.

If you can bring these fleeting impressions into more concise awareness, you can ask yourself: "Am I hopeless about deserving happiness because I, possibly quite justifiably, dislike certain traits in me?" But don't you then also believe that these traits mark and define your person. That is the great struggle, my friends: You erroneously believe that what is most obnoxious to you is you. This, at the same time, is the cause for the great resistance, inherent in all human beings, against changing. For, since you do not believe that you can essentially be anything else but that which you dislike, you have to hold on to it nevertheless, because you do not wish to cease existing. That is the crux of this dualistic confusion. This is why you so inexplicably hold on to destructive traits.

You hold on because you genuinely believe this is you; you are in a fixed state, and any change is impossible because you do not realize that all possibilities exist in you. You are already what you think you would have to produce artificially, laboriously, and through forcibly contorting your very nature. But since you will not believe this, you cannot give up holding on to the very facets you so dislike, for they seem to represent your essence.

This is indeed a vicious circle, for true self-esteem can, of course, come only by your sensing your capacity to love, to give of yourself. Yet this capacity cannot be known when you take it for granted that it simply does not exist; when you believe that any state other than the one you express now is alien to you—intrinsically alien, and your real, final, fixed self is what you dislike. As long as that is the case, you remain trapped in a vicious circle.

In order to come out of this circle, life must be understood in its essence. No matter how fixed your life may appear, it is only one tiny part of the whole story, my friends. Underneath all these personality traits you believe are fixed, final things, the fluid life exists like a winter stream under the snow. It is constant; feelings branch out of it in all directions, spontaneously and wondrously forever self-renewing. Its life pulsates vibrantly; it is movement itself. Above all, it is a life in which you are free at any moment to think new and different thoughts that create a new and different life expression and personality.

You see, as long as you ignore the true state of life, hence your own true state, you cannot give yourself the fundamental respect that you deserve as a human creature. As long as you confuse life with death, with inanimate matter, you will despair. And even inanimate matter, as you now know from present-day science, has an intrinsic life and incredible movement, once this life is released. Think about this, my friends. Even an apparently dead object is not dead; it contains life, movement, and utter change. Think of the movement, life, and change in every atom of the deadest-seeming matter.

So, nothing in the universe actually exists that is lifeless. How much less so with consciousness! Your thinking is a constant movement. The only trouble is that you have conditioned yourself to let it ruminate in habitual negativity, self-rejection, and needless limitation. But once you decide to use your thinking in a new way, you will experience the truth of life's hopeful changeability, its endless possibilities to move in new directions. You can constantly expand your thinking, take in new ideas, embrace new realizations, and therefore bring to yourself new will-directions, new expansions, new aims, new energies, new feelings. All of this is personality change. Without your being quite aware of it, these new ways of thinking and feeling change those attitudes you now dislike so much.

When I talk about new ways of being, I want to make it quite clear that this does not mean they have not existed in you as a dormant essence. They are only new as far as your awareness is concerned, for they are all there, constantly ready to be used for the asking. But as long as you enclose yourself within the narrow framework of your limited perceptions of yourself and of life, you cannot use what is already there. Perceive yourself as fertile soil before the seeds are planted. Fertile soil contains incredible power to bring about new expressions of life. The potentials seethe in it, whether or not the seeds are actually put in. Your entire consciousness and aliveness are the most fertile soil imaginable. The fertile soil is constantly there with incredible power to bring forth new expressions of life in your thinking, your feeling, your willing, your energies, your possibilities of action and reaction.

Each situation you are in contains new possibilities for reaction. You have choices all the time. You can be in a new situation and automatically fall into the old conditioned reflexes, your negative approach, without paying attention to what you are doing. Perhaps you moan about the misery of life because this or that has happened to you that you do not like, and you never see the connection between your discontent and failures on the one hand, and your one-sided, negative automatic reactions on the other. As long as you assume that this habitual approach is the only one possible, you will not grasp the possibilities and powers in your life.

Thus, when you feel unhappy or hopeless, question yourself: "Do I not have another way to react to this situation that seems to befall me out of nowhere and to which I choose to react negatively, destructively, making myself hopeless, complaining and feeling angry about it?" This choice is yours. Your anger and complaints against the world are wasted, for all that energy could do so much to build new life for you if it were used properly. You cannot change others, but you can certainly change your own attitudes and your thinking. Then life offers its limitless possibilities to you.

First, your thinking and your attitudes change; then the feelings follow suit; then your actions and reactions begin to respond to new spontaneous impulses. And these, in turn, bring forth new life experiences. The more you experience the chain reaction of this process, the more you also perceive that you are a living, moving, endlessly changing unit of life expression. And no trait merits evaluating and rejecting your whole self because of it. Once you perceive this, you can afford the wonderful, relieving luxury of calmly admitting any undesirable, ugly trait, without in the least disliking yourself for it; without in the least losing your sense of being a divine expression, no matter what the traits may be. Then, and only then, can you really transform these traits.

Paradoxical as this may seem, the total self-rejection, the destructive kind of guilt under discussion is incapable of overcoming anything. You will not understand why, my friends, unless you see that it is impossible to overcome anything when you believe you are a fixed, unchangeable blob. You have heard that according to your belief you must experience, but when you have built a false belief system you cannot see beyond it. Your actions then are determined by your beliefs and must thus provide proof of their veracity, no matter now mistaken those beliefs are and how many other alternatives exist in reality.

Thus, if you are convinced that you cannot change, you cannot even take a meaningful step in the direction of change. Therefore, you cannot experience change and must be convinced that change is impossible. The negative conviction makes it also impossible to summon the necessary effort for bringing change about. The energy, the discipline, the stamina, the initiative essential for effecting a change will be comparatively easy to muster when you know a change is possible; when you know that change merely means bringing out your dormant qualities. When you know that, no matter how ugly the traits may be, you will not despair about being unlovable. You will make available the powers in you to surge forward; you will be able to dip into the resources of your innermost being that enable you to overcome any ugly destructive trait.

The power that created the universe, with everything in it, including all that you are, possesses the strength to change anything. For even the things that should be changed were created by that same power and must, in essence, be something other than they appear now. This power is also you and is manifest once you contact it deliberately. This can be done only when you know of the source within you, which is forever changing, moving, and expanding with infinite possibilities.

Reconnection with the Instinctual Life

You see, my friends, the life that is inherent in nature is also in you. Bare will and intellect are sterile, as you well know. Only the feeling of life, the natural life, can indeed bring you the fulfillment without which life is a sorry affair indeed. This is what we have been talking about and aiming for on this path. Now why has humanity lost touch with the source of its own life, the source of its feelings, the source of its instincts, the source of its own nature, deep inside the self? Only because you are so terrified of your destructiveness and do not know how to handle it. So civilization has for millennia denied the instinctual life in order to preserve itself from its dangers. But by doing so humanity has cut off its connection with the essence of life itself. It had not realized that there are other ways to eliminate the distorted, perverted, natural forces, ways that need not deny life itself. The instinctual life has always been wrongly equated with destructiveness. Only as humanity matures is it capable of learning that the instinctual life does not need to be denied in order to avoid evil. Indeed, it should not be denied, for doing so defeats life every bit as much as the feared evil itself. Only within the deep core of the instincts can God be found because only there can true aliveness be found. Thus humanity must find another means to handle its destructive instincts if it is not to annihilate itself by different but just as fatal ways as giving vent to those negative instincts.

This lecture will give you an additional tool to meet your destructive side. You will learn to value and nurture the deep instincts you have always so distrusted and to find the truth of the living creative spirit in and through them. You will then joyfully further your instinctual life, unfold and integrate it.

You will believe and trust in it. Do not deny and fear it because you still have difficulties accepting and meeting your undesirable destructive traits. If you truly look at them in a dispassionate, objective way, you will always find that fear and denial really oppose the life of the instincts. The instincts are simple and innocent in themselves; your destructiveness is always a result of pride, selfwill, fear, vanity, greed, separateness, lovelessness, one-upmanship.

In this way, you will find it more and more possible to meet, acknowledge, admit, and accept anything in you, no matter how ugly, and never lose for one second the sense of your intrinsic beautiful aliveness, and of deserving your own esteem. This inner state will be the springboard from which change becomes possible. It will not only be a possibility in the abstract, but an effective way of living, day in and day out, a constantly growing movement.

Any one of you who can truly bring this important topic to bear upon whatever state you are in at this moment will overcome an important hurdle. Many of you may be stuck just in this painful inner confusion. Some of you may not know this consciously; others may feel it vaguely; still others may be quite aware of this struggle. Most human beings are totally oblivious of the fact that this very same battle rages in them; that this battle has created the instinctual restrictions and fear, the self-alienation, the aridity and impoverishment of the souls who cannot thrive in a climate of self-rejection. People also ignore that all the religious commands to love cannot be fulfilled until this dualistic split is healed and unification found, so that self-liking is no longer confused with self-indulgence, and honest self-confrontation need not bring self-loathing. You can find peace only when you can truly accept the ugliest in you and never lose sight of your intrinsic beauty.

Now, are there any questions?

QUESTION: *I feel a terrific battle going on right now in relation to my self-esteem. It feels like an atomic explosion. I realize I'm stuck in my own limitations. I realize that I can't stand pleasure. Coming from my habitual state of unpleasure, pleasure almost seems unnatural.*

ANSWER: If you can conceive of yourself as the essence of life, with all its incredible powers, possibilities, and inherent potentials, you will indeed know that you are deserving of your own esteem and acceptance. You will be able to see the traits you hate and still not lose sight of who you essentially are.

I also suggest a specific exercise you might find quite helpful. Put down in writing everything that you dislike about yourself. Have it down in black and white. Look at those traits when they are written down. Then feel into yourself and ask: "Do I really believe that this is all there is to me? Do I really believe that I must be these traits all my life? Do I believe I have the possibility to love? Do I hold forces locked up in me that contain all the good imaginable?" By raising these questions seriously, you will get an answer on a deeply feeling level, a level where the answer is more than a theoretical concept. You will experience a new power in you that you do not need to fear, and a new gentleness and softness that does not need hostility or other defenses. Then you will know how much there is in you to love and respect.

Unifying Love and Pleasure

You have recently come across, in your personal pathwork, a very specific misconception that makes loving impossible as long as you harbor it. When you mistakenly equate loving with the terrible danger of being totally impoverished, even robbed of your very life, how can you want to love? How can you let yourself love? According to this false idea, giving of yourself means losing what you give without ever being replenished. If this were true, love would indeed be impossible and giving a folly. Is it now conceivable for you to see that this is not so; that reality is different? And if you can see that love comes from the same inexhaustible well as wisdom, as all life does, can you further perceive that you will not need to deny your own natural instinct that wants to reach out, that wants the pleasure of feeling love, warmth, and giving of yourself? And can you still foresee the next natural, organic step in the chain, which is that if you can love, you will inevitably love yourself? This is the reason why you fear pleasure. For pleasure not only seems entirely undeserved, but love and pleasure are interchangeable. True pleasure is loving, and without loving pleasure just does not exist. If you harbor love feelings your whole body is in a blissful vibration, with certainty, with security, with peace, with stimulation, with excitement in the most relaxed, pleasurable way. That cannot come through anything that is given to you when you are merely a recipient. It comes when you vibrate with this feeling. Nor does this mean that you do not also receive love. The giving and receiving become so interchangeable that it can often no longer be discerned which is which. Both become indistinguishable in one movement.

But if your nature is as yet incapable of allowing the feeling of love, you must fear bliss, since bliss and loving are the same thing. The misconception that giving is losing causes you to close up and contract in all situations that might bring forth your natural instincts. When you deny love and pleasure, you must inevitably also deny your self-esteem. Your key must lie in seeing that your inability to love is not an inborn aspect that you alone harbor forever. It is a temporary block to loving, based on some false premises that exist on a deeper level of your emotional experience. You can change this misconception any moment you truly and fully look at it.

Be blessed, every one of you. Be in peace. Be what you are, honestly and truly, so that God manifests more and more in you.

14

Meditation for Three Voices: Ego, Lower Self, Higher Self

In this meditation, specifically geared to self-transformation, we engage the conscious ego to facilitate a dialogue between the higher self and the lower self, so that what is in the unconscious reveals itself to the conscious mind. Doing this, and noting down what comes to the surface because it needs to be acknowledged and transformed, can be an invaluable daily practice. With the strength thus acquired, we can learn the art of positive life-creation.

∽

Greetings, all my friends here. Love and blessings, help and inner strength are coming forth to sustain you and help you open up your innermost being. I hope you will continue and cultivate this process, so that you bring to life your entire being—creating wholeness in you.

There are many different kinds of meditation. Religious meditation consists of reciting set prayers. There is meditation in which the main emphasis is put on increasing the powers of concentration. In another type of meditation spiritual laws are contemplated and thought through. There is also meditation in which the ego is made totally passive and will-less and the divine allowed its own flux. These and other forms of medita-

183

tion may have more or less value, but my suggestion to the friends who work with me is rather to use the available energy and time for confronting that part of the self that destroys happiness, fulfillment, and wholeness. You can never create the wholeness you truly aspire to, whether or not this aim is articulated, if you bypass this confrontation. This approach includes giving voice to the recalcitrant aspect of the egotistical, destructive self that denies happiness, fulfillment, and beauty for any reason.

To really understand the dynamics, the meaning, and the process of meditation and derive the maximum benefit from it, you must be clear about certain psychic laws. One of those is that if meditation is to be truly effective, three fundamental layers of personality must be actively involved in it.

These three fundamental personality levels we may call:

(1) the *conscious ego level,* with all conscious knowing and willing;

(2) the *unconscious egotistical child level,* with all its ignorance, destructiveness, and claims to omnipotence; and

(3) the *supraconscious universal self,* with its superior wisdom, power, and love, as well as with its comprehensive understanding of events in human life.

In effective meditation the conscious ego activates both the unconscious, egotistical, destructive self and the supraconscious, superior, universal self. A constant interaction among these three levels must take place, requiring great alertness on the part of your conscious ego self.

The Ego as Mediator

The conscious ego must be determined to allow the unconscious egotistical self to reveal itself, to unfold, to manifest in awareness, to express itself. This is neither as difficult nor as easy as it may seem. It is difficult exclusively, my friends, because of the fear of not being as perfect, as evolved, as good, as rational, as ideal, as one wants to be and even pretends to be, so that on the surface of consciousness the ego becomes almost convinced of being the idealized self-image. This surface conviction is constantly counteracted by the unconscious knowledge that this image is untrue, with the result that secretly the whole personality feels fraudulent and terrified of exposure. It is a significant sign of self-acceptance and growth when a human being is capable of allowing the egotistical, irrational, outright destructive part to manifest in the inner awareness, and acknowledges it in all its specific detail. This alone will prevent a dangerous *indirect* manifestation of which the person's consciousness is not aware because it is not connected with it, so that the undesirable results seem to come from outside.

So the conscious ego has to reach down and say, "Whatever is in me, whatever is hidden that I ought to know about myself, whatever negativity and destructiveness there is should be out in the open. I want to see it, I commit myself to seeing it, regardless of the hurt to my vanity. I want to be aware of how I deliberately refuse to see my part wherever I am stuck, and how I therefore overconcentrate on the wrongs of others." This is one direction for meditation.

The other direction must be toward the universal higher self, which has powers that surpass the limitations of the conscious self. These higher powers should also be called upon to expose the destructive little self, so that resistance can be overcome. The ego-will alone may be incapable of accomplishing this, but your conscious self-determining ego can and must request the higher powers to help. The universal consciousness should also be asked to help you to understand the expressions of the destructive infant correctly, without exaggeration, so that you do not go from ignoring it to making it a monster. A person can easily fluctuate from an outer self-aggrandizement to a hidden, inner self-deprecation. When the destructive infant reveals itself, one could fall prey to believing that this destructive self is the ultimate, sad reality. For a complete perspective on the revelation of the egotistic infant, one needs to ask constantly the guidance of the universal self.

When the infant begins to express itself more freely be-cause the ego allows it and receives it as a non-judgmental, in-terested, open listener, collect this material for further study. Whatever reveals itself should be explored for origins, results, further ramifications. Ask yourself what underlying mis-conceptions are responsible for the hate, spite, malice, or whatever negative feelings come to the surface. When the misconceptions are recognized, guilt and self-hate diminish proportionately.

Another question to ask is, what are the consequences when for the sake of a momentary satisfaction you give in to the destructive impulses? When questions like these are clearly worked out, the destructive aspects weaken—again in proportion to the understanding of the particular cause and effect. Without this part of the pathwork, the task is only half done. Meditation must deal with the entire problem of uncon-scious negativity step by step.

The interaction is threefold. The observing ego must ini-tially want it and commit itself to reaching in and exposing the negative side. It has also to ask for the help of the universal self. When the infant reveals itself, the ego should *again* ask for the help of the universal self to strengthen the conscious-ness for the further work, which is the exploration of the un-derlying misconceptions and the heavy price paid for them. The universal self can help—if you allow it—to overcome the temptation to give in again and again to destructive impulses. Such giving in does not necessarily result in action, but man-ifests in emotional attitudes.

The Meditative Attitude

Such meditation requires a great deal of time, patience, perseverance, and determination. Remember that wherever you are unfulfilled, wherever there are problems, wherever there is conflict in your life, your attitude should not be to concentrate with woe on others or circumstances outside your control, but to reach into yourself and explore the causes em-bedded in your own egocentric childish level. Meditation is an absolute prerequisite here: It means *ingathering yourself;* calmly, quietly wanting to know the truth of this particular circumstance and its causes. Then you need to quietly *wait for an answer.* In this state of mind, peace will come to you even before you fully understand why you have a particular negativity. This truthful approach to life will already give you a measure of the peace and self-respect you lacked as long as you held others responsible for what you had to suffer.

If such meditation is cultivated, you will discover a side of yourself that you have never known. In fact, you will come to know two aspects: The highest universal powers will communicate themselves to you to help you discover your most destructive, ignorant side, which needs insight, purification, and change. Through your willingness to accept your lower self, the higher self will become more of a real presence in you. In fact, you will increasingly experience it as your real self.

Many people meditate, but they neglect the two-sidedness of the endeavor and therefore miss out on integration. They may indeed actualize some of the universal powers that come into play wherever the personality is sufficiently free, positive, open, but the unfree, negative, closed areas are neglected. The actualized universal powers will not, by themselves, enforce an integration with the undeveloped part of the self. The conscious ego-self must decide for this integration and fight for it, otherwise the universal self cannot get through to the blocked-off areas. Partial integration alone with the universal self may lead to even greater self-deception if the consciousness is deluded by the actually existing partial integration with divine powers and becomes even more prone to overlook the neglected side. This makes for lopsided development.

The Changes Effected by the Pathwork Meditation

When you go through the entire process, a tremendous strengthening of your whole self takes place. Several things begin to happen within your personality, my friends. In the first place, your conscious ego-personality itself becomes stronger and healthier. It will be stronger in a good, relaxed sense, with more determination, awareness, meaningful directed-ness and a greater power of concentration with one-pointed attention. Second, you will cultivate a much greater self-acceptance and understanding of reality. Unreal self-hate and self-disgust will go away. Equally unreal claims for special-ness and perfection also stop. False spiritual pride and vanity as well as false self-humiliation and shame disappear. Through the steady activation of the higher powers, the self feels less and less forlorn, helpless, lost, hopeless, or empty. The whole sense of the universe in all its marvelous possibili-ties reveals itself from within, as the reality of this wider world shows you the way to accept and change your destruc-tive inner child.

This gradual change enables you to accept all your feel-ings and let the energy flow through your being. When you accept your small, petty, mean side without thinking that it is the total, final reality, then the beauty, love, wisdom, and in-finite power of the superior self become more real. Dealing with your lower self leads to balanced development, integra-tion, and a deep, reassuring sense of your own reality. Realis-tic, well-founded self-liking must result.

When you see the truth in yourself and it becomes second nature to want and commit yourself to this truth, you will de-tect an ugly side in you, which until this point you were too resistant to see. Simultaneously, you also detect this great, uni-versal, spiritual power that is in you and that in fact *is* you. Paradoxical as it may seem, the more you can accept the mean little creature, the ignorant little infant in you without losing your sense of self-worth, the better you will perceive the great-ness of your innermost being, provided you truly do not use your discoveries about the little self to beat yourself down. The lower self wants to seduce the conscious ego to stay within the narrow confines of neurotic self-beating, hopelessness, and morbid capitulation, which always cover unexpressed hatred. The conscious ego must prevent this stratagem using all its knowledge and resources. Observe this habit of self-beating, hopelessness, and capitulation in yourself and counteract it—not by pushing it underground again, but by using what you know. Talking to this part of yourself you can bring to bear on it all the knowledge of your conscious ego. If this is not sufficient, request the powers beyond your consciousness to come to your help.

As you get to know both the lowest and the highest in you, you discover the function, the capacities, but also the limitations of the conscious ego. On the conscious level the ego's function is wanting to see the full truth of both the lowest and highest in you, wanting with all of its strength to change and give up destructiveness. The limitation is that the ego-consciousness cannot execute this alone and must turn for help and guidance to the universal self and wait patiently without doubting or impatiently pushing. This waiting needs an open attitude about the way the help might manifest. The fewer preconceived notions one has, the faster help will come forth and be recognizable. Help from the universal consciousness may come in an entirely different manner than your concepts may make room for, and this might prove to be an obstacle. An open, waiting, accepting, and positive attitude is also necessary, though recognizing its absence, however, can also become a constructive acknowledgment of where the self is at the moment.

The Reeducation of the Destructive Self

So far we have discussed two phases of the meditation process: first the recognition of the unconscious, destructive egotistical self and then the understanding of the underlying misconceptions, the causes and effects, the meaning and the price to be paid for the present destructive attitudes. *The third phase is the reorientation and reeducation of the destructive part of the self.* The destructive infant is now no longer entirely unconscious. This infant with its false beliefs, its stubborn resistance, its spitefulness and murderous rage, must be reoriented. Reeducation, however, cannot take place unless you are fully aware of every aspect of this destructive

infant's beliefs and attitudes. This is why the first part of meditation—the revealing, exploratory phase—is so fundamental.
It goes without saying that this first phase is not something one
gets over with, so that then the second, and later the third
phase can begin. This is not a sequential process; the phases
overlap.

What I will say now must be taken with great care, otherwise the subtleties involved will not be communicated. Reeducation might very easily be misunderstood and lead
toward a renewed suppression or repression of the destructive
part that is beginning to unfold. You have to take great care
and deliberately aim to avoid this, without, however, allowing the destructive part to engulf you. The best attitude toward the unfolding destructive part is one of detached
observation, of unjudging, unharried acceptance. The more it
unfolds, the more you must remind yourself that neither the
truth of its existence, nor its destructive attitudes are final.
They are not the only attitudes you have, nor are they absolute. Above all, you have the power inherent in you to change
anything. You may lack the incentive to change when you are
not fully aware of the damage the destructive part of you does
to your life when it goes unrecognized. It is therefore another
important aspect of this phase of pathwork meditation to look
deeply and widely for indirect manifestations. How does unexpressed hate manifest in your life? Perhaps by making you
feel undeserving and afraid or by inhibiting your energies.
This is only one example; all indirect manifestations have to be
explored.

It is important here to remind yourself that where there
is life, there is constant movement, even if this movement is
temporarily paralyzed: Matter is paralyzed life-stuff. The frozen blocks of energy in your body are momentarily hardened,
immobilized life-stuff. This life-stuff can always be made to
move again, but only consciousness can do it. For life-stuff is
filled with consciousness, as well as energy; whether this
energy is momentarily blocked and frozen or whether this
consciousness is momentarily dimmed does not matter. Meditation must mean, above all, that the part of you that is al-

ready conscious and moving actually intends to make blocked energy and dimmed consciousness moving and aware again. The best way to do this is to allow the frozen and dimmed consciousness first of all to express itself. Here you need a receptive attitude, instead of a reaction that what comes forth is devastating and catastrophic. The panicky attitude toward one's own unfolding destructive infant does more damage than the destructive infant itself. You must learn to listen to it, to take it in, to calmly receive its expressions without hating yourself, without pushing the infant away. Only with such an attitude can you come to understand the causes of its underlying destructiveness. Only then can the process of reeducation begin.

The denying, panicky, frightened, self-rejecting, and perfection-demanding attitude you usually have makes every part of this meditation impossible. It does not permit unfoldment; it does not permit exploration of the causes of what might be unfolded; and it certainly does not permit reeducation. It is the accepting and understanding attitude that enables the conscious ego to assert its benign dominion over violently destructive and stagnant psychic matter. As I have said many times, kindness, firmness, and deep determination against your own destructiveness are necessary. It is a paradox: Identify with the destructiveness and yet be detached from it. Accept that it is you, but also know that there is another part of you that can say the final word if you so choose. For this you need to widen the limitations of your conscious ego expressions to include saying at any moment: "I will be stronger than my destructiveness and will not be hampered by it. I determine that my life will be at its best and fullest and that I will and can overcome the blocks in me that make me want to remain unhappy. This determination of mine will bring in the higher powers that will make me capable of experiencing more and more bliss because I can let go of the doubtful pleasure of being negative, which I now fully recognize." This is the task of the conscious ego. Then and then only can it also call into play the powers of guidance, wisdom, strength, and a new inner feeling of love that comes from being penetrated by the universal self.

For reeducation, too, has to proceed through the relationship of the three interactive levels, just as it was necessary for making the destructive side conscious and exploring its deeper meaning. Reeducation depends on the efforts of both the conscious ego, with its instructions to and dialogue with the ignorant egotistical child, and on the intervention and guidance of the universal, spiritual self. Each in its own way will effect the gradual maturing of this infant. The ego determines its goal to change the consciousness of the negative inner child by wanting this and committing itself to it. This is its task. Full execution of this task is made possible by the spiritual influx from the deeper personality that has to be deliberately activated. Here the consciousness must again adopt a twofold approach: One is activity that asserts its desire to transform the self-defeating aspects, leading the dialogue and calmly but firmly instructing the ignorant child. The other is a more passive, patient waiting for the final, but always gradual, manifestation of the universal powers. It is they who bring about the inner change when the feelings lead to new, more resilient reactions. Thus good feelings will replace those that were negative or dead.

Rushing and pressuring the resisting part is as useless and ineffective as accepting its direct refusal to budge. When the conscious ego does not recognize that there is a part of the self that actually refuses every step toward health, unfoldment, and the good life, a counteractive movement may be one of hurried, impatient pressure. Both derive from self-hate. When you feel stymied and hopeless, take it as a sign for you to search for that part in you that says, "I do not wish to change, I do not wish to be constructive." Set out and find this voice. Use the meditative dialogue here again, to explore and let the worst in you express itself.

You can see my friends, how expressing the negative part, exploring its meaning, cause and effect, and reeducating it must be a constantly fluctuating process, alternating and often simultaneous. See how the three levels of interaction combine in the effort of purification and integration. Meditation functions here as a constant articulation of what was previously unarticulated. It is a threefold communication and confrontation: from the ego toward the destructive self and from the ego toward the universal self, so that the universal self can affect both the ego and the destructive self. Your own sensitivity will grow day by day to feel what exactly is needed at any given point on your evolutionary path.

A Way to Begin Meditation

Each day brings forth new tasks, exciting tasks, beautiful tasks. They should not be approached in a spirit of wanting to get it over with, as if only then could life begin. On the contrary, the meditation process is living at its best. You may begin each meditation by asking yourself, "What do I really feel at this moment about this or that issue? In what respect am I dissatisfied? What is it I may be disregarding?" Then you may request the universal spirit in you to help you find these particular answers. Wait trustingly for what may unfold. Only when some part of you unfolds can you have a direct confrontation, communication, or dialogue with it and ask it further questions, as well as instruct it. With patience and determination you can remold the distorted part, but only after it has fully expressed itself. You can re-form, reorient stagnant psychic energy with your willingness to be totally honest, totally constructive, loving, and open. If you find an unwillingness in this regard, then that must be confronted, explored, and re-educated.

This is the only meaningful way in which meditation can move your life toward the resolution of problems, toward growth and fulfillment, and toward unfolding your best potential. If you do this, my friends, the time will come when trusting life will no longer sound like a vague, faraway theory that you cannot put into personal action. Instead, your trust in life, as well as self-love in the healthiest sense, will fill you more and more, based on realistic considerations, instead of wishful thinking.

Reconciliation of the Paradoxes of Your Life

As your consciousness expands, the paradoxes and opposites that constantly puzzle you in life will be reconciled.
Let us examine first the paradox of desire. Both desire and
desirelessness are important spiritual attitudes. Only to the
dualistic, separated mind do they seem like opposites leading
to confusion about which is right or wrong.

Human beings desire, for only desire can bring you to the
fourth aspect of meditation. This is the expansion of your
conscious concepts in order to create new and better life-
substance, hence life experience. If you do not desire a better
state of being and more fulfillment, you will have no material
to create and mold life-substance. Visualization of a fuller
state presupposes desire. These concepts must be fostered by
the conscious ego, and the universal consciousness must inter-
vene to help create a more expanded state.

If you see desire and desirelessness as mutually exclusive,
you cannot grasp or feel the necessary attitude. Desire must
exist for one to believe in new possibilities and to unfold into
greater states of fulfillment and self-expression. But if desire is
tense, urgent, and contracted, it forms a block. Such desire
implies, "I do not believe that what I want can happen,"
which is, perhaps, the result of an underlying, "I really do not
want it," because of some misconception or unjustified fears,
or an unwillingness to pay the price. This underlying denial
creates too tense a desire. Therefore a kind of desirelessness
must be present that could be expressed as the statement, "I
know I can and will have such and such, even if it is not realizable right now, in this or that specific form. I trust the universe and my own good will sufficiently that I can wait and
will strengthen myself along the way to cope well with the
temporary frustration of this desire."

What are the common denominators of healthy desire
and healthy desirelessness that make meditation and indeed all
life-expression real and beautiful? First there is an absence of
fear and the presence of trust. If you fear frustration, unful-

fillment, and their consequences, the tension of your soul movement will prohibit the fulfillment you want. Eventually you will even give up all desire. Then desirelessness will be distorted, misunderstood, and of the wrong kind because too much tense desire is present. In the final analysis such tense desire comes from fear caused by the infantile belief that you will be annihilated if you do not have what you want. Hence you do not trust your ability to cope with lack of fulfillment, which makes you inordinately frightened of it. So the vicious circle continues. The fear induces a cramp that becomes a denial of desire. These very subtle, obscure attitudes need to be explored in your meditation, so that you can come to the fourth stage of meaningful meditation. In this stage you express your desire with confidence in your ability to cope with both non-fulfillment and fulfillment, and therefore with a benign universe, capable of yielding to you what you long for. The obstacles along the way can be dealt with when you know that the ultimate state of bliss will be yours anyway. Then desire and desirelessness will not be irreconcilable paradoxes, but complementary attitudes.

Similarly, it seems paradoxical to postulate that both involvement and detachment must exist in the healthy psyche. Again there must be a twofold approach to the understanding of this seeming contradiction. If detachment is indifference because you are afraid to be involved and unwilling to risk pain and scared of loving, then detachment is a distortion of the real attitude. If involvement means merely an expression of a super-tense will that your infantile insistence on having what you want right away generates, then the healthy, productive version of involvement is inverted.

I will choose a third example of apparent opposites that make a comprehensive whole when not distorted. Let us take the inner attitudes of *activity and passivity*. On the dualistic level these two seem to be mutually exclusive. How can you be both active and passive in a harmonious way? The right inner interaction includes both these inner movements. For instance, meditation, as I have explained it here, must include both. You are active when you explore your inner levels of consciousness; you are active when you commit yourself and struggle to recognize and overcome resistance; you are active when you question yourself further to let the previously un-admitted destructive side express itself; you are active when you have a dialogue and reeducate the infantile, ignorant aspects of yourself; you are active when you use your ego-consciousness to enlist the help of the spiritual consciousness; you are active when you create a new concept of life experi-ence, as opposed to an old, limiting one. When the ego deals with both other "universes" to establish a connection, you are active. But you must also learn to wait passively for the un-foldment and expression of both these other levels. Then the right blend of activity and passivity prevails in the psyche. The universal powers cannot come to fruition in a human being unless both the active and the passive movements are present.

These are very important concepts to understand, to use, and to observe within yourself. Find where they are distorted and where they are functioning well. When the three-way in-teraction within yourself takes place, there is always a harmo-nious blend between desire and desirelessness; between involvement and detachment; between activity and passivity. When this balance becomes a steady state, *the destructive infant grows up*. It is not killed or annihilated. It is not exor-cised. Its frozen powers resolve themselves into live energy, which you will actually feel, my friends, as a new, *living force*. This infant must not be slain. It must be instructed so that salvation can come to it, liberating it, bringing it to growth. If you work toward this goal, you will steadily move closer to unifying the ego level and the universal self.

This is powerful material. Be blessed, be in peace, be with God.

15

Connection Between the Ego and the Universal Power

Energy and consciousness manifest as the un-divided power of the universe. This power is the creative life principle residing within all of us. However, human beings often lose conscious contact with this creative, divine power and trust the limited ego more than the higher self within. What is the fear behind this separation? How can we detect our shame of what is best in us, and how can we give over to the universal power within?

∽

Greetings, my dearest friends. May this lecture give you renewed insight and strength, so that your attempts to find yourself—who you are, where you belong, and how to fulfill yourself—become a little easier. May you find a new shaft of light through these words by truly opening up to new aspects of ideas you have perhaps heard before but that have not as yet become personally experienced truth for you.

The Universal Life Principle and the "Forgetful" Ego

The meaningfulness and fulfillment of one's life depend, in the last analysis, entirely on the relationship between your

197

ego and the universal life principle—the real self as we also call it. If this relationship is balanced, everything falls into place. The universal life principle is life itself. It is eternal consciousness in its deepest and highest sense, eternal movement and pleasure supreme. Since it is life, it cannot die. It is the essence of all that breathes, moves, vibrates. It knows all, for it constantly creates and perpetuates itself, because it cannot be untrue to its own nature.

Every individual consciousness is universal consciousness—not just a part of it, for a part implies only a little—but wherever consciousness exists, it is the original consciousness. This original consciousness, or creative life principle, takes various forms. When in the process of individualization an entity passes the point of remembering its connection with its origin, a disconnection occurs. The particular consciousness continues to exist and to contain the universal consciousness, but it becomes oblivious to its own nature, its laws, and its potentials. This, in short, is the state of human consciousness as a whole. The part that has forgotten its connection to the life principle we call the separate ego.

When you begin to become aware of the life principle, you discover that it has always been there but you have not noticed it because you were under the illusion of existing separately. It is therefore not entirely accurate to state that the universal consciousness "manifests." It would be more correct to say that you begin to notice it. You may notice the life principle's ever-present power as autonomous consciousness or as energy. The separated ego-personality possesses both, but the ego intelligence is inferior by far to the universal intelligence whether or not you can recognize it and put it to use. The same applies to the energy. *Consciousness and energy are not separate aspects of universal life; they are one.*

One of the universal life principle's basic characteristics, whether expressed as autonomous consciousness or as energy, is that it is spontaneous. It cannot possibly reveal itself through a laborious process or a cramped, overconcentrated state. Its manifestation is always an indirect result of effort. Effort needs to be expended for the sake of seeing the truth about oneself, of giving up a specific illusion, of overcoming a barrier to wanting to be constructive rather than destructive, and not for an as yet theoretical process called self-realization that promises to feel good.

Each step toward seeing the truth in the self, with a genuine desire for constructive participation in the creative process of life, frees the self. This is how the spontaneous processes begin. They are never consciously volitional. The more you fear the unknown, the letting go, the involuntary processes in your own body, the less you can experience the spontaneous life principle in the self.

The life principle may manifest as previously unimaginable wisdom in solving one's personal problems or in cultivating one's creative talents. It can become a new vibrant way of experiencing life, giving a new flavor to all one is doing and seeing. The life principle is always safe, always holds out justified hope that will never be disappointed. There is never any fear in this new life experience, yet it cannot be pushed and forced. It comes about exactly to the degree that you no longer fear the involuntary processes, those inner mechanisms that are not under the direct control of the ego.

The Conflict Between Yearning For and Fearing the Real Self

Humanity finds itself in the paradoxical position of deeply yearning for the fruits of these involuntary processes, yet fearing and battling them. The conflict is terrible and tragic, and it can be resolved only when you let go of the fear.

All psychological problems come, in the final analysis, from this much deeper existential conflict, far beyond those individual personal difficulties the child experiences that later cause inner problems and misconceptions. All life moves toward resolving this basic conflict. But such resolution can only happen if first the individual neurotic conflicts are found and understood. You need to learn to see and accept whatever is real and true in yourself, in others, in life. Honesty must prevail to stop one's attempts to cheat life, no matter how subtly.

All character defects have to be removed by fully acknowledging and objectively observing them without plunging into despair or denying them. This attitude in itself removes the defects infinitely more effectively than any other approach. Only then is one able to perceive the existential conflict between the ego and the universal consciousness.

Misinterpretations of the Universal Life Principle in Religion

The spontaneously manifesting universal consciousness has nothing to do with religious precepts of a removed deity, or a life beyond this physical life. These are misinterpretations that occur when a person senses the universal life principle and gropingly tries to convey this experience to those whose ego is still in conflict with it. Such misinterpretations must alienate you from your immediate self and from your practical daily life.

People wish to find a compromise between their yearning, which comes from the deep sense of the present possibilities available to them, and their fear. They have created it in every formalized religion that removes God from the self and from daily life, that splits human nature into the spiritual and the physical being. Thus total fulfillment is perforce removed from the *now* into a life after death. All such views and approaches to life are nothing but a compromise between what one senses could exist and what one fears. This fear goes beyond the neurotic fears that stem from misconceptions and personally experienced traumas.

What is this basic fear of letting go of the outer ego and letting the universal processes unfold and carry you? It is the misunderstanding that giving up the ego means giving up existence. In order to get a little better understanding of this problem, let us consider how the ego formed itself out of universal life.

Individuation is an integral aspect of the universal life force. Creative life is always moving, reaching out, expanding and contracting, finding new areas of experience and branching into new territories. It finds forever new ways to experience itself. As an individual consciousness separates itself further and further from its original source, it "forgets" its essence and becomes oblivious of its own principles and laws until it seems to be a totally separate entity. Individual existence is, in its present state, associated only with separate existence. Giving up the ego must then appear to the individual as an *annihilation* of its unique personal existence.

This is the current condition of human beings. You live under the illusion that life, the sense of "I am," can be found only in your "separate" existence. This illusion has brought death into the human realm, for death is nothing but this illusion being carried to its final absurdity.

The realization that the separate ego-existence is an illusion constitutes an extremely important step in the evolution of humanity. Any work of self-actualization brings this issue into very clear focus. As you look deeply at the immediately available truth of yourselves as individuals, you will find that you and the creative life principle are one. The more you look at yourself in truth and shed your illusions about yourself, the more you will realize that individual existence is not surrendered when the involuntary processes of the creative life principle are allowed to take over and integrate with the ego functions.

Those who have begun to experience the immediacy of this greater life in a renewal of energy find, paradoxically, that the more they give of their energy, the more renewed energy they generate within. For that is the law of the universal life principle. The separated state operates dualistically; it seems "logical" that the more one gives, the less one has and the more depleted one becomes. This comes from the illusion that the outer ego is all there is to individuality. The root of the fear to let go of all tight ego defenses is precisely this misconception.

Those who begin to experience these powers and energies also begin to notice the influx of an inspirational intelligence that seems to be much vaster than anything they know in their outer intellect as opposed to inner wisdom. Yet it is essentially their "best self." It first seems to be a foreign power, but it is not. It only seems so when these channels have become clogged due to one's ignorance. This vaster intelligence manifests as inspiration, guidance, and a new form of intuition that comes not in a vague feeling, but in concise words, in definite knowledge, graspable and translatable into daily living.

The discovery of this new life reconciles the apparent opposites of being an individual and being at one with all others, an integral part of a whole. These are no longer irreconcilable opposites, but interdependent facts. All such opposites, all apparently mutually exclusive alternatives that cause so much heartache to humanity, begin to fall into place when the ego connects with universal life.

How to Let Go of the Ego

When I speak of letting go of the ego, I do not mean its annihilation, or even disregarding its importance. The ego has made itself a separated part of the universal life that can be found deep within the self. It is immediately accessible if so desired, when the ego is ready to reconnect itself to its original source. When the ego becomes strong enough to take the risk to trust faculties other than its limited conscious capabilities, it will find a previously undreamed-of new security.

Before it can take this new step, the ego fears that it will be crushed, fall into nothingness, and cease to exist. Holding on to unmoving, petrified psychic substances seems to alleviate this fear. The unmoving seems safe; the moving, perilous. To want to hold on makes life scary, for life is eternally moving. When you find that the movement is safe because it carries you, you have found the only real security there is. All other security—trust in, or leaning on, the static—is illusory and breeds forever more fear.

Analogy with the Law of Gravity

The principle is the same as the one that moves the planets, which do not fall into space. At the core of the human predicament there always lies the feeling, "If I do not hold on to myself I endanger myself." Once you are conscious of this feeling, you possess an important key, for you can consider the possibility that it is an error. There is nothing to fear; you cannot be crushed or annihilated. You can only be carried, as the planets are carried in space.

As I so often say, the state of humanity's present consciousness creates the world you live in, including its physical laws. You are so used to putting effect first and cause later, because in your dualistic state of mind you are unable to see the whole picture and tend to think in an either/or manner. The truth is you are not relegated to this sphere; rather, this sphere, with all it contains, is an expression of humanity's overall state of consciousness. One of the physical laws expressing this state of consciousness is the law of gravity. It is a special law that pertains only to your dualistic consciousness. The law of gravity parallels, or expresses on the physical level, the emotional reaction to and the apprehension of falling and crushing when the ego is given up as the sole form of individual existence. Spheres of consciousness that have transcended the dualism of this plane have different physical laws, corresponding to their overall consciousness. The science of space proves this, because in outer space there is no gravity. Your earth is not the last and only reality.

This analogy is more than merely symbolic. It is a sign that could widen your horizon in thinking about, and inwardly experiencing, new boundaries of reality, thus diminishing your fear and your illusory, isolated ego-existence.

How to apply this, my friends, to where most of you are in your search for your real self? Look at the various layers of your consciousness. The more you succeed in making previously unconscious material conscious and consequently reorienting the faulty reflexes of previously unconscious material, the closer you come to the reality of the universal life principle within you. The universal life principle then becomes freer to disclose itself, and you become freer from fears, shames, and prejudices, until you can open yourself up to its availability. Anyone can corroborate that as more courage is summoned to look at the naked truth of oneself, it becomes easier to connect with a vaster, safer, more blissful life within. The more connected you become with something that removes all uncertainty and all conflict, the more you will feel a security and an ability to function that you never knew could exist within you. Here are functions of power, of energy; functions of intelligence that resolve all conflict and furnish solutions to apparently unsolvable problems. All ifs and buts in daily practical living are loosened up—not through outer magical means, but through your increasing capacity to cope with everything that happens as an integral part of yourself. Moreover, you develop an increased ability to experience pleasure, as you are meant to. To the extent you have disconnected yourself from universal life, you must yearn for this way of living.

During our discussions we have come face to face with many aspects of this triad. I have spoken before of a frequent phenomenon, namely, that people are often ashamed of their higher selves—of the best in them. This shame of your higher self is a very important feeling, connected with the fear of exposing the real self. A specific personality type feels this shame primarily about good qualities, about giving and loving. Such people resist giving into society's demands, believing that thereby they would lose the integrity of their individuality. They fear their submission to and dependency on the opinions of others and therefore feel ashamed of any genuine impulse to please others. They feel more "themselves" when they are hostile, aggressive, cruel.

The Human Reaction to the Real Self—Shame and Falsification

All human beings have a similar reaction to their real self. This does not apply only to their actual goodness and loving generosity, but also to all other real feelings and ways of being. This strange shame manifests as embarrassment and a sense of exposure about the way one really is. It makes one feel as though one were naked and exposed. This is not the shame of one's deceits and destructiveness, nor of one's compliance. This shame is on an entirely different level, and of a different quality. Whatever one really is feels shamefully naked—regardless of good or bad thoughts, feelings, or behavior. The shame is felt most acutely when it comes to being what one is in the moment.

Because of this feeling, people pretend. This is a different kind of pretense than the one that covers up lack of integrity, destructiveness, and cruelty. This different kind of pretense is deeper, more subtle. You may pretend things you actually feel. You may really feel love, but to show this real love feels naked, so you create a false love. You may really feel anger, but the real anger feels naked, so you create false anger. You may really feel sadness, but you feel mortified to acknowledge this sadness even to yourself, so you create false sadness, which you can easily display to others. You may really experience pleasure, but this, too, is humiliating to expose, so you create false pleasure. This even applies to elements like confusion and puzzlement. The real feeling seems naked and exposed, so you create a false one. This falsification appears like a protective garment that no one but one's deepest, usually unconscious, self knows of. This "protective garment" anesthetizes one to the vibrancy and buoyancy of life. All such imitations build a screen between you and your life center. This, too, separates you from reality, for it is the reality of your own being that you cannot stand and feel compelled to imitate, thereby counterfeiting your very existence. The moving stream of life seems dangerous, not only as far as your safety is concerned, but also as it affects your pride and dignity. But all this is stark and tragic illusion. As you can only find true safety when you unite with the source of all life within you, so you can find true dignity only when you overcome the shame of being real—whatever this may mean at the moment.

Sometimes annihilation seems a lesser evil than the strange sense of shame and the exposure of one's real being. When you recognize this shame and do not push it away as inconsequential, you take a tremendous step, my friends. Feeling this shame is the key to finding a numbness that causes despair and frustration, because it leads to self-alienation and disconnectedness of a particular kind. This feeling is not translatable into rational language, because only the flavor of the experience and its quality distinguishes the real from the false. The imitation feelings are often subtle and so deeply ingrained that they have become second nature. Therefore it takes a deeply sensitive letting go, letting yourself be, and letting yourself feel, as well as wanting to be discerning about your discoveries. All this is necessary before you become acutely aware of the apparent sense of exposure and nakedness the real feelings cause in you. The subtle imitation not only reproduces other, or opposite, feelings from those you register, but also, and just as frequently, the identical ones. The next step is then the intensification, which serves as a measure to make the false appear real.

When you do meet the momentary real self, it is far from "perfect." This is not a dramatic experience—yet it is crucial. For what you are now contains all the seeds you will ever need in order to live deeply and vibrantly.

You are already this universal life power. When you have the courage to be your real self, a new approach to your own inner life can begin, after which all pretenses fall by the wayside.

The Biblical Symbolism of Nakedness

The shame of one's own nakedness in showing one's self, as it is in the now, is explained by the deep symbolism of the story of Adam and Eve. *The nakedness of reality is paradise*. For when that nakedness is no longer denied, a new blissful experience can begin—right here and now, not in another life in the beyond. But it takes some acclimatizing after one has become aware of the shame and of the ingrained subtle habits with which one covers up one's inner nakedness. But once you learn to uncover yourself, you will finally step out of your protective shell and become more real. You will be the naked you, as you are now—not better than you are, not worse than you are, and also not different from the way you are. You will stop the imitation, the counterfeit feelings and ways of being, and venture out into the world the way you happen to be.

Are there any questions in connection with this lecture?

QUESTION: *How can you determine whether your feelings are real or put on?*

ANSWER: The only one who can determine it is you, by seriously probing and, first of all, considering the possibility that your feelings may be put on, and by not being frightened of this. For people are terrified of the thought that their feelings are fake—even in a subtle way. They fear that if these feelings are not real then they have no feelings. They fear their own emptiness. And this fear is devastating. It exerts a subtle pressure to go on pretending. But there is always a point inside where you say, "No, I do not want to feel." Whether this stems from childhood and personal traumatic experiences, or connects with the deeper human problem applying to all individuals that I discussed in this lecture, there must always be a wish not to feel. This wish is often totally unconscious, so that one is disconnected from it and helpless about the result— which is, of course, no feelings. The terror is infinitely greater when the conscious self that wants feelings is ignorant of the side of the self that fears feelings. The terror of being unable to feel cannot be compared to any other. It is therefore of enormous help to realize that no one is really without feelings and these feelings cannot ever die permanently. Life and feelings are one; where there is one, there must be the other, even if one is inactivated at the moment. Knowing this makes it possible to search within and ask, "Where have I decided not to feel?" The moment you become acutely aware of your fear to feel, you will cease to fear that you have no feelings. It is then possible to reactivate your feelings with the help of reason, through realistic and rational evaluation of the circumstances.

I have given you a lot to think about. This is quite a bit

of material, which you can fruitfully use in the continuation of your pathwork.

Be blessed, every one of you. May your endeavors succeed to become real, to find the courage to be nakedly real without any false covers. You cannot help but succeed if you really want to. Those who do not move and grow and liberate themselves do not want to—and it is important to know this and find in you the inner voice that refuses to move. May all your false layers fall away because this is what you really want and decide. You will then discover the glory of living. Be in peace, be in God!

16

Consciousness: Fascination with Creation

*In addition to presenting to us the universal
laws governing positive creation with consciousness,
the Guide also explains how negative creation came
into existence. The allegory of the "fall of the angels" is here expressed in terms accessible to the
modern mind. To put our resources into the service
of positive creation by recapturing our original God-
consciousness is our goal, and the Guide in this lecture points out the steps to be taken for its recovery.*

∾

Greetings, all my friends here, who receive tangible
blessings in the form of energy currents containing consciousness and strength. They flow toward you and permeate you.
They are a reality that can be perceived as your own consciousness grows and ventures forth.

I would like to talk about aspects of consciousness and its
significance in the scheme of creation. Creation is indeed a result of consciousness and not, as generally assumed, the other
way around. *Nothing can exist unless it occurs first in consciousness.* It makes no difference whether the source is the
universal or the individualized self. Whether your consciousness perceives, creates, and formulates something important,

world-forming, or just a passing insignificant attitude, the principle is the same.

You need to understand the tremendous significance of your conscious creations; your disconnection from them causes real suffering. No suffering is as acute as the one that is felt when you do not know that you have created what you experience. This applies, to a lesser extent, even to positive experiences. For if you do not know that you have created your experiences, you will always feel helpless in the hands of a power you cannot comprehend. This power is truly your own consciousness, my friends.

Knowing, Feeling, and Willing as Tools of Creative Consciousness

Now let us understand a little better some of the most outstanding attributes of consciousness. Consciousness is not only the power to think, to discriminate, and to choose; that is obvious. It is not only the power to know, to perceive, and to feel. It is also the ability to *will*. Willing is a very important aspect of consciousness. Whether you will with awareness or whether you disconnect from your will makes no difference. Your will is an aspect of your consciousness and hence of what you continually create. Willing is an ongoing process, just as knowing and feeling are. Where consciousness exists, knowing, feeling, and willing always exist as well.

Often a number of contradictory will currents short-circuit on the surface, manifesting as a lack of awareness or numbness. Consciousness is diminished on the surface but continues below the surface. Its products manifest as tangible life experiences and you feel at a loss, believing that what life brings is totally independent from your own willing and knowing. Any path of genuine development must bring all the confused and contradictory desires, beliefs, and inner knowing to the surface so that life circumstances appear in their true light as the creation of the self. This awareness gives you power to recreate.

Willing, determining, formulating, knowing, and perceiving are all tools of your creative consciousness. Humanity can be divided into those who know this and use these tools deliberately, creatively, constructively; and those who are unaware of it and are constantly creating destruction without ever knowing it.

Humans are the first entities on the upward evolutionary scale who can deliberately create with their consciousness. You, my friends, who search for your true identity must come to experience your power to create and, specifically, how you have created whatever you have or do not have now. You can then see how fighting against your own creations augments the pain and tension in your being. This is inevitable when you are not yet aware, generally and specifically, of how your life is the outcome of your own mental activity. What you do not like you will invariably rebel against, never knowing that you actually tear yourself apart even more. The rebellion may not be entirely conscious either; it may manifest as vague discontent with life, hopeless longing, a sense of futility and frustration from which you see no way out. The discontent, too, is a kind of rebellion.

To understand the nature of consciousness in still greater depth, you need to see what positive and negative directions consciousness can take. You have within you the purest wisdom, flowing toward ever-expanding bliss, an infinite variety of new life expressions. This is the universal spirit. I am not saying that the universal spirit is in you; I am saying that *you are it*, but most of the time you do not know it. You also harbor within you the distorted expression of your creative consciousness with which you will negative and destructive results. One could also say that this is the eternal fight between God and the devil, between good and evil, between life and death. It does not matter what you call these powers; whatever you name them, they are your own powers. You are not a helpless pawn in anyone's hands. This is the all-important fact that truly alters your entire self-perception and attitude toward living. Not knowing this will make you feel constantly victimized by circumstances beyond your control.

Three Conditions of Experiencing Yourself as the Universal Spirit

In order to perceive and experience your true identity as being the universal spirit, three basic things are necessary:

1) *That you tune in to it.* You activate the universal spirit by your deliberate attempt to listen to it. You must become very quiet within yourself and allow it to happen. This is not as easy as it may sound, for the tumultuous static of the busy mind keeps blocking this possibility. Your mind requires training to become sufficiently calm without producing involuntary thoughts. Once you have accomplished this to some degree, you will experience an emptiness. You will then seem to listen into nothingness that may even be frightening or disappointing. Finally, the universal spirit will begin to manifest—not because it "decides" to because you were a "good child" who now "deserves" it, but because you begin to perceive its ongoing presence, which you will then know was always there and immediately accessible—almost too near to perceive.

The first manifestations may not come to you as a direct voice, a direct inner knowing, but through detours—through other mouths, or as apparently coincidental ideas that suddenly occur to you. If you are alert and sensitive, attuned to reality, you will know that these are the first signs of establishing contact with the universal self. Later the emptiness will prove to be a tremendous fullness impossible to express in words. Its immediacy also hinders you from perceiving the universal spirit's constant presence. The immediacy is, of course, wonderful. When you discover that you harbor this presence within yourself at all times, it will fill you with safety, with strength, with the knowledge that you never need to feel inadequate and helpless again, for the source of all life supplies you with every smallest detail of living that is important to you. This inner source fills you with rich feelings; it stimulates and calms you; it shows you how to handle problems. It offers solutions that unify decency, honesty, and self-interest; love and pleasure; reality and bliss; fulfillment of your duties without diminishing your freedom in the least. It contains everything. However, this wonderful immediacy presents problems at first, because you believe that all this can be sought only very, very far away. Since you were geared to experience the universal spirit only as a remote reality you find it impossible to experience its nearness.

2) It is necessary *to fully experience and comprehend the negative part of your consciousness* that has become destructive. This is not easy, precisely because, once again, you are geared to believe that your life is a fixed mold you were put into and you must learn to cope with it, independently of your inner abilities to think, will, know, feel, and perceive. As you can now appreciate, it requires a great deal of honesty, discipline, and effort to overcome resistance to make this all-important switch in your entire approach to life: from feeling helpless to seeing life as your own creation in all respects. It is not really possible to activate the presence of the universal self when you are still blind to your negative creations. Sometimes certain channels happen to be unobstructed, but where the blocks, the blindness, the imagined helplessness persist, you cannot contact your universal self.

3) *Your conscious thought processes are the first handle on the universal spirit.* You create with your conscious thoughts just as much as with your unconscious thinking and willing. Your thinking ability is actually exactly the same as the creative processes of the universal mind. Though your consciousness is a separated fragment of the whole, it has the same powers and possibilities. The separation is not even real; it exists only because this is how you experience yourself at this time. The moment you discover the immediacy of this presence, you will no longer feel a separation between your thoughts and those of the greater Being. Eventually they will merge and you will realize that the two have always been one. It becomes evident that you have not availed yourself before of

your innate powers. You left them unused, or even misused them in your blind state.

You can finally begin to experience yourself as the universal spirit by using your conscious thoughts in a deliberate, constructive way. You can do this in two steps. First, you must clearly see how you have unknowingly used your mental processes negatively, thereby creating destructively. Then you can formulate what you now wish to produce in your life. You do this by stating that this is possible and by perceiving, knowing, and willing it with a relaxed attitude. This also includes the willingness to change faulty and dishonest inner attitudes, for otherwise you will block what you want.

By building creative thoughts you can tap the rich source within your own being. You begin with conscious thinking, which requires focusing attention on your thinking processes, observing how you use them, how they create both what you do have and do not have. Once you can reverse this process you have discovered a means of creation; you become truly your real self, for you are the universal spirit who created the world. You are constantly creating your own world right now: It is the life you lead.

Self-Observation and Purification on Three Levels

Paying attention to your inner processes will reveal that much of what you thought was unconscious is really not hidden at all. Observe this especially when you find yourself in a disturbing situation. See how you take so much for granted that you gloss over your most obvious attitudes, exactly those that will give you clues to understand how your creative power works; although in this case, of course, they are inverted, manifesting negatively. Considering every detail of the situation, turning your attention to a fresh approach will bring you the insight you had been lacking so far.

This self-knowledge is purification in the truest sense, because ultimately it establishes your awareness of your power to create your own life. Discovering how you have created destructively is never a really bad experience, for it becomes immediately obvious that you also have the power to create beautiful life experiences for yourself. You become immediately aware of your own eternal nature with its infinite power to expand.

So you see, my friends, we are dealing here with three levels. All of them must become accessible. They are all equally difficult to perceive. It would be an error to believe that your everyday thought processes are easier to perceive than either your destructive will or your divine nature with its endless power and wisdom. They are all equally near—and seem far only because your vision is turned away from them. Both the willful destructiveness and the great creative spirit you really are, are "unconscious" only because you do not give their existence the benefit of the doubt as a first step toward discovering them. Practically the same is the case with your daily mental activity, which goes on unobserved without critical evaluation, so you are completely unaware of how your thoughts continue to run in unproductive negative channels. Nor do you see that you continue to derive a sort of satisfaction from allowing the inattention to go on.

When you observe your negative thoughts, it is important to realize (a) what they do to you, how they connect with the very results you deplore most in your life; and (b) that you have the power to alter them and find new avenues of expression for your thoughts. These two realizations will make all the difference in the world, because they bring true liberation and self-finding, the coming into one's own we speak so much about. The discovery of your true identity indeed brings glad tidings. But first you must see yourself pursuing negative thoughts. See yourself brooding in the same vicious circles; see yourself almost willfully pursuing the same roundabout, narrowly confined channels of thinking and never venturing beyond them.

Let us suppose that you are convinced you can experience only this or that negative manifestation in life. Once you observe the tenacity with which you take this for granted, you can ask, "Does it really have to be so?" The moment you raise this question you begin to open a crack in the door. But being unaware that you are convinced of having only this one narrowly confined possibility makes it impossible for you to imagine further alternatives. You can actually venture into them—only by first formulating your thoughts as the blueprints of creating. Then the world begins to open. This opening must be achieved to begin with, by thinking and then saying to yourself, "It does not have to be this way, it can be another way. I want this other way. I would like to eliminate whatever stands between me and this more desirable way. I have the courage to face it and go beyond the life experience I have given myself until now by taking for granted that it cannot be any other way." On this conscious level you must see how you took it for granted that a certain negative manifestation had to be experienced by you.

Perhaps you want a positive result, but simultaneously do not wish to accept certain logical consequences that follow from what you wish. This is due to your misconception that these consequences are undesirable for you. Here you have a childish resistance to give of yourself, a distorted attempt to cheat life and gain more than you wish to give. Life cannot comply with such unfair desires, and you feel cheated and resentful because you have not really clearly examined the issue. Nor are you aware of your false reasoning when you resist giving of yourself. Thus you create errors and distortions that stand in the way of unfolding your possibilities.

So you can see that your level of conscious thinking is influenced by both your destructive side and the universal spirit. You can choose consciously in which direction to shape your thoughts once you are aware of their habitual patterns. This self-determination is your key to liberation.

You will see more and more clearly that your destructive side is also something you choose; it is not something that befalls you. Once you have truly progressed on this path you come to the point where you can finally admit this deliberate desire to choose destructive attitudes. You can see that you are unhappy, actually forsaking happiness, fulfillment, bliss, fruitful living. You may be terribly unhappy about the result, but you nevertheless insist on hanging on to your negative will. You can see how all-important it is to find this out.

The Origin of "Sin" or Evil

The age-old question is: What brought all this about? Why do human beings harbor these utterly senseless desires? Why does the mind want to take this direction? Religion calls it sin or evil. Psychology calls it neurosis or psychosis, among other things. Whatever name you give it, it is indeed a disease. In order to heal this disease it is necessary to understand it to some extent. This is done, primarily, by following your own erroneous assumptions and beliefs to the emotions and will-direction they create. This can be done only to a certain degree without also understanding the dynamics of mental creativity, both in the positive and negative sense.

People often ask, "How does evil come into existence?" Or, "Why did God put evil into us?"—as though someone else had "put" anything anywhere. Once you have sufficient self-awareness and your own rejection of happiness is on the surface, the same puzzling question may be raised, "Why do I do it? Why can't I want what feels good for me?" This question has been asked here, as well as elsewhere in the world, many times, wherever spiritual teachings are being given. Once, a long time ago, at the beginning of this contact, I even gave an allegorical account of the so-called fall of the angels, about a spirit who was once utterly constructive and expanding into forever greater realms of light and bliss, then deviated from this course, separated himself from his innermost Godself, and became fragmented. How did he turn into those dark, destructive channels? Any account, such as I have given and has been given elsewhere, is very easily misunderstood because it is always interpreted as a historical event that has taken place in time and space. I shall venture now to give another explanation about how destructiveness comes into being in an utterly constructive consciousness. I shall try to find a different approach that may perhaps reach you on some level and give you a deeper understanding of this all-important topic. You can then meet your own destructiveness with a new understanding and eventually come out of it.

Picture, my friends, a consciousness, a state of being, in which there is only bliss and infinite power to create with one's own consciousness. Consciousness is, among other things, a thinking apparatus. Thus it thinks—and lo, something comes into existence. It wills—and lo, what is willed and thought, is. Life is endlessly filled with these possibilities. Creating starts with thinking, then the thinking takes on form, becomes a fact in the life beyond the confines of the ego, the consciousness that is free-flowing and free-floating. There the thought immediately takes form and becomes deed. It is only in the human ego that thought seems separate from form and deed. The less awareness an entity has, the more separated thought, form, and deed appear, to the extent that the form seems entirely independent from the deed, the deed from the thought or the will. None of these three stages seem connected.

An essential part of raising one's consciousness lies precisely in making this connection. No matter how separate in time and space they may appear, thought and will, deed and action, form and manifestation, are all one unit. In the state of being, where there is no confinement, where there is no tight structuring, this unit is experienced as a living reality. In the experience of this lies an indescribable bliss and fascination. The whole universe is open for exploration, for new ways of self-expression and self-finding, giving form to forever more worlds, more experience, and more effects. The fascination of creating is endless.

Since the possibilities are infinite, the consciousness can also explore itself by confining itself, by fragmenting itself to "see what happens," as it were. To experience itself it contracts instead of expanding; it wants to see how it is to feel and experience darkness. *Creating is pure fascination*. This fascination is not eliminated simply because what is created is at first perhaps only slightly less pleasurable or blissful or brilliant. Even in that may lie a special fascination and adventure. Then the creation begins to take on a power of its own. For everything that is created has energy invested in it and this energy is self-perpetuating. It takes on its own momentum. The conscious being who has created these pathways may experiment longer, and go beyond more than what is "safe" because it no longer leaves itself enough power at the moment to reverse the course. Thus the consciousness may get lost in its own momentum, and be unwilling to stop. Later, it no longer sees how to stop. Creation then takes place in a negative sense, until the results are so unpleasant that the conscious being seeks to get a hold on itself and counteract the momentum by "recalling" its knowledge of what could be. At any rate, it knows there is no real danger, for whatever suffering you human beings feel is truly illusory in the ultimate sense. Once you find your true identity within, you will know it. It is all a play, a fascination, an experiment, from which your real state of being can be recaptured, if only you will truly try.

Now, many human beings still find themselves in the state in which they do not yet want to really try. They still find fascination in the exploration of negative creation, at least to some extent. Some separated entities have never gone beyond the point where they lose the immediate awareness of who they really are and their power to redirect their explorations. Others have temporarily lost this awareness. But they will find it again the moment they really want to. It is well that all of you should remember this.

The momentum of creating contains incredibly powerful energies. These energies have impact; they impress the all-pervading creative substance—the stuff that responds to creative mind. This substance then is molded into form, event, object, state of mind, or whatever. The imprints in the soul substance are so deep that nothing but the greater power of molding mind can erase false imprints, which govern your life events. Mind or consciousness impresses; life substance is impressed upon. Everything around and within you participates in both the masculine principle of a determining, etching consciousness and the feminine principle of a molded, responding life substance. Find this truth within you, and the universe will become yours all over again, as it once was.

Thus if the creative consciousness does not alter the course at a certain point, it becomes caught within its own processes. Part of the power and momentum of consciousness is the quality of being "self-imitating." It is very hard to convey this aspect of creative energy. Human beings frequently experience the urge to imitate others. This takes on many forms and applies to self-imitation as well. It is a process of deeply imprinting something upon the substance of life.

Let me give you an example of the power of imitation and creating new experiences. Many of you have experienced the strange urge you have when you see cripples who limp, perhaps, or those who have a facial tick, to imitate their postural or facial aberrations. Haven't you experienced the sometimes irresistible desire to imitate something that is highly undesirable for you? At the same time there is a kind of revulsion and fear of doing this because you sense somehow that by doing it you set something in motion that you might imitate again and again and cannot stop doing. The power and the energies of creation have this self-perpetuating effect that only consciousness, with its knowing, will, and determination, can alter. Creating becomes so involving, and the pleasure of it so engrossing, that once set in a negative direction, the pleasure continues to keep the soul in its spell until the consciousness steps in with its deliberate counter-force. Even if what is created is painful, the pleasure of creating is difficult to abandon as long as the individual ignores that positive creation is also possible.

As negative creations proceed, consciousness seems to become more and more fragmented—not really, my friends, but your awareness cannot experience your connection with the world spirit, which you are.

I do not know to what extent these words can reach you. But if they can, they will prove, as you meditate and think about them, of tremendous help for you. They will help you not only to comprehend, but find the right way to eliminate the destructiveness within you. It is the power of your mind that creates the negative. This force is even stronger when it is used for the positive because in the negative there are always conflicts, contrary longings, and will directions that weaken the force. In the constructive, expanding direction, this need not be so. Once the switch is made, something will "click" in your mind. Your consciousness will flow into a new direction that comes more easily and naturally, without the torture that negative creation always entails.

The more consciousness has separated itself from the whole, the more fragmented it becomes, the greater the structure it creates. But the wholeness of consciousness is unstructured; it is the state of being in all its blissfulness. Once fragmentation has occurred, lost consciousness gradually works toward a state of self-consciousness. This state needs structure to protect it from the chaos of negativity and destruction. When negativity is met and eliminated, unstructured, blissful consciousness is attained again.

The Way Out of Negative Creation

The ego, with its confinement, is the structure that protects the entity from its own destructive creating. It holds the destructive urges in check. Only when consciousness expands in bliss and truth can the structure be removed. So, at one point in your evolution, you were chaotically unstructured. As you grow and evolve, the structuring walls off this chaos, so that at least for a while consciousness is protected from the inner chaos.

The available thinking processes can then become the tools to show the way out of negative creations and confining structuring. Looking beyond the structure and into the chaos, comprehending it, realizing the power of the mental processes constantly in use, affords you the possibility to reverse the downward curve that makes you constantly seek ways to deny life, love, pleasure, happiness; to court decay, waste, and pain. The part of your universal self that has remained whole knows the pain is short and illusory, but the part of you that is in chaos does not know this and suffers.

Let us review. Conscious processes can swing the pendulum from destructive creating to the original state of consciousness, an expanding blissful creating. The confining structure will dissolve, and the ultimate state of being, unstructured consciousness and experience, energy and blissful being, will reinstate themselves and become your existence. This is where it is all going, my friends. Part of your attempts must therefore go in the direction of bringing order into the confusion of the workings of your mind, its self-involvement, its blindness to itself and its tendency to get lost to itself. It is not the world outside yourself that confuses you; it is the world within your own consciousness that does so.

You can now begin to contemplate how you can deliberately *will* creative construction; you can do it by consciously formulating, thinking, and willing a state of happiness, aliveness, fulfillment, truth, love, growth, both in general and in particular detail. The climate of this may first seem strange and unfamiliar. You need to acclimatize yourself to it. Picture yourself in such states and call upon the universal power within to fortify your conscious mind with the necessary creative energy. The will to happiness must become so strong that the causes for unhappiness must be seen and eliminated, and this, too, must truly be wanted. Then the creative power will grow; the divine self will inspire you and show the way. You will learn to recognize it and receive it in your conscious brain.

Make use of what I have said here. I mean *actively* make use, not just reading this as a beautiful theory, but deeply knowing its immediate value and applying it every day of your life. On the day when you see your destructive creating and then deliberately change it, you will indeed have done something wonderful. The will to be happy and to unfold in life is the foundation of your power to create. The more concisely this is formulated and the greater your willingness is to eliminate attitudes that hinder the result, the more effective your creation will become.

Be blessed. Receive the power that is streaming forth, and increase it by your conscious, deliberate, willing expressions and formulations. Express your willingness to grow, to be happy, to be constructive. Do this not by willing in a tight, insistent, constricted way, but in a relaxed, confident way, contemplating that all possibilities exist as potential realities, realizable the moment you know and will this with all your being. The power is there, it is in you. All you have to do is tap it, use it, build with your conscious mind the channels that can free it, and become very quiet and calm. Listen and tune in on it. It is there forever and ever, in its grandiose power, in its wonderful wisdom, in its ultimate knowledge that there is nothing but bliss, already now, within you.

17

Creative Emptiness

In order to reach the greatest heights of spirituality, we need to learn to become receptive channels for the God-consciousness. We cannot achieve such a state without knowing how to still the outer mind. This is yet another step into the unknown, into a temporary sensation of inner emptiness. The reward for taking it is the opening of a channel through which we can always contact the voice of God within.

∽

My most beloved friends, blessings for every one of you. A golden force is flowing through your inner being now and forever, if you open yourself to it.

I have spoken to you about the coming of a new era. This event requires that many human beings be ready for it. For many years, you on this path have worked for that purpose, whether or not you were aware of it. You have filed away impurities, and you still do. And you make yourself available for a powerful force that has been released in the universe—the inner universe.

Many spiritual teachers and channels know this, but many have misinterpreted this event. They believe it will bring geological cataclysms with effects on a human level. As I have said before, this is not true. The changes that are al-

224

ready in progress are changes in consciousness. And you are working at this. You see, as you develop and purify yourself, you become more and more ready for an inner enlightenment that has not yet occurred and is indeed self-perpetuating in its force. It is unprecedented, for there was no other time in human history when this power was as available as it is now.

What you increasingly experience is the result of this power's coming upon a receptive channel. If this power hits an unreceptive channel, a crisis arises, as you well know. Even if only a part of you blocks the creative forces that could make you thrive in an entirely new way, you put yourself under great psychic, emotional, and spiritual stress. This must be avoided.

On your path you have learned to contact the deep levels of intentionality where you deny truth and love as well as a greater power that operates differently from the outer ego power you so strive for. Real truth and love, real power, come from within.

How to Open Up to the New Consciousness

I will now speak about the importance of being receptive to this force, this energy, this new consciousness: the Christ consciousness that is spreading through human consciousness wherever possible. To become receptive to it, you also need to understand another principle: that of creative emptiness.

Most human beings create an agitated mind because they are frightened that they may be empty, that there may be nothing within to sustain them. This thought is rarely conscious, but on a path such as this the time comes when you do become conscious of this fearful thought. Then the first reaction is very often, "I do not even want to acknowledge that I am afraid of this. I'd rather continue busying my mind in order not to face the terror that I am nothing inside, that I am only a shell that needs sustenance from without."

This self-deception is obviously futile. It is of utmost importance that you face this fear and deal with it openly. You need to create an atmosphere within yourself in which you allow this emptiness to exist. Otherwise you perpetually deceive yourself, which is very wasteful because the fear is unjustified. How can you ever live in peace with yourself if you do not know what you fear and therefore make it impossible to find out that what you fear is not so?

As a result of a process that has continued for centuries, humanity has conditioned itself to make the outer mind a very busy place, so that when that busyness ceases temporarily, the resulting quiet is confused with emptiness. It indeed seems empty. The noise will recede, and you must indeed embrace and welcome the emptiness as the most important channel through which to receive your innermost Godself.

The Way Leads Through Seeming Contradictions

There are several psychic and spiritual laws you need to comprehend in order to nurture this emptiness and make it a creative venture. Some of these laws seem to be contradictory. Let me put it this way: If you cannot let yourself be empty, you can never be filled. Out of the emptiness a new fullness will arise, yet you cannot disregard your fear. It must, like everything else, be gone through. My advice is that you challenge that fear, and at the same time welcome the emptiness as the doorway to your divinity. This seems contradictory, but it is not. Both attitudes are necessary.

Another apparent contradiction: It is extremely important that you be receptive and expectant, yet without preconceived ideas, impatience, or wishful thinking. This seems very hard to explain in human words. It is something you have to feel into. There must be a positive expectancy that is yet free from preconceived notions of how and what should happen.

Still another related apparent contradiction: You need to be specific, yet this specificity must be light and neutral. You must be specific in one way, but not in another. If this seems confusing now, ask your inner being to relay the comprehension to your mind, rather than trying to understand directly with your ego-mind.

The workings of the greater self so far surpass the mind's imagination that specificity would be a hindrance. Yet the mind must know what it wants, be prepared for it, reach for it and claim it, know that it deserves what it wants and will not misuse it. The outer mind must make constant changes in order to adapt itself to the greater scope of the inner God-consciousness. Your outer mind must become empty and receptive, yet it must hold itself poised for all possibilities. Thus it will be able to mate with the inner stillness and what appears at first as emptiness.

A New Fullness Begins to Manifest

As you do this, in a spirit of patient, persevering, positive expectancy, yet empty in mind and soul, a new fullness can manifest. The inner stillness will begin to sing, as it were. From the energetic point of view, it will convey light and warmth. Strength you never knew you possessed will arise. From the point of view of consciousness, guidance will come for the biggest and smallest issues in your life.

Receptive, creative emptiness must truly be nurtured. Listen with an inner ear, and yet you must not do this with urgency but become receptive to when and how you will be filled. This is the only way, my friends, to find your inner sustenance, to find your divinity, and become a receptacle for the great universal power that is being released and will manifest in your life, even more than you have already experienced.

This is an important time in the history of evolution, and you are all needed to comprehend and perpetuate a great change in thinking and perception regarding the laws and values that the Christ consciousness is spreading. The way must be open from within and from without to create as many receptacles as possible.

The mind can be a hindrance or an aid to this process. You all know that your mind is limited only by your own concept of its limitations. To the degree you limit your mind, you cannot perceive what is beyond it. The mind is finite and it must aim to spread the boundaries of its finiteness until it measures up with the infinite that is beyond the mind and that is within yourself, right here, right now. Then the mind merges into the infinite consciousness of your inner universe, in which you are one with all that is, and yet infinitely your personal self.

As it is now, you carry your mind with you almost as a burden because it has become a closed circuit. Inside that circuit there is a certain leeway for ideas, opinions, and possibilities you have made room for in your life as a result of your education and the mores of your society. That circuit contains what you have chosen to learn and adopt as knowledge, both as part of the group consciousness and as your personal experience. To the degree you have grown and expanded, the closed circuit of your mind has widened; however, it is still a closed circuit. You are still burdened with limiting ideas about yourself and your world. It is therefore necessary, in order to elicit creative emptiness, that you visualize the boundaries of your mind by questioning yourself about all the things that you think are impossible for you. Where you are hopeless and frightened there must be an idea of finiteness that is simply locked into your mind; thus you lock out the great power that is here for all those who are ready to receive it honestly.

Puncturing the Closed Circuit of the Mind

Again we have an apparent contradiction. On the one hand, it is necessary that this limited mind open itself up to new ideas and possibilities, as you have already learned to do in your meditation. You have seen infallibly that where you have made room for a desirable new possibility, it has indeed come into your life. You have also seen that when it does not come into your life, you deny that it can, for whatever reason. It is therefore necessary that you begin to puncture that closed circuit. You cannot immediately dissolve it; you live with a mind and you need your mind. But where you puncture your mind, the flow of new energy and consciousness can penetrate. Where it is not punctured, you stay locked within its narrow confines, which your spirit is fast outgrowing. On the other hand, your mind must rest, not hold opinions, be neutral, in order to be receptive to the great new force sweeping the inner universe of all consciousness.

But let us return to the process of puncturing the limited mind. How do you do that? First tell yourself that you do hold limited beliefs, instead of taking them for granted. The next step is to challenge them. This requires taking the trouble to walk through, in the well-practiced attitude of self-observation and self-confrontation, your limited beliefs and to truly think about them. Sometimes it is not just that you have a false belief, and possibly a negative intentionality in holding on to it, but you can also see that you keep the circuit closed and deprive yourself of the inner plenitude you yearn for.

Another law of great importance for this purpose is that the opening to the greater universal consciousness must not be approached in a spirit of magic that is supposed to eliminate the growing and learning process. Now, this ultimate power is supposed to fill and sustain you; however, your outer mind must go through the steps of acquiring whatever knowledge is necessary. You all see this in the arts and sciences. You cannot be inspired as a great artist, no matter how much genius you have, unless you learn the craft and the technical dexterity. If the childish lower self wants to use the channel to the greater universe in order to avoid the initial tedium of learning and becoming, the channel will remain closed. For this amounts to cheating, and God cannot be cheated. When you cheat, the personality may become seriously doubtful that anything beyond the mind exists, because no inspirational response comes forth when using "magic" to coddle your laziness and self-indulgence. The same is true of science or any other field.

Now how about this same law with respect to inspiration for your personal life and decisions? Here, too, you must not fail to go through the work that the outer ego-self has to do in order to become a proper channel for the God-consciousness. You do this in pathwork. You need to truly know yourself, your weaknesses, your lower self, where you are corruptible, where you are dishonest or tend to be. As you all know, this is hard work, but it needs to be done. If you avoid it, the channel will never really be reliable and may contain a lot of wishful thinking, stemming from your "desire nature," or it may reveal "truth" that is based on guilt and fear and is thus equally unreliable.

Only when you work in this fashion on your development will you come to a point when you no longer confuse gullibility and wishful thinking with faith, or doubt with discrimination. As a great pianist can be a channel for higher inspiration only when he goes through the finger exercises and the hours of practice that make his playing finally effortless, so must God-inspired people work on their purification process, on deep self-knowledge and self-honesty. Only then does the receptacle become commensurate with higher truths and values, fit to be influenced and used for higher purposes to enrich the world and the self.

At the same time you need to cultivate a neutrality. Your devotion to fulfilling the will of God must include an attitude that whatever comes from God is all right, whether you desire it or not. Too much desire is as much a hindrance as the absence of all desire, which manifests as resignation and hopelessness. The refusal to endure any kind of frustration creates an inner tension and defensive structure that close up the vessel of the mind and maintain the closed circuit. In other words, you, as a receptacle, need to be neutral. You need to give up the strong, tight, selfwilled yes or no to make way for a flexible trust guided by your inner God. You need to be willing, pliable, flexible, trusting, and forever ready for another change you had not contemplated. What is right now may not be right tomorrow.

There is no fixedness when it comes to the divine life that springs from within your innermost being. This idea makes you insecure, for you believe that security lies in fixed rules. Nothing could be further from the truth. This is one of those beliefs that need to be challenged. Envisage that in the idea of forever meeting every new situation by being inspired anew, there lies a new kind of security that you have not found as yet. What is right in one situation may not be right in another.

This is one of those laws of the new age that is opposed to the old "stable" laws according to which what is fixed and unchangeable is secure.

The laws that pertain to this new venture into your inner creativity and life need to be studied very carefully; you must work with them. These are not just words to listen to; you need to make them your own. These laws are apparently full of contradiction. You need to acquire knowledge, the mind must be expanded, it must be able to conceive of truthful possibilities, and yet you must make your mind neutral and empty. This seems contradictory from the point of view of the dualistic consciousness, but from the point of view of the new consciousness that is spreading through your inner universe, these are not contradictions at all. For years I have tried to show you in many areas how this principle works: Something that is in truth and commensurate with the higher laws of life conciliates opposites that are mutually exclusive on the lower level of consciousness. What is conflict-producing on the lower level is mutually helpful and interactive on the higher level.

Making Your Mind an Instrument of Unification

More and more you will discover the truth of unification, where dualities cease to exist and contradictions no longer contradict; where you experience two previous opposites as valid aspects of the same truth. When you begin to comprehend this principle and apply it to your own life, your outlook and values, then you are indeed ready to receive the new consciousness released in realms far beyond your own.

When I say that you must not approach your divine channel with the attitude that it should save you the work of living and growing, I am not contradicting the necessity of being passively receptive. It is simply a shift of balance: Where you have been overactive with your mind, you now need to quiet down and let things happen; where you insisted on taking the controls, you must now relinquish them and let a new inner power take over. On the other hand, where you before tended to be lazy and self-indulgent and looked for the line of least resistance and therefore made yourself dependent on others, you now need to take over and actively nurture the principles that help to establish the channels to your inner God. You also need to actively express its messages in life. Thus, activity and passivity need to be reversed.

Your mind will thus become an instrument. It will open up, puncture its limitations, and acquire new concepts— lightly, not tightly—with which to "play around" for a while. This attitude of lightness in your perceptions, of flexibility, of motility of mind, will make you the most receptive to your apparent emptiness.

Now, my friends, as we approach this emptiness, how does it feel? What is it all about? Again, the human language is extremely limited, and it is almost impossible to squeeze this kind of experience into the context of language. I will try my very best to give you some tools, however.

As you listen into your inner "chasm," it seems at first to be a black gulf of emptiness. What you feel at this point is fear. This fear seems to fill you up. What is this fear? It is as much a fear of finding yourself to indeed be empty as of finding yourself with a new consciousness, with a new being evolving within you. Although you yearn for this, you also fear it. The fear exists in both possibilities: You want the new consciousness so much that you fear disappointment, and yet you also fear finding this consciousness because of all the obligations and changes that this might impose on you. You must travel through both these fears. On this path you have received the tools to deal with such fears by questioning your lower self.

Going Into the Emptiness

But the time comes when you are ready, notwithstanding the fear, because you have already made the connections. You know, for example, what your lower self wants and why you have negative intentions. The time comes when, in spite of the fear, you decided calmly and quietly to go into the emptiness. So you empty your mind in order to meet the emptiness deep within. Lo and behold, very soon that very emptiness will feel, not full the same way you are used to, but it will contain a new aliveness that the old artificial fullness of your mind made impossible. In fact, you will soon find out that you made yourself artificially dull by packing yourself tight: tight in the mind because of its noise, and tight within your channel by contracting your energy into hard knots of defense. You had killed your aliveness with this artificial fullness. So you became needier because without your inner life you could not be fulfilled in a real sense. A vicious circle was established as you strove to get fulfillment from outside, since you refused to go through the necessary steps to make fulfillment first manifest within.

In one sense you fear the aliveness more than the emptiness. And perhaps you had better face that. When you make yourself sufficiently empty, the first initial response is an inner aliveness, and you tend to immediately shut the lid tight again. Yet by denying your fear you also deny that you are really very unhappy about your lack of aliveness. But lack of aliveness comes from fearing it. You can make the fear give way to aliveness by letting yourself be creatively empty.

The Actual Experience

You will experience your whole inner being, including your body and your energy, as a vibrantly alive "inner tube." Energy goes through it, feelings go through it, and something else is vibrantly coming to the fore that you cannot as yet name. If you do not shy away from that unnameable something, it will sooner or later turn out to be constant inner instruction: truth, encouragement, wisdom, guidance, specifically destined to your life right now, wherever you need it most. That emptiness, that vibrant alive emptiness, is God talking to you. At any moment of the day it is talking to you where you need it most. If you really wish to attune to it and hear it, you will discern it, first vaguely, later strongly. You need to condition your inner ear to recognize it. As you begin to recognize the vibrant voice that speaks in wisdom and love—not in generalities, but specifically to you—you will know that this voice has always existed in you, but you have conditioned yourself not to hear it. And in that conditioning you have tightened and packed up that "inner tube" that will fill you with the vibrant music of the angels.

When I say the "music of the angels," I do not necessarily mean this literally, although that, too, may exist. But what you need more is the guidance for every decision about what opinion or attitude to adopt in a given situation. That instruction is truly comparable to the music of the angels in its glory. This fullness cannot be described in its wonder; it is a treasure beyond all words. It is what you constantly look and yearn for, but most of the time you are not aware of this searching and project it on substitute fulfillments that you expect to come from outside.

Refocus on what has always existed within you. Your mind and outer will have confused and complicated your life, so this new contact is like finding your way out of a maze—a maze you have created. You can now recreate your inner landscape without that maze.

The New Person as the Receptacle of the Universal Intelligence

Now, my dearest friends, I would like to say a few words about the new person in the new era. What is the new person? The new person is indeed always a receptacle of the universal intelligence, the divine consciousness, the Christ consciousness, that permeates every particle of being and of life. The new person is not functioning from the habitual intellect. For many centuries the intellect had to be cultivated to fulfill its role as an important stepping stone in humanity's evolution. By now, the overemphasis has gone on too long. This does not mean you should revert to the purely blind, emotional "desire-nature," rather, it means you should open up to a higher realm of consciousness within you and let it unfold.

There was a period in evolution when it was as hard for people to find their ability to think, to weigh, to discriminate, to retain knowledge, to remember, in short, to use all the faculties of the mind, as it now seems hard to find contact with the higher self. The new person has established a new balance in the inner system. The intellect must not be left out; it is an instrument that must serve, become unified with the greater consciousness. For many ages people believed that the intellectual faculties were the highest form of development, and some still believe this now. So they make no attempt to journey further and deeper into their inner nature to find greater treasures. On the other hand, there are many spiritual movements that practice discarding and inactivating the mind altogether. This is equally undesirable because it creates splits rather than unification.

The Function of the Intellect in the New Person

Both these extremes are half-truths, though they can have relative validity. For example, in the past, people were like beasts, undisciplined and irresponsible as far as their immediate desires were concerned. They were totally driven by emotions and desires, regardless of ethics and morality. So for that stage the development of the intellect fulfilled its function. And the intellect also fulfilled its function as a very sharp tool of learning, of discriminating. But when it ends there it becomes futile. People become pitiful when they cannot become animated by their divinity. By the same token, the practice of leaving the mind temporarily inactive is advisable, and I recommend it myself. But to treat the mind as if it were the devil and to oust it from your life is missing the point.

In either extreme, people lack something; they need all their functions in working order to express their divinity. Without a mind, you become a passive amoeba; when the mind is deemed the highest faculty, you become a hyperactive robot. The mind then becomes a computerized machine. True aliveness exists only when you wed the mind with the spirit and allow the mind to express the feminine principle for a while. Until now the mind has been very much linked with the masculine principle: action, drive, control.

Now the mind has to express the feminine principle: receptivity. This does not mean that you will become passive. In a sense, you will be more active, more truly independent than you were before. For when the mind receives inspirations from the God-consciousness, they must be put into action. But this putting into action is harmonious, effortless, not like a cramp. When your mind is receptive, it can be filled with the higher spirit within you. Then the functioning becomes totally different, forever new and exciting. Nothing becomes routinized, nothing becomes stale, nothing becomes redundant. For the spirit is forever alive and changing. This is the energy and experience you have increasingly in your community, where the new influx is working so strongly.

The new person makes all decisions from this new consciousness after working his or her way through to becoming truly receptive to the spiritual being within. The results would sound utopian for someone who has not begun to experience this. I am happy to say that quite a number of you are already part of this strong cosmic movement for which you have made yourself available. You experience hitherto undreamed-of expansion and joy, resolutions of problems that you never thought possible. And it continues. There are no limitations to your fulfillment, to the peace, to the productivity, to the creativity of living, to joy, love, and happiness, and to the meaning your life has acquired as you serve a greater cause.

Entering the New, Greater Life

The time has passed for each individual to live only for a selfish, immediate little life. This can no longer continue. Those who insist on this way lock themselves out from a power that would turn destructive in a mind that is still geared to selfishness. For that selfishness comes from the false belief that you are happy only when you are selfish, and unhappy when you are unselfish. That false belief is one of the first myths you need to explore and challenge.

You are creating a new life for yourself and your environment, of a kind that humanity has not yet known. You are preparing for it, others are preparing for it, here and there, all over the world, quietly. These are golden nuclei that spring up out of the gray, dark matter of untruthful thinking and living. So further that channel in you. It will bring you the excitement and the peace you always wanted. Enter this new phase, my dearest friends, with courage and affirmation. Rise up and become who you truly are, and experience life at its best.

All of you are blessed, my very dearest ones. The blessings will give you the sustenance you need to go all the way with all of yourself and become enlivened, activated, actualized by the God within. Be in peace.

The Voice Within: A Meditation from the Guide

. . . If you make yourself still and listen into your inner self, you will hear its voice. It will say, with variations:

I am the ever-loving God,
the ever-present Creator
living within you
moving through you
expressing as you in myriad forms—
as you, and you, and you—
as the animals
as the trees and the sky and the firmament
as everything that exists.

I shall dwell in you
and if you allow Me to act through you
to be known through your brain
to be felt through your feelings
you will experience My power that is limitless.

You will not fear this power
that manifests on all levels.
The power is great, but give in to Me.
Give in to this power
to this stream that surges forth,
that will make you cry

238

*and that will make you laugh
both in joy.*

*For you are Me and I am you.
I cannot act on this level
without your being an instrumentality for Me.
And if you listen to Me,
I will guide you through every step of the way.*

*Whenever you are in darkness,
you are away from Me.
And if you remember this,
you will make steps to come back to Me.
I am not far away.
I am right here, in every particle of your own being.*

*If you thus fulfill My will,
you and I become more one,
and I can fulfill your will.*

Background: The Guide, Eva, and the Pathwork Foundation

The Guide never identified himself by name. He maintained that his identity was not important, that no matter what he said, we would not be able to verify that identity anyway. All that we should be concerned with were his teachings. Even those we should not believe merely because they come from a spirit entity. We should consult our hearts, and only if we find an echo inside that affirms their truth should we accept his words.

Eva Pierrakos was born in Vienna in 1915, daughter of the well-known novelist Jakob Wassermann. She grew up among the intellectual elite of Vienna; her first husband was the son of another famous writer, Hermann Broch. A bright, outgoing young woman, Eva loved to dance and ski; she later became a dance instructor. The last thing she would have imagined was to be chosen to serve as an instrument for spiritual communication.

Eva managed to leave Austria before the Nazi takeover. She received a United States visa and moved to New York. It was, however, in Switzerland, where she lived for a while, that her psychic talent began first to manifest in the form of automatic writing. By meditating for long hours, changing her diet, and making the commitment to use her gift only for helping people—even taking the risk of losing her friends, who thought she was losing her wits—she eventually succeeded in becoming a pure channel so that a spirit entity of high wisdom like the Guide was able to manifest through her and offer us the gift of his teachings.

When Eva moved back to the United States, a small group formed around her. She gave individual "Guide sessions," and twice a month a lecture or a question-and-answer session.

She was a dark-haired, small woman with luminous dark eyes and a dancer's body. Usually sun-tanned, she was very healthy-looking, and had a wonderful capacity for enjoying herself. When John Pierrakos, a psychiatrist working in the Reichian tradition, and co-founder of bioenergetics, met her, both his work and Eva's became enriched. Their marriage, in addition to bringing personal happiness, helped John to transform his practice of bioenergetics into core energetics by incorporating into it the Guide's teachings. In turn, the introduction of the energetic element into the practice of the Pathwork process contributed to its effectiveness.

More and more people were drawn to the teachings of the Guide, and a home for the Pathwork was found in one of the secluded valleys in the Catskills, where deep transformation work can be done in the beauty and stillness of nature. In 1972, the Pathwork was incorporated as a not-for-profit educational foundation.

Eva died in 1979, leaving us a rich heritage of channeled material. In addition to the 258 lectures delineating the Pathwork, there are hundreds of recorded question-and-answer sessions and private consultations with the Guide.

By now tens of thousands have read the lectures—they are available individually—and thousands of people have been following this path, though the Pathwork has not sought wide publicity. There are a number of very active Pathwork Centers in North and South America and Europe, and a network of many groups which study and work with the Guide lectures around the globe.

We welcome the opportunity to support you in connecting with others who are interested in exploring this material further. For more information please contact the following regional centers:

California & Southwest:
Pathwork of California, Inc.
1355 Stratford Court #16
Del Mar, California 92014
(619) 793-1246
Fax (619) 259-5224

Path to the Real Self/Pathwork
Box 3753
Santa Fe, New
   Mexico 87501-0753
(505) 455-2533

Central:
Pathwork of Iowa
24 Highland Drive
Iowa City, Iowa 52246
(319) 338-9878

Great Lakes Region:
Great Lakes Pathwork
1117 Fernwood
Royal Oak, Michigan 48067
(810) 585-3984

Mid-Atlantic:
Sevenoaks Pathwork Center
Route 1, Box 86
Madison, Virginia 22727
(540) 948-6544
Fax (703) 948-5508

*New York, New Jersey,
   New England:*
Phoenicia Pathwork Center
Box 66
Phoenicia, New York 12464
(914) 688-2211
Fax (914) 688-2007

Northwest:
Northwest Pathwork/
   Core Energetics
811 NW 20th, Suite 103C
Portland, Oregon 97209
(503) 223-0018

Philadelphia:
Philadelphia Pathwork
910 S. Bellevue Avenue
Hulmeville,
   Pennsylvania 19407
(215) 752-9894

Southeast:
Pathwork of Georgia
1765 Blue Pond Drive
Canton, Georgia 30115
(770) 889-8790

Brazil:
Aidda Pustilnik
Rua da Graviola #264, Apt.
1003
41810-420 Itaigara, Salvador,
Brasil
Ph. 71-247-0068
Fax 71-245-3089

Canada:
Ottawa/Montreal Pathwork
Roddy Duchesne
604-222 Guigues Ave.
Ottawa, Ontario K1N 5J2
Canada
Ph. (613) 241-4982

Germany:
Pfadgruppe Kiel
Rendsburger Landstrasse 395
24111 Kiel, Germany
Alf Girtler   Ph. 0431-69-74-73
Paul Czempin
Ph. 0431-66-58-07

Italy:
Il Sentiero
Raffaele Iandolo
Campodivivo, 43. 04020
Spigno
Saturnia (LT) Italy
Ph. (39) 771-64463
Fax 39-771-64693

Luxembourg:
Pathwork Luxembourg
Maria van Eyken
21 rue de Capellen
L-8279 Holzem, Luxembourg
Ph. 0/352-38515

Mexico:
Andres Leites
Pino 1, Col Rancho Cortes
Cuernavaca, Mor 62130
Mexico
Ph. 73-131395
Fax 73-113592

The Netherlands:
Padwerk
Johan Kos
Boerhaavelaan 9
1401 VR Bussum, Holland
Ph/Fax 02159-35222

Argentina:
Claudia Boatti
Editorial Primera Linea
S.R.I. Ballarco 353 1-B
Buenos Aires, Argentina
54-1-3422296
Fax 54-1-3433344

List of Pathwork Lectures*

1. The Sea of Life
2. Decisions and Tests
3. Choosing Your Destiny
4. World Weariness
5. Happiness as a Link in the Chain of Life
6. God as Father-Image—Negative Attachment to Matter
7. Asking for Help and Helping Others
8. Mediumship
9. The Lord's Prayer
10. Male and Female Incarnations: Their Rhythms and Causes
11. Know Yourself
12. The Order and Diversity of the Spiritual Worlds—The Process of Reincarnation
13. Positive Thinking
14. The Higher Self, the Lower Self, and the Mask
15. Influence Between the Spiritual and the Material Worlds
16. Spiritual Nourishment
17. The Call
18. Free Will
19. Jesus Christ
20. The Communication of Spiritual Truth to Humanity— God and the Creation
21. The Fall
22. Salvation

*The missing numbers indicate Question and Answer sessions.

You can order any of these lectures for $2.50 each, plus postage and handling, from any of these regional centers:

California & Southwest:
Pathwork of California, Inc.
1355 Stratford Court #16
Del Mar, California 92014
(619) 793-1246
Fax (619) 259-5224

Path to the Real Self/Pathwork
Box 3753
Santa Fe, New
    Mexico 87501-0753
(505) 455-2533

Central:
Pathwork of Iowa
24 Highland Drive
Iowa City, Iowa 52246
(319) 338-9878

Great Lakes Region:
Great Lakes Pathwork
1117 Fernwood
Royal Oak, Michigan 48067
(810) 585-3984

Mid-Atlantic:
Sevenoaks Pathwork Center
Route 1, Box 86
Madison, Virginia 22727
(540) 948-6544
Fax (703) 948-5508

New York, New Jersey,
    New England:
Phoenicia Pathwork Center
Box 66
Phoenicia, New York 12464
(914) 688-2211
Fax (914) 688-2007

Northwest:
Northwest Pathwork/Core
    Energetics
811 NW 20th, Suite 103C
Portland, Oregon 97209
(503) 223-0018

Philadelphia:
Philadelphia Pathwork
910 S. Bellevue Avenue
Hulmeville, Penn-
    sylvania 19407
(215) 752-9894

Southeast:
Pathwork of Georgia
1765 Blue Pond Drive
Canton, Georgia 30115
(770) 889-8790

Brazil:
Aidda Pustilnik
Rua da Graviola #264, Apt.
 1003
41810-420 Itaigara, Salvador,
 Brasil
Ph. 71-247-0068
Fax 71-245-3089

Canada:
Ottawa/Montreal Pathwork
Roddy Duchesne
604-222 Guigues Ave.
Ottawa, Ontario K1N 5J2
 Canada
Ph. (613) 241-4982

Germany:
Pfadgruppe Kiel
Rendsburger Landstrasse 395
24111 Kiel, Germany
Alf Girtler   Ph. 0431-69-74-73
Paul Czempin
            Ph. 0431-66-58-07

Italy:
Il Sentiero
Raffaele Iandolo
Campodivivo, 43. 04020
 Spigno
Saturnia (LT) Italy
Ph. (39) 771-64463
Fax 39-771-64693

Luxembourg:
Pathwork Luxembourg
Maria van Eyken
21 rue de Capellen
L-8279 Holzem, Luxembourg
Ph. 0/352-38515

Mexico:
Andres Leites
Pino 1, Col Rancho Cortes
Cuernavaca, Mor 62130
 Mexico
Ph. 73-131395
Fax 73-113592

The Netherlands:
Padwerk
Johan Kos
Boerhaavelaan 9
1401 VR Bussum, Holland
Ph/Fax 02159-35222

Argentina:
Claudia Boatti
Editorial Primera Linea
S.R.I. Ballarco 353 1-B
Buenos Aires, Argentina
54-1-3422296
Fax 54-1-3433344

Index

Conscious ego, 184, 185, 187,
188–189, 191
Consciousness
components of, 174, 210,
218
creation and, 218–221
creative consciousness,
210–211
dualistic plane, 58
state of consciousness,
174–175
unequal development of
parts, 92–93
unified plane, 58
willing and, 210–211
See also New conscious-
ness.
Cosmic feeling, 51–52
Creativity
creative consciousness,
210–211, 218–221
creative emptiness,
225–226, 227, 232–233
distorted aspect of,
162–166
feelings and, 105
God and, 54–56
momentum of creating,
218–221
negative creation, 219–222
Crisis
avoidance of, 149
death as, 149–150
degree of pain and, 146
divine help and, 155–157
and end of negative self-
perpetuation, 148–149

meaning of, 145
message of, 154–157
necessity of, 146
outer and inner crisis,
150–151
readjustment and,
145–146, 149
taking cover, 158

D

Danger, emotions as,
118–119
Dark aspects of self, 15
Death, as crisis, 149–150
Dependency
dependent child, existence
in adult, 135–136
forcing-current and, 137,
138, 139
hiding dependency,
134–135
liberation from, 142–144
and paralysis of being, 139
reorientation to life and,
140–141
as vicious circle, 137–139
Depression, vicious circle of,
147–148
Desire, ideal state of,
194–195
Desirelessness, 194–195
Destructive self
choice and, 216–217
effect of meditation on,
189–192
Divine laws, 52–54
Divorce, 90

About the Author

EVA PIERRAKOS was born Eva Wassermann in 1915 in Austria. She grew up in Vienna during the political unrest of the post-World War I years, while the darkness that was about to descend and culminate in World War II was gathering over Europe. However, Eva loved life, nature, animals, the pleasures of dancing and skiing and of friendship. She was able to leave Austria and lived for a while in Switzerland before settling down in New York. During this time she became the channel for a highly-developed spirit guide who gave the series of lectures from which this volume was compiled. Hers is the perennial story of transmitters of spiritual truth: first, astonishment at the manifestation of the gift, then reluctance to accepting it, finally, humbly taking on the task with total commitment. Quietly, she drew to herself an ever-growing number of people who became attracted to the path of self-transformation taught by the Guide. From the materials of these lectures Eva Pierrakos developed *The Pathwork*, a psychological method which leads to the Godself through facing and transforming the lower self.

Eva died in 1979, leaving behind her the rich legacy of 258 Guide lectures, two flourishing Pathwork centers, and thousands of students and followers of the teachings which she transmitted with such devotion for twenty-five years.